Praise for Phil Zuckerman's *Living the Secular Life*

"An insightful mixture of academic research on shifting American religious views, his own experience as a parent, and interviews with others facing moral crises without God . . . this book is a humane and sensible guide to and for the many kinds of Americans leading secular lives."
—Susan Jacoby, *The New York Times Book Review*

"Zuckerman is a sociologist who in this groundbreaking book writes clearly, offers unobtrusive statistical support, and provides a persuasive and comprehensive look at the growing contemporary phenomenon of people who choose to live without religion, but with ethics and meaning in their lives." —*Publishers Weekly*, A Best Book of 2014

"As secularism becomes more prominent and self-confident, its spokesmen have more insistently argued that secularism should not be seen as an absence—as a lack of faith—but rather as a positive moral creed. Phil Zuckerman, a Pitzer College sociologist, makes this case as fluidly and pleasurably as anybody in his book *Living the Secular Life*."
—David Brooks, *The New York Times*

"In this fascinating work, Zuckerman (*Faith No More: Why People Reject Religion*), professor of sociology and secular studies at Pitzer College, explores the moral and ethical foundations of secularism, addressing the question of whether you can live a good life without God or religion. Anecdotal evidence abounds; interviews with former religious adherents who have moved into secularism, both within and outside their religious communities, offer a compelling argument for the non-necessity of God in the pursuit of a moral life." —*Publishers Weekly*

"With recent polls reporting 30 percent of Americans are nonreligious, while other studies find atheists the least-trusted people in the country, isn't it high time to blow away the myths about the nonreligious? Answering affirmatively, the sociologist founder of the first secular-studies program at Pitzer College presents real secular people as peaceable, productive, and living happily. . . . He also shows that secularism isn't bipolar—believer or nonbeliever—but includes many with some supernatural beliefs but who aren't religiously observant. And there's not a proselytizer or zealot among this group—the point being that secular people are not all—indeed, hardly ever—Christopher Hitchens or Madalyn Murray O'Hair. May one more prejudice fall." —*Booklist*

"The author brilliantly weaves stories and reflections together with empirical sociological research to create a rich portrait of secular America . . . Highly recommended for all readers, both religious and nonreligious, seeking a more accurate understanding of this ever-growing segment of the American population." —*Library Journal*

"Phil Zuckerman is without a doubt the leading American sociologist of secularism. And with America secularizing more rapidly and profoundly now than in any previous era in our history, Zuckerman's work has become essential reading for everyday people who want to understand religion—and the nonreligious—in this country. *Living the Secular Life* represents the next big chapter in a centuries-old story, so if you've ever taken an interest in Dawkins, Harris, Hitchens, et al., you certainly need to pick this book up and find out where things are headed."
—Greg M. Epstein, humanist chaplain at Harvard University; author of *Good Without God*

"Since coming out as a post-Christian minister, I've discovered all kinds of people sincerely pursuing goodness without the nurture, encouragement, and mutual support most church folks take for granted. These folks are hungry for fellowship and pastoral care, but even hungrier for a thoughtful, positive way to communicate their values and commitments to friends and family members instinctively distrustful of anyone who doesn't believe in God. For them—and for me—Phil Zuckerman is a genuine hero, and *Living the Secular Life* is a wonderful gift. Here at last is a clear, concise, and compassionate guided tour of the world's fastest-growing way of life. Zuckerman isn't trying to prove everyone else wrong. On the contrary, he's helping the secular community better understand and comport itself, and helping the rest of humanity understand that we're on their side too."
—Bart Campolo, author of *Things We Wish We Had Said*

"For secular people seeking deeper insight into their own worldview, or religious people seeking to better understand the rise of irreligion in society today, this book is indispensable. An engaging, powerful read."
—Peter Boghossian, professor of philosophy, Portland State University; author of *A Manual for Creating Atheists*

PENGUIN BOOKS

LIVING THE SECULAR LIFE

Phil Zuckerman is a professor of sociology and secular studies at Pitzer College in Claremont, California. He is the author most recently of *Faith No More* and *Society Without God* and blogs for *Psychology Today* and the *Huffington Post*. In 2011 Zuckerman founded an interdisciplinary Department of Secular Studies at Pitzer College, the first in the nation.

Living the Secular Life

NEW ANSWERS

TO

OLD QUESTIONS

Phil Zuckerman

PENGUIN BOOKS

PENGUIN BOOKS
An imprint of Penguin Random House LLC
375 Hudson Street
New York, New York 10014
penguin.com

First published in the United States of America by Penguin Press,
a member of Penguin Group (USA) LLC, 2014
Published in Penguin Books 2015

THE LIBRARY OF CONGRESS HAS CATALOGED THE HARDCOVER EDITION AS FOLLOWS:
Zuckerman, Phil.
Living the secular life : new answers to old questions / Phil Zuckerman.
pages cm
Includes bibliographical references and index.
ISBN 978-1-59420-508-8 (hc.)
ISBN 978-0-14-312793-2 (pbk.)
1. Secularism—United States.   2. United States—United States.   I. Title.
BL2747.8.Z83   2014
211'.60973—dc23   2014009785

Printed in the United States of America
1   3   5   7   9   10   8   6   4   2

Designed by Chris Welch

Names and other descriptive information of the individuals represented
in this book have been changed in several instances.

For Stacy, Ruby, Flora, and August

Contents

Living the
Secular Life

Introduction

And there it was again: the whole notion of "nothing." It came at me twice in the same week, and from two different people. The first time it came up was with Jill. We were standing and talking on the curb outside the studio where her son and my son both take cello lessons. Jill is in her early forties, from San Francisco, and she recently sold her modern furniture store in order to be at home more with her kids. We often chitchat when cello lessons are over and our sons are busy playing in the nearby bushes.

The other day as we were talking, religion came up. That was when Jill expressed what I've heard so many times before: "I just don't want my kids to be 'nothing.'"

Jill is one of tens of millions of Americans who are nonreligious. Her mom was Buddhist and her dad was Catholic, and she was raised with a fair amount of both traditions. But by the time she got to college, she knew that she didn't believe in God. Sure, maybe there's something more out there—who can say? But religion just wasn't her thing. Her husband felt the same way. And all was fine for several years.

But lately, with her kids being three and six, things have somehow started to feel different. Jill is a little worried. She told me that she was considering sending her kids to some church, perhaps the local Catholic church. But I could tell that she was conflicted. When I asked her why she was contemplating sending her kids to church if she didn't feel 100 percent about it, she said, "I want them to get some morals. I think that's important."

"But your children can develop a healthy, durable morality without religion," I replied.

"Yeah, I guess you're right. But still . . ."

Being a secular parent myself, and having studied the hills and dales of secular culture for some time now, I know what gnaws at Jill. I'm quite familiar with the angst that many such secular Americans experience: the feeling that maybe one is making a mistake by raising one's kids without religion. Even though Jill is living a meaningful, thoughtful, and ethical life without religious faith or affiliation, she nonetheless feels that if she doesn't impart some sort of religious identity to her kids—if they lack religious involvement—then they will be . . . *nothing*.

Oh, and immoral to boot.

A few days later, the matter of "nothing" confronted me again. This time it came from a religious woman. Her name is Beverly. She is in her late sixties. She describes herself as "just Christian." We met at a picnic being thrown by mutual friends at a park near Pasadena. She asked me what I did for a living. I said that I was a professor at a small liberal arts college. She then told me that she was the programming director at the religious center of a large university, a place where students from all walks of faith can find community, attend services, meet with clergy, and so on. Beverly loves her job. She helps arrange religious events, she coordinates panels and discussions, she sets up volunteering and charitable opportunities, among other things.

When Beverly asked me what I studied, I said, "Secular people."

Pause.

"You know," I continued, "people who live their lives without religion. . . ."

And then she calmly replied, "Well, without religion, you've got nothing."

Now, mind you, there was nary of hint of snark or derogatoriness in her comment. It was said kindly and openly, a genuine expression of this woman's lived experience, inner faith, and personal orientation. To Beverly, life without religious faith and involvement would be empty, desultory.

This association of secularity with nothingness runs deep. Many people assume that a life lived without religion is not only somewhat void, but intrinsically problematic. After all, how does one deal with death without religion? How does one cope with life's troubles? Develop morals and ethics? Find community? Experience a sense of transcendence? These are extremely fair questions. And yet the idea that religion is the best and/or only option out there when dealing with such matters is simply untenable. The glaring truth is that millions of people live their lives without religion—and they do so quite well. They aren't living aimlessly, adrift in a vacuum of nihilistic nothingness.

Jill may not know it, or she may not conceive of it in terms of clearly articulated precepts, but her secular lifestyle is actually very moral and deeply grounded in ethical conduct. How she interacts with those around her on a daily basis, the choices that she makes as a mother, wife, neighbor, businesswoman, and citizen, and the ways she reacts to and appreciates the world around her—all of these are linked to developing and expressing an empathetic spirit, caring about others and the wider world, being responsible and upstanding. And they are very much linked to the secular sensibility. For as the stories of the many nonreligious men and women presented in this book will illustrate, there are actually specific key virtues of secular living, and prominent pillars of secular culture, that enhance moral rectitude and promote human decency.

As for Beverly, while I didn't want to get into it at the picnic, what I would want her to know is that religion is definitely not the only avenue for people to live good, meaningful, or inspired lives. There are other, secular options.

A life lived without religion is not "nothing." There are common attributes, characteristics, traits, and values one finds among nonreligious people, and within secular culture, that directly enhance individuals' ability to cope with life's troubles, allow for moments of fulfillment and existential awe, and even increase societal well-being.

Indeed, the foundational components of a secular orientation are both abundant and laudable: from encouraging pragmatic, reasonable problem solving to fortifying oneself against groupthink and a herd mentality, from deepening our attachment to the people and things of this world to sparking a soulful appreciation for the majesty of nature, from encouraging scientific inquiry to manifesting a humane empathy, from fostering a mature morality to engendering a serene acceptance of mortality, secularity offers individuals a rich, proud wellspring of both wisdom and wonder. And as the many men and women you'll meet in the pages that follow will attest to, being secular is an affirming worldview and positive, purposeful life stance.

What it means to be secular—and the cardinal virtues of secular living—are thus deeply important matters to recognize and understand, and their importance is all the more timely given that the number of nonreligious Americans is precipitously rising. Indeed, the recent spike of secularity has been a truly remarkable phenomenon, unprecedented in our nation's history.

BACK IN THE 1950s, fewer than 5 percent of Americans were nonreligious. By the 1990s, that figure was up to 8 percent. Then it jumped to 14 percent in 2001, 16 percent in 2010, 19 percent in 2013, and as of the latest national surveys, it is up to 30 percent today. This means that the number of nonreligious Americans has increased by well over 200 percent over the last twenty-five years, making it the fastest-growing "religious" orientation in the country.

More than a third of Americans between the ages of eighteen and twenty-nine now claim to be nonreligious. In the early 1970s, only 9 percent of Americans said that they *never* attended religious services; today, nearly 25 percent say as much. And there are currently more people in this country who were raised in secular homes—without any religion—than there are African Americans. Such a surge of people eschewing religion is truly remarkable, and helps explain why *Time* magazine recently cited the dramatic increase of Americans claiming "none" as their religion as one of the ten most significant trends changing American society.

I am fascinated by this trend. And in my work as a sociologist and professor of secular studies, I have sought to thoroughly explore secular people's approaches to life, to probe the ramifications of their worldviews and perspectives, and to shine a light on their experiences, joys, and challenges. I've done all of this with an eye toward connecting such information to the broader social scene, both here in America and in the world at large.

My primary investigative method has been to conduct in-depth interviews with nonreligious people from all over the country and from all walks of life, representing a variety of races, ethnic groups, ages, occupations, sexualities, and class backgrounds. And I've purposely sought out people exhibiting a wide array of secular orientations, from the firmly convinced to the mildly befuddled, from the staunchly atheistic to the serenely indifferent. I've interviewed people who have devoted their lives to secularism as well as people who have hardly given it a thought prior to our discussion, and many others in between such extremes.

I have found my interviewees through every imaginable channel: by searching secularist Web sites to find potential informants, by going to humanist gatherings of various shapes and sizes and getting to know the people involved, by pursuing individuals I've come in contact with at various conferences, by tracking down people from stories I've read in the newspapers, and by pursuing any and all leads that come my way via professional and personal contacts and networks. Such qualitative research, especially when corroborated by relevant statistics and bolstered with quantitative data, offers the best possible window into people's lives and worldviews, allowing their contoured stories and personal reflections to come forth—stories and reflections that are unique to each man and woman, and yet simultaneously relevant for countless others.

What I have learned, and what shall be illustrated throughout the chapters ahead, is that while secular Americans may have nothing to do with religion, this does not mean that they wallow in despair or flail about in hapless oblivion. To the contrary, they live civil, reasonably rational, and admirably meaningful lives predicated upon sound ethical foundations.

Secular Americans are undoubtedly a remarkably diverse lot, exhibiting a wide spectrum of identities, beliefs, dispositions, and proclivities. But as I've been able to glean through my research, most do share certain key traits and values, such as self-reliance, freedom of thought, intellectual inquiry, cultivating autonomy in children, pursuing truth, basing morality on the empathetic reciprocity embedded in the Golden Rule, accepting the inevitability of our eventual death, navigating life with a sober pragmatism grounded in this world (not the next), and still enjoying a sense of deep transcendence now and then amid the inexplicable, inscrutable profundity of being.

For most nonreligious men and women, to be secular ultimately means living in the here and now—with exuberance, relish, passion, and tenacity—because this is the only existence we'll ever have. It also means being committed to making the world a better place, because this world is all we've got. Being secular means loving family and friends rather than a deity or savior. Being secular involves seeking to do good and treating others right simply because such behavior makes the world a better place for all. Being secular is about finding joy, splendor, and fulfillment in newborn babies and thunderstorms, peaches and tears, harmony and inner thighs, algebra and forgiveness, squid and irony, without attaching any supernatural or divine masking tape to such inexplicable wonders of life.

And in line with what one of the leading lights of American secular humanism, Paul Kurtz, emphasized in his many books, essays, and speeches, most secular folk deeply believe that education and scientific discovery have the potential to enhance life, that democracy and respect for human rights are essential elements of a good society, that justice and fairness are ideals worth enacting, that the earth is to be valued and protected, that honesty, decency, tolerance, integrity, love, altruism, and self-responsibility are attributes to be cultivated, that creative and artistic expression are vital to the human experience, and that life, though at times beset with horror and despair, is intrinsically beautiful, wonderful, sublime.

No doubt most religious people can wholeheartedly agree with the above sentiments. But many of them—perhaps people like Beverly— don't know that secular individuals actively advocate and embody such principles and beliefs. And many others—perhaps people like Jill—

don't quite understand just what it is about being secular that strengthens and emboldens these principles and beliefs.

THERE HAVE BEEN countless books extolling the philosophical rigor of atheism or polemically assaulting, deriding, and/or condemning this or that aspect of religious life. But what I offer here is something altogether different: a positive view and encouraging vision of real secularity that is developed "on the ground," in ordinary life, by and among ordinary people. I will explore how secular Americans get on and how they get by, how they confront death without the promise of eternal life, how they face tragedy and confront life's difficulties without the comfort of religious faith, how they find community beyond the walls of church, synagogue, temple, or mosque, how they raise their kids—in sum, how secular people navigate their lives.

Of course, many secular Americans have rejected religion for very specific and staunch reasons; they are ideologically, philosophically, or politically motivated to embrace the secular life and they know its value and promise. However, many other nonreligious people are more passively secular, with less pointed intention or self-reflective awareness. People like Jill. And thus for the less consciously secular, or the newly secular, or the reluctantly secular, I hope that this book offers some guidance—a road map of sorts—that can ideally help such people navigate life lived without God or congregation. For those Americans out there living secular lives but feeling not quite sure just what that even means or ultimately entails, may the pages that follow be of use, for matters both existential and practical.

But I also hope that this book will be illuminating for the majority of Americans out there who are happily religious—people like Beverly. I hope that the stories and experiences of the people profiled in the pages ahead, as well as the concomitant analysis, will positively influence the way that they make sense of and understand their neighbors, colleagues, and relatives who, for whatever reasons, do not or cannot share their religious faith and involvement. And in this vein, I further hope that the information, data, and discussion that follow will serve to counter some of their negative stereotypes and shake up a few of the many misconceptions out there concerning atheists, agnostics, humanists, skeptics, and other such freethinkers.

For example, a lot of religious Americans don't like or trust people who don't believe in God because they assume that atheism is the same thing as being without morals. This assumption is so widespread that in many surveys atheists come in at last place when Americans are asked to rank members of certain racial, ethnic, or religious groups as potential spouses for their kids. And a recent national poll found that 43 percent of Americans said that they would not vote for an atheist for president, putting atheists in last/worst place, behind Muslims (40 percent of Americans said they wouldn't vote for a Muslim for president), homosexuals (30 percent wouldn't), Mormons (18 percent wouldn't), Latinos (7 percent wouldn't), Jews (6 percent wouldn't), Catholics (5 percent wouldn't), women (5 percent wouldn't), and African Americans (4 percent wouldn't).

Many other studies conducted in recent years have shown just how disliked the nonreligious are. For example, psychology professor Adrian Furnham found that people gave lower priority to patients with atheist or agnostic views than to Christian patients when asked to rank them on a waiting list to receive a kidney; legal scholar Eugene Volokh has documented the degree to which atheist parents have been denied custody rights in the wake of a divorce; psychologist Marcel Harper has found that many Americans consider secular people to be selfish and immoral; psychology professor Will Gervais found that many Americans consider atheists to be untrustworthy; and finally, sociologist Penny Edgell found that nearly half of all Americans would disapprove of their child wanting to marry an atheist, and when compared to other religious or minority groups such as African Americans, Mormons, Muslims, and Latinos, "atheists are at the top of the list of groups that Americans find problematic."

All of the above needs to be contended with—and countered. An initial goal of this book, then, is to disabuse Americans of their dislike or distrust of the secular, not just because I am secular myself, but because the reality of secular men and women's lives and values indicates just how wrongheaded the dislike or distrust of nonreligious people truly is. People who don't believe in God are not immoral; most have very sound ethical orientations and moral principles, and in fact, on certain measures, secular people appear more tolerant, more law-abiding, less prejudiced, less vengeful, and less violent than their religious peers.

It is by stepping into this important arena—looking at how secular individuals construct and experience their morality, and what actually constitutes the primary ethics that undergird life without religion—that we'll begin our foray into the world of contemporary secular life and culture.

Chapter 1

Morality

My father was recently getting his teeth cleaned. The friendly dental assistant, Brittany, was chatting to him about the weather, her boyfriend's new paintball gun, and the Kardashians. Somehow, religion came up. She asked my dad what church he goes to. He said that he didn't go to church. She asked him why not. He said because he was Jewish. She asked him if he went to synagogue. He said no. She asked him why not. He said because he was an atheist. The twinkle in her eye immediately flickered out. She was crestfallen.

"But if you don't believe in God," she said, dental instruments held pensively in midair, "how can you be a good person?"

"Well," my dad replied. "Remember Jiminy Cricket? I let my conscience be my guide." Brittany couldn't quite remember who Jiminy Cricket was, but she did like the idea of my dad having a conscience. And yet she just couldn't quite wrap her brain around the idea that my father could be a good person without religion. In her mind, being moral and having a conscience were only *possible* with an abiding faith in God.

It is a widespread, all-too-common, taken-for-granted "truth" among many Americans today: morality comes from religious faith and involvement. The corollary to this belief is the assumption that without religion, one can't be moral. In other words, to be secular (or an atheist, heaven forbid) means that you must be immoral. This notion is not only held by dental assistants like Brittany, but is put forth by professors such as James Spiegel of Taylor University in Indiana, who in his book *The Making of an Atheist* argues that atheism is essentially, integrally predicated on immorality. Supreme Court justice Antonin Scalia recently shared his opinion that atheists favor "the devil's desires." And as broached in the introduction, various national surveys consistently report that a majority of Americans associate a lack of belief in God with a lack of personal morals.

And yet, as I suspect you already know, it simply isn't so. No one who is secular themselves, or has any good friends or relatives who are secular, could ever cling with any tenacity to the notion that secular people are intrinsically or inevitably immoral.

How Can You Be Moral Without Faith in God?

Even if one doesn't hold to the prejudice that secular people are immoral, it is nonetheless a fair matter for inquiry: What *does* underlie secular morality, at root? How do individual men and women navigate their moral lives without a religious compass? And as Brittany's dismay implies, if secular people don't believe in God, or divine judgment, or heaven or hell, how do they construct their notions of ethical conduct, decency, and goodness?

In beginning to answer these questions, we can start with the words of George Jacob Holyoake—the man who first coined the very term "secularism" back in 1851. Holyoake was from Birmingham, England. He worked as a schoolmaster, lecturer, writer, and magazine editor. He was also an atheist, and he even spent six months in jail for giving a speech deemed hostile to Christianity. According to Holyoake, secularism is not about being *against* religion. Rather, it is something positive, a personal orientation predicated on a this-worldly ethos—that is, guiding beliefs and principled ideals that are concerned with the here and now, people and nature, life and existence. As he explained in a publication from 1896, "Secularism is a code of duty pertaining to this life, founded on considerations purely human, and intended mainly for those who find theology indefinite or inadequate, unreliable or unbelievable. Its essential principles are three: (1) The improvement of this life by material means. (2) That science is the available Providence of man. (3) That it is good to do good. Whether there be other good or not, the good of the present life is good, and it is good to seek that good."

It is good to do good. Nice enough. But what is good? For contemporary secular people, the answer to that is simple: the Golden Rule. Being good means treating others as you would like to be treated. That is the bedrock of secular morality. Not harming others—and helping or assisting others, should they seek such assistance or help—is pretty much it. For the nonreligious, morality *isn't* about abstaining from sex or avoiding alcohol, or doing what someone in authority tells you to do, or not doing something because you fear the otherworldly consequences if you do. Rather, secular morality hinges upon little else than not harming others, and helping those in need, both of which flow easily and directly from the Golden Rule's basic, simple logic of empathetic reciprocity.

Given its easy applicability and inherent reasonableness, it shouldn't be surprising that the Golden Rule is remarkably widespread the world over. And it is also ancient, predating many of the famous moral precepts one finds in Christianity. Though it was undoubtedly articulated countless years prior, a version of the Golden

Rule was first written down by the ancient Egyptians; a piece of papyrus from as far back as 600 BCE contains an inscription stating, "That which you hate to be done to you, do not do to another." The Golden Rule was also recorded in ancient China, among the teachings of Confucius (551–479 BCE), who in his *Analects* taught, "Do not impose on others what you do not desire others to impose upon you," and "What you would require of your friend, first apply in your treatment of him." In ancient Greece, Thales (c. 624–c. 546 BCE) argued that humans live most virtuously and justly when "we never do ourselves what we blame in others," and Isocrates (436–338 BCE) reasoned that "those things which provoke anger when you suffer them from others, do not do to others." The rabbi Hillel of ancient Israel, living in the first century BCE, preached that "what is hateful to you, do not do to your neighbor." All of these formulations predate Jesus's teachings, found in the Gospels, that "all things whatsoever ye would that men should do to you, do ye even so to them," and "as ye would that men should do to you, do ye also to them likewise."

Although we find other versions of the Golden Rule within all of the world's religions, from Buddhism to Islam and from Jainism to Bahaism, not a single one of these religious articulations of the Golden Rule requires a God. All that is required is basic, fundamental human empathy.

But how is basic, fundamental human empathy developed? Simply by living among other empathetic humans. As the great English philosopher John Stuart Mill so wisely quipped, "Though direct moral teaching does much, indirect does more." In other words, while people can certainly be taught to be considerate of others via sermons, lectures, bedtime stories, and so on, what really does the trick is actual lived experience. That's the "indirect" and yet far more effective way of developing morality. People learn, understand, and develop empathy as a result of what they observe in and experience from those around them. Sure, preaching and teaching morality are fine. But they don't hold a candle to day-to-day interactions.

Children who are raised by considerate, fair, empathetic people generally grow up to be considerate, fair, and empathetic themselves. Children who grow up in stable, safe, and supportive environments generally develop the capacity to be kind, sensitive, and humane toward others. No philosophical proofs, theoretical arguments, logical axioms, Bible stories, or theistic beliefs are necessary. As Kai Nielsen, author of *Ethics Without God*, has stated, "What makes us moral beings is not so much the theoretical belief systems we inherit . . . but the way we have been nurtured from very early on. If we were fortunate enough to have had good moral role models, that is, kind, tolerably wise, and understanding parents, and to have lived in conditions of security where our basic needs were stably met, the chances are reasonably good that we will have those desirable moral characteristics ourselves."

For many secular people, questions such as "Why be moral?" or "How can you be moral without faith in God?" are almost nonsensical. The very questions implicitly suggest that one "chooses"—in an intellectual, purely cognitive manner—to be moral based on certain theories, logical proofs, ideologies, beliefs, or on one's faith in a divine being. And yet for most secular people their morality is something much more experiential, much more visceral, even automatic. It has to do with the way they were raised, what they observed as they were growing up, what they unconsciously absorbed through their socialization—not this or that idea, theory, belief, dictum, or doctrine.

I've talked to many secular people about their morality, specifically questioning them about where it comes from and how it works. And in response to my queries, I've heard a lot of interesting philosophical speculations, anecdotes, enthusiastic references to this or that book or film, and plenty of personal reflections. But two responses particularly stand out that I'd like to share here. One comes from a man named Milton Newcombe, from Pennsylvania, the other from a woman named Sonja Weiss, from Massachusetts. I find the way that they were able to articulate their thoughts on secular morality to be especially compelling.

WE CAN CALL it the "matter of moral outsourcing," and it comes from Milton, age forty-six. Milton's take on secular morality goes something like this: people who base their morality upon their belief in God, or who think that morality comes from God, are guilty of "moral outsourcing." Morality, according to secular people like Milton, is essentially about the decisions and choices one personally makes for oneself, based on contemplation, the weighing of options, understanding alternatives, accepting possible consequences, and navigating complex life questions via one's own conscience. Morality is about listening and adhering to one's inner moral compass concerning what is right or wrong, just or unjust, compassionate or cruel, and then acting accordingly in relation to others. But if God is the source of morality, a person doesn't need to consult his or her own inner moral compass—one simply looks to God for direction. And looking to God for guidance about how to be moral is basically absolving oneself of doing the heavy lifting of moral deliberation. It is obediently deferring to a higher authority. It is seeking moral guidance elsewhere, outside of one's self.

And according to many secular men and women, that is a major abdication. A serious eschewal of ethical duty. A deep deferment of moral decision making. It is, in short, a cop-out. Secular morality allows for no such cop-outs. Godlessness means that *you* have to make your own choices about how to treat others and how to live your life in a way that reflects your conscience. That, many secular folk will argue, is true morality. In the words of philosopher and humanist Stephen Law, "It is our individual responsibility to make our own moral judgments, rather than attempt to hand that responsibility over to some external authority."

By predicating his morality upon his own conscience rather than looking to God or a pastor or the teachings of an ancient text for guidance, Milton gets by quite well, or at least as well as most of us. And one obvious benefit to the secular morality embraced by people like Milton—at the larger, societal level—is that it is less likely to lead to blind obedience to those in positions of authority, or herdlike behavior, or a mob mentality. As history has repeatedly shown, when too many people in a society look for moral guidance outside of themselves, ignoring their own conscience in favor of heeding some external source of moral instruction, the results are often quite unsavory, if not downright bloody. An orientation such as that of people like Milton who refuse to outsource their morality and instead rely on their conscience is more likely to foster independent thinking, personal responsibility, skepticism toward hegemonic propaganda, and a sober self-awareness of why one chooses to do right over wrong—all of which are virtues highly compatible with and indeed essential for a healthy democracy.

A SECOND ARTICULATION of the value of secular moral reasoning is what I would call the "eye in the ceiling." This comes from Sonja, age sixty-two. During our interview, Sonja presented me with a hypothetical situation in order to illustrate what she thinks reveals the superiority of secular over God-based morality.

Here's the scenario: Imagine that there is a room, and in the middle of the room, perched on a small table, is a beautiful, amazing, intricate piece of art. It contains all sorts of colorful levers, golden pulleys, shimmering crystals, silver balls, cute bells, spiked wheels, red spokes, brittle branches, webbed wires, all arranged in a psychedelic, fanciful way that is truly spectacular to behold. But this piece of art is extremely fragile. And it is the only one in existence. And the artist who made it is dead.

Okay, so now let's say we take two nine-year-old kids. We say to the first kid, "Go into this room and look at this wonderful piece of art. You will have ten minutes in there, all to yourself. No one will be in the room but you. But please do not touch the piece of art. It is extremely delicate, very fragile, and it is the only one in existence. If you were to touch it, you might accidentally break, stain, or alter it, which would possibly cause irreparable damage, and then other kids won't be able to see it as it should be seen. Now, if you do touch it, and if you do accidentally break it, we won't punish you—but we'd be quite sad, and so we'd just really like you to not touch it." The kid goes in, looks but doesn't touch, and comes out. Great.

Now here comes the second kid. But we say something quite different to this kid. We say, "Go into this room and look at this wonderful piece of art. You will have ten minutes in there, all to yourself. No one will be in the room but you. And please do not touch the piece of art. It is extremely delicate, very fragile, and it is the only one in existence. Now, there will be a small hole in the ceiling, and through that hole, the principal of the school will be watching you. His eye will be on you at all times. If you touch that piece of art, he will see it, and he will be very angry, and you will be severely punished when you come out of the room. However, if you don't touch it, he will see this as well, and he will be very pleased, and he will reward you with something wonderful when you come out." The kid goes in, looks but doesn't touch, and exits. Fine.

Now, for many secular people, such as Sonja, the first scenario represents secular morality: the kid who makes a choice not to touch the piece of art does so because she understands the risks and she understands the potential consequences, and she understands the value of what is before her. She chooses to do what is right, but not out of fear of punishment, or hope of reward, or because she is ever mindful of that eye in the ceiling watching her. The second kid represents religious morality: he makes a choice not to touch the piece of art largely because he is aware of the eye in the ceiling, and he doesn't want to be punished, and he wants a reward at the end. That isn't morality, Sonja argues. That's just being obedient, or merely fearful, or prudent, or greedy.

To be sure, both kids in Sonja's hypothetical scenario did the right thing. But the underlying motivations were quite distinct. And I would agree with Sonja that if we as individuals, when placed in morally ambiguous or potentially precarious situations, make choices because we think the Eye of God is watching us, and we seek to avoid punishment while attaining personal rewards, we aren't being truly moral. But if we make moral choices on our own volition, based on our understanding of what is at stake and what might be gained or lost and who might be harmed or helped, and not because we are being prudently mindful of a cosmic eye waiting to punish or reward us, well, that's *truly* moral.

But there's more. In Sonja's scenario, the child who is only acting morally because of the eye in the ceiling engages in exactly what Milton described: moral outsourcing. He is not relying on his own conscience. He is not depending on his own sense of morality that has been developed through making his own decisions, mistakes, and good choices. Rather, he simply adjusts his behavior because of that eye. But what happens if, at some point down the line, this child begins to doubt the existence of that eye? Well, now we're stuck with an actively immoral individual, who can't rely on himself to do the right thing. The child raised within a secular framework does not risk such a crisis, since her morality is not predicated upon belief in an all-watching eye to begin with.

Such a secular orientation to morality has concrete benefits in the real world: when people make decisions based on their understanding the ramifications of their actions, weighing harm to others versus personal pleasure, without reliance upon or fear of a deity whose existence we can't even be sure of, such a moral orientation is not only more durable—requiring no leaps of faith—but it also lends itself to reasoned decision making, unavoidable self-reflection, and, perhaps most important, an empathetic disposition.

Secular Morality in American Society

In order to see the real-world benefits of secular morality in action, we need not rely on thought experiments. Many recent studies are available that reveal the tangible degree to which secular men and women harbor ideals and exhibit ethical orientations that evidence a deep valuing of life, empathy for the suffering, desire for fairness, and hatred of injustice and cruelty.

For example, consider racism. In a landmark paper published by then Duke University professor Deborah Hall and associates, fifty-five separate studies were carefully analyzed to reveal the relationship between religion, irreligion, and racism. The most interesting finding of this impressive meta-analysis was that strongly religious Americans tend to be the most racist, moderately religious Americans tend to be less racist, and the group found to be the least racist of all are secular Americans, particularly those espousing an agnostic orientation. As psychologists Ralph Wood, Peter Hill, and Bernard Spilka note, basing their assessment upon decades of research, "As a broad generalization, the more religious an individual is, the more prejudiced that person is." Perhaps this helps explain why secular white people were more likely than religious white people to support the civil rights movement, and why secular white South Africans were more likely to be against apartheid than religious white South Africans.

How about feelings about torture? In the aftermath of 9/11, President George W. Bush began allowing for the torturing of prisoners suspected of terrorism. This decision to make government-sponsored torture legal was met with great debate. And in a national survey from 2009, it was found that those Americans who were the most supportive of the governmental use of torture were the most strongly religious, while those who were most opposed to the governmental use of torture were the most secular. The same holds true for support of the death penalty: the more religious tend to be the most supportive of it, favoring vengeance over forgiveness, while the more secular tend to be the most against it, manifesting a more merciful orientation.

Not only are secular people less likely to be racist or vengeful, on average, than religious people, but they are also less likely to be strongly nationalistic. And when we look specifically at militarism, we see that the more religious among us tend to be more in favor of attacking and invading other countries, such as Iraq or Vietnam, while the most secular among us are the least supportive of such military aggression. Secular people are also much more tolerant on all fronts than their religious peers, being more likely to support the civil liberties of people they strongly disagree with or even oppose politically. And as for protecting the environment, religious Americans (especially the most strongly religious) tend to be the least in favor, while atheists and agnostics are the most supportive, and secular Americans are more likely to understand and take seriously the catastrophic threat of global warming than religious Americans. They are also more likely to support women's equality. In fact, secular Americans are much less likely than their religious counterparts to believe that wives should obey their husbands. And what about gay rights? As to be expected, the religious are most likely to be opposed, while the secular are most likely to be supportive. How about the hitting of children? Religious people are, on average, much more supportive of corporal punishment, while secular people are much more likely to be against it. As for the status of illegal immigrants in the United States, the secular are far more supportive of offering a path to legal citizenship status than the religious, who are more likely to insist that there *isn't* any more room at the inn. The secular are also more likely to be concerned with the suffering of animals than the religious.

In sum, when it comes to a host of issues and positions—from torture to war, from global warming to the welfare of animals—secular people clearly feel that it is good to do good in this known lifetime.

Admittedly, secular men and women don't outshine their religious peers in every way. For example, when it comes to generosity, volunteering, and charitable giving, secular men and women fall short, with religious people being more likely to donate both their time and their money. However, as for what is perhaps the ultimate indicator of moral behavior (or lack thereof), namely, violent crime, we know that atheists are grossly *under*represented in our prisons today, with some reports suggesting that atheists make up less than half of 1 percent of all Americans behind bars. A similar underrepresentation of secular folk in prison is found in the United Kingdom as well, suggesting that this is no fluke. As professor of psychology Benjamin Beit-Hallahmi has concluded, "Ever since the field of criminology got started and data were collected of the religious affiliation of criminal offenders, the fact that the unaffiliated and the nonreligious had the lowest crime rates has been noted."

Brian and Paula: Good Without God

The findings of social science, when it comes to revealing the degree to which secular people can be moral without faith in God, are important—nay, essential. The survey data, statistical averages, and opinion polls summarized above provide concrete evidence concerning contemporary secular moral predilections and proclivities.

But in order to get a richer, deeper, and more personable sense of lived secular morality, I'd like to shift away from sociological averages and surveys and introduce you to two living, breathing individuals: Brian Mackelroy and Paula Hendricks. They are both ER nurses who spend their days caring for others in need. Their lives illustrate some profound truths and realities concerning the nature of secular morality.

I'll begin with Brian, who works as an ER nurse at a hospital in one of Wisconsin's larger cities. Brian is thirty-seven years old, married, and the father of twin boys. He was raised a Catholic but started having doubts about his faith in his late teens. And then, when he was twenty-one, he took a philosophy course on existentialism at the University of Wisconsin. At the heart of existentialism is the insistence that each individual, through her own consciousness, must create her own meaning in her life, and there is in fact no grand meaning to the world other than what we ourselves give to it. While it is certainly possible to be an existentialist and also a Christian believer, many people, like Brian, find existentialism to be inimical to traditional religion. "After reading this philosophy, I was, like, 'Oh, wait a minute!'" he says, laughing. "I've been an agnostic with atheist leanings ever since."

Brian's loss of faith did not result in feelings of alienation or despondence—quite the opposite. "It was actually very liberating, losing my faith. It made me want to seize the day more." And his sense of responsibility toward others only strengthened. "We are social creatures. We are interdependent. I think it is just part of our evolved human nature to want to be with each other and to help each other."

The other day at work, Brian tended to a woman who was so drunk that she was essentially unconscious; when she arrived at the ER, her pants and underwear were down below her knees and her body was covered in bruises. The day before that, a man came in with diabetes and advanced cancer—large tumors all over, including his liver and spine. The day before that, a man came in who had been shot by a shotgun at point-blank range; his left shoulder was gone, and his left lung was collapsed. The day before that, a woman came in who had been stabbed multiple times. Day in and day out, Brian helps and comforts people in literal life-and-death situations. "Just recently a woman came in—she had a history of ulcers and colitis. She came in with a perforated bowel—one of the ulcers in her colon ruptured . . . huge infection, lots of internal bleeding . . . and we said, 'We've got to get you to the operating room immediately and we can save you. . . .' And she said, 'No, thank you.' She was about fifty-five. Her sisters had come in, and they were just pleading with her to have the surgery. And she said, 'No.' So I watched this woman exercise her most profound right—the right to decide her own fate. She just kept saying, 'I've had a good life. And up until recently it's been really good. But now I am suffering. I don't want to live like this. I've had a good life, and I am prepared to die.' So I watched her die. And it wasn't a pretty death. Her two sisters were in the room just bawling—really freaking out. And when she died, she just threw up tons of blood—all through her mouth—it was an ugly situation. Fecal matter, blood, the whole thing. And I cleaned her up, gave her sisters as much time as they needed, checked in with them frequently, told them they could have as much time with their dead sister as they wanted. That's really intense, right? But I actually feel privileged to experience such things. It's life. It's death."

Yes, and it's really heavy. It's got to take a toll. How does he keep at it? What keeps him going?

"It gives me real job satisfaction to have positive interactions with people day after day, and I love the amazing sense of teamwork that takes place when someone comes in and they are in real dire need of care—when it is a life-or-death situation—and we're on it and we help them. It can be really heated and really intense, and you can't take things personally at those times—but the interdependence is incredible, and it all comes together. And of course, it seems sort of obvious to say, but it feels really good just working with and helping people. Just helping people. The helping aspect. I enjoy that."

What underlies Brian's personal morality? What's the source?

"I don't know the exact answer to that, to be perfectly honest. But I look at the world through the lens of evolutionary biology. I got my degree in biology. And if you're asking how I can be ethical—how we can have ethics without religion, or without it all being handed down by the word of God—from a natural selection viewpoint, we are social creatures, and in small communities, way back when, people needed to work together and contribute to the greater good, to the group, which was the key to survival."

But if there is no God—no ultimate divine being that establishes morality—then how do we live according to a moral system?

"I would argue that the Golden Rule prevailed long before we decided that it came from a God. And for me, I just look at it in terms of our human evolution. If you take a group of humans living in a situation where they need to work together, need to band together in order to defend themselves from predators and find food and water and shelter, and you throw in the mix someone who tries to manipulate the system for his own good and rob or steal, I think, sure, he may thrive for a little while, but if suddenly more such people emerge and grow and now you have a community of people who are *only* inclined to rob and steal from one another, well, that community is going to fail. They're not going to be able to get their food, water, and shelter. And they're going to be preyed upon. So natural selection has selected for humans who believe 'I'll watch your back if you watch mine and I'll do unto you as I want you to do unto me and if we don't, we're fucked.' To me, that's how human morality started and that's what we've inherited. Being a moral person means not screwing over my fellow tribe members, because I wouldn't want them to screw me over. It's that simple. I don't need to complicate the issue with the notion of a God."

When Brian speculates about the natural, adaptive evolutionary underpinnings of human morality, he is in good company: a growing number of developmental psychologists, evolutionary biologists, historical anthropologists, and primatologists are discovering more and more evidence that bolsters just such a perspective. For example, Matt Ridley, in his book *The Origins of Virtue: Human Instincts and the Evolution of Cooperation*, shows how human trust, mutual aid, and ethical cooperation naturally evolved over time and that such primal instincts helped early humans survive, both as individuals and in groups. In his book *Good Natured: The Origins of Right and Wrong in Humans and Other Animals*, Frans de Waal similarly argues that primate morality, both among humans and our closest primate relatives, is indeed a naturally evolved trait, and that cooperation and humane behavior have been evolutionarily key to our success as a species. De Waal adds more depth in his latest book, *The Bonobo and the Atheist*, arguing that human morality does not come down to us from the heavens, but develops within us naturally as a product of evolution.

Additionally, Cristopher Boehm, in his book *Moral Origins: The Evolution of Virtue, Altruism, and Shame*, asserts that while selfishness certainly has its evolutionary advantages, so too does cooperation. Boehm analyzes the evolutionary role of altruism, arguing that selflessness and mindfulness of others' needs have most definitely played positive roles in the evolution of human thriving. Such research is mushrooming at the moment, and as scientists J. Anderson Thomson and Clare Aukofer sum up, this new research indicates that human morality developed as "an adaptive strategy handed down to us by natural selection." For as psychology professor James Waller explains, since the small social group has been one of the few constants in our evolutionary history, that means that we "have evolved in the context of group living. . . . What are some of the psychological adaptations that enhance the fitness of individuals within a group . . . ? Love, friendship, cooperativeness, preferential and reciprocal altruism, nurturance, friendship, compassion, communication, a sense of fairness . . . in short, the things that hold society together." For any social species, be it early humans or bonobos, the rewards of being part of a group that shares, cares, and looks out for one another generally outweigh the benefits of selfishness.

WHEN IT COMES to caring and looking out for one another, Paula Hendricks is as good a human specimen as they come. Paula is from New Jersey; she is fifty-three years old, divorced, with one daughter. She has worked as a trauma and ER nurse for more than twenty-five years. Like Brian, Paula was raised with religion and definitely believed in God as a child, but by the time she was in her early twenties she wanted nothing more to do with faith, church, or religion.

Working at a hospital in a large city in New Jersey with very high rates of crime and poverty, Paula has seen her share of traumatic cases: stabbing victims, shooting victims, rape victims—and she's seen lots of people die. Sometimes those deaths are peaceful, but sometimes they are painful, prolonged, and gut-wrenching. The many years of such work, however, have not in any way sapped Paula's passion for what she does. "I love being a nurse. A day doesn't go by when I don't love being a nurse. And I feel like every patient is a gift, every interaction is a gift, every experience is a gift. It is a gift about learning about myself and learning about what it means to be human. And that happens, as a nurse, every day, all day long. . . . I'm grateful for the moments I have helping people, that I am able to share with people, every day."

If Paula is ever depressed or distressed about anything, it is the inability of the large hospital she works at to help more people. She feels terrible about the current inadequacies of the American health care system, and how so many people are left unassisted or poorly handled. "We are so overwhelmed—just the volume. Some days I am just so overwhelmed—because what is happening is that people, because they've lost their jobs and they've lost their insurance—we often just can't handle the load of people coming to us for treatment. And some days we have ambulances lined up at the door—and we don't have enough beds. And I always feel like I am fighting to give each patient the very best care, and there's always someone pushing me to move quicker, move on to the next one, that you don't get to give *care*. You're just quickly performing tasks. I hate those days. Because being a nurse is not just about performing tasks. It's about being there for people, talking to them, listening to them. You know, the best thing I can hear is when a patient says to me, 'I just feel so safe in your care.' I want people to feel safe."

Perhaps the hardest times for Paula are when children come in who have been the victims of violence. "I've seen a lot of children—sodomized, abused—just bad, bad things. Just bad. And there's nothing you can appreciate, there's no 'silver lining.' It's just bad." Sometimes, when several such cases come in a given week, she takes a day or two off in order to deal with the sadness and feel good again. But these times are uncommon. Generally, she feels wonderful about what she does, even though it involves encountering so much suffering and death. "I appreciate life so much after I see people die. It is always just such a reminder that every moment—this is all we have. This is it. I don't know if there is anything before or after, but *this* is what we do know. This is it. There are no guarantees for anything else. So we have to always, always appreciate."

Paula's career—her very life's purpose—is deeply moral. It is about tending to those in need. What could be more loving?

So if she doesn't believe in God, where do her morals come from?

"I can't really answer that and I don't think about it that much because, well, I guess I just don't know any people who say things like that or think like that. Yeah, I hear it on the news, and it scares me: 'God says that this is how things should be!'—I can't stand that. I mean, seriously? For me, morality is just about being human. I don't know how else to account for it. It is about people. It is about dignity. It is about pulling up a blanket on someone who is cold. You don't need God for that. You just look at people and think, 'What if this was your mother? Your father? How would you want them to be treated?' I don't know. I guess I just don't really think about it that much. It's just the right thing to do. And I would say that in my entire life this has never come up as much of an issue."

Felix and Gwen: Religionless

Both Brian and Paula were raised with religion. And so perhaps their admirable devotion to others, and the underlying orientation that propels this devotion, were largely shaped or caused by the religion they experienced as children, even if they rejected that religion as adults.

But what about people who were raised without any religion at all, ever? How do they develop their morality, and what compels them to be good? These are important questions, given that the number of people raised without any religion whatsoever, although still quite small, has been steadily increasing in America for many years. Today, nearly 11 percent of American children are raised without any religious influence at home.

Are the children raised in such secular homes disproportionately criminal or malevolent? Absolutely not. No study exists that even suggests that kids raised in secular homes are disproportionately immoral, unethical, or violent. As Benjamin Beit-Hallahmi has observed, "Having no religious affiliation is the best predictor of law-abiding behavior," and "lifelong atheists have been found to be well-socialized . . . and nonviolent."

Felix Campanella is twenty-nine years old. He's from Maryland, but currently lives in Florida with his fiancée. He works as a waiter during the day, and at night he works on his dissertation, which is a critical treatise on the contemporary construction of ethics. His goal is to eventually become a professor. Although a nonbeliever in God for all his life, Felix doesn't like to label himself an atheist. "It just makes it seem like my identity is formed in response to questions about the existence of God, and that's just not true. It would be more accurate to call myself a backpacker or scuba diver or snowboarder—these are much more central to my identity than not believing in God."

Felix explains that his understanding of morality came simply from living. "I lived life. I experienced other people. I've seen people get hurt by other people. I've seen family disputes. I've experienced turmoil. I've seen what *not* caring for other people can do. I've simply learned from experience that when you do genuinely care about others, more good comes from it. So my sense of morality comes from my experiences in life. And having good role models—my parents are good, genuine people."

What would he say to those who insist that we need a divine, transcendent source of ultimate moral authority in the form of God?

"I think it's pretty ludicrous. It takes all of the humanity out of it. It takes our experiences with other people out of the equation. If you're just doing something or not doing something for the pure fact that you were told to do so, or not to do so—it completely ignores the experiences we have, and the pain and suffering that people experience as a result of certain actions. And if people don't see that—if people don't see those connections for themselves, that certain actions lead to certain consequences—then that cheapens our sense of what morality is. To just obey some rules put forth by an invisible deity? No. Morality must stem from our humanity, and from our experiences with other humans. That's it."

EVERY NOW AND THEN I interview people who are so completely secular that they literally have nothing to say about religion, let alone God. And even their being secular is such a nonissue for them that the topic itself elicits little commentary or reflection. For such individuals, religion and secularity have about as much importance, or take up about as much thought in their life, as the latest advances in furniture upholstery, or the political situation in Tajikistan. Whenever I sit down with such a person for an interview, we have our cups of tea steaming before us, the vibe is pleasant enough, and then I turn on the tape recorder, but when I start asking questions about being religious or irreligious, there just isn't that much to say.

That's how it was with Gwen Li. Gwen is twenty-two, and about to graduate from one of America's top liberal arts colleges. Her major is molecular biology. Her senior thesis is on the aging process of hydra—microscopic freshwater organisms that appear to be immortal. After graduation, she'll be attending one of America's most prestigious graduate programs, and her ultimate goal is to do biomedical research in a university lab. Gwen grew up in Iowa, but when she was ten her parents got jobs in Minnesota, where she spent the rest of her childhood. Her mother is a cilia geneticist, and her father is a computational biologist.

Gwen's family never went to church, temple, or mosque. They never prayed. They never did any religious rituals. They never discussed God. They never spoke of spirituality. They never talked about an afterlife. Nor did they ever criticize or speak against such things. Rather, they simply lived their lives without any reference to or discussion of religion—or secularity. Gwen was never told that she was secular, nor did her parents ever say that they were atheists. Thus both religion and its absence were simply nonissues. "One of my best friends in the third grade was Jewish, and that was the first introduction I ever had to people having religion—and all I really got was that they had some special kind of dinner every Friday night. But I didn't know anything more than that."

Today, Gwen has no qualms about identifying herself as an atheist. And for her, given her thoroughly secular, utterly godless upbringing, she understands morality as all boiling down to compassion. And she is quick to point out that she doesn't think being moral is such a big deal or rare phenomenon—nearly everyone she knows, including all her friends and family members, are people whom she would describe as moral. "I don't really know any horrible, immoral people."

How does she feel about the idea that people need religion, or faith in God, to be moral? "I think that completely misses the point. You can easily teach children moral rules independent of such things. And I think that most moral impulses are just pretty intuitive. Even if you aren't taught, you'll figure it out by simply acting immorally— and soon everyone will hate you. Kids can pretty much figure out that they shouldn't steal or lie. You don't need God to make those things obvious."

But if she doesn't think the Eye of God is watching her at all times, what keeps her from doing immoral things, especially if she knows that she could get away with it? For example, if she was alone in the dorms one day, and she saw a purse on the ground with some cash sticking out, and no one was around, why not just take the cash? "I guess I just think that if it were my purse and my money, I would hope that someone would find it and then give it back to me with the money. I think there is just a way that people should behave if they want to be a part of society, and so I try to act that way in how I live. If I want people to help me, I should help them. I mean, it's pretty basic."

When religious people face a moral dilemma, they can pray about it. They can turn to God for direction. But not secular people like Gwen. So I wondered, has she ever faced a real moral quandary? And if so, who or what did she turn to, if not God?

"One time I had a good friend tell me something that she didn't want me to tell other people. She had confided in me, and begged me to keep it a secret. But I felt like I needed to tell other people. She had an eating disorder. It was pretty bad, and could have been really dangerous. I was worried about her. But I had also sworn to her that I wouldn't tell anyone about it. But I felt like she needed help. So I didn't know what to do. I didn't want her to feel betrayed by me, but at the same time, she needed serious help. So I ended up going to another friend that I trusted, and I told her, and then we just tried to figure it out together. We ended up, the two of us, going to this friend together and talking to her and urging her to tell someone, and she eventually went and got help."

As Gwen has gotten older, she's met more and more people who are religious. And she's lived with various religious people in fairly close quarters in the dorms at her college. The question of morality has come up now and then. And this has, on at least one occasion, presented Gwen with a problem. "I just didn't know what to say when this Christian girl asked me where my morals come from. Her answer to that question was really straightforward. She said, 'I get my morals from God.' Or maybe she said, 'I get my morals from the Bible.' Something like that. And that was it. But when she asked me where I get my morals from, I didn't—I was sort of stumped because I didn't have a quick, you know, simple answer."

Secular Morality, Simply Put

Many nonreligious men and women have faced the same dilemma as Gwen. I've heard it from numerous people I've interviewed that when they have been asked where they get their morals from, they've suddenly found themselves tongue-tied. I myself have been questioned by earnest students in class, or I've gotten into it with a colleague, or I've been in public debates with religious believers, and this question of "Where do you get your morals?" has sapped my ability to reply with any sort of aplomb. Where does one even begin to start to answer that? How does one reply to such a query with as pat, succinct, and staunch an answer as the one typically offered by the religious?

The bald truth is, secular morality *doesn't* have a simple, observable, obvious origin. Secular men and women *don't* get their morals from some singular, readily citable source or supernatural deity. Rather, our morals are complex creations. They are the outcome of numerous forces, factors, and influences working simultaneously—many of which we aren't even fully aware of, at least most of the time.

Social science is quite insightful—if not downright stubborn—on this front, revealing just how much our morals are the inevitable result of intrinsically dynamic and often obfuscated processes. For example, we know from the discipline of psychology that our ability to manifest empathy or feel sympathy, shame, guilt, trust, or honor is heavily determined by our early childhood experiences, not to mention innate aspects of our personalities, which can be to varying degrees genetically or hormonally based. From the discipline of neuropsychology, we know how fundamental the intricacies of the brain are in our developing the ability to possess any sense of morality at all. The neuronal wiring of our brain has evolved to give us the capacity to learn, remember, understand, imagine, and thus be empathetic, kind, concerned, and altruistic. But when this wiring is damaged, dysfunctional, or atypical, our ability to employ moral reasoning is hindered, destroyed, or functionally disabled.

From the discipline of sociology, we know that socialization—the informal, often unconscious process of learning how to be, based on what we experience and observe while young—is fundamental to our development as thinking, caring, and loving human beings. The people who raise, nurture, feed, and love us, and all of the experiences we have and the people we interact with and observe as we grow up, shape us to an undeniably strong degree, in both conscious and unconscious ways, so that our very sense of self—and that includes our morality!—is inexorably tied to these unavoidable dynamics of socialization.

From the discipline of anthropology, we know that culture shapes us, defines us, and confines us at all times. Culture is to humans what water is to fish: essential, ever present, and yet all too often invisible. But culture molds much of how we see, interpret, label, and experience the world: our goals and aspirations, our fears and worries, our loyalties and loathings are intrinsically cultural things. And thus no development of individual morality is even possible without culture. And we know that different cultures exhibit different norms, mores, and values—sometimes dramatically different—and thus our own sense of wrong and right is exceedingly, excessively, unavoidably determined by the cultural water within which we swim, whether we like it or not.

From the discipline of criminology, we know that systemic poverty, violence in the home, alcohol and drug abuse, access to firearms, poor nutrition, lack of employment opportunities, and a host of other institutional, economic, and societal factors can all crack a person's moral compass. And finally, from the discipline of history, we know that constructions of morality change and develop over time quite significantly, so that simply *when* a person lives can have an incredible influence on their sense of good and bad, right and wrong, justness and evil, morality and immorality.

Complicated indeed. And as my colleagues within the various disciplines of the social sciences can attest to, what I've just offered above is actually quite cursory, truncated, underdeveloped, and woefully insufficient. For trying to adequately account for "where humans get their morals" is an almost endless endeavor, given the complexity of the sources and processes involved, which are social, psychological, neurological, anthropological, evolutionary, historical—and then some.

But if I could offer a suggestion to Gwen, or any other secular individual out there who'd like a pat, simple answer to the question at hand, I'd offer the following: "I get my morals from the people who raised me, the culture within which I live, the kind of brain that I have, and the lessons I have learned from things I experience as I navigate life."

Of course, in the end, where an individual "gets" his or her morals is of less importance than how those morals are enacted in daily life. If religious people develop their morals through believing in a god, and the result is compassion, kindness, honesty, and altruism, that's wonderful. For secular people, no such deity is necessary, or even intelligible. The Golden Rule—in all its simplicity and universality—suffices.

———

DEBATES ABOUT the costs or benefits of secular versus religious morality have always gotten a lot of lively play in the academic halls of philosophy. And related considerations, or loaded insinuations, frequently flare up within just about any culture war, be it over gay marriage or abortion. But what is new here is the *social* significance of secular morality, because for the first time in history huge chunks of large modern societies are affirmatively secular, with millions of men and women navigating their lives without religion or faith in a divine source of moral guidance.

How are such highly secularized societies faring? Does the existence of more and more secular people in society result in societal decay? Is increasing secularization a menacing threat to the social order?

The answers to these questions may surprise you.

Chapter 2

The Good Society

S
everal years ago, my best friend got stabbed and my mother-in-law fell down half a flight of particularly hard stairs. As you can imagine, these two unfortunate events caused me a good deal of worry and concern. But they did more than that. They provided me with a clear opportunity to reflect upon the underlying relationship between personal life occurrences—be they good or bad—and the wider societal context within which they occur.

Put simply: when bad things happen to people living in dysfunctional, poor societies, those bad things are, well, really bad. Or worse than they need or ought to be. But when bad things happen to people living in well-functioning, affluent societies, those bad things can be dealt with and responded to in such a way that they often aren't as bad as they might have been. So if you happen to suffer a violent assault in a struggling society with underfunded medical facilities, then your chances of being well tended to are obviously less than ideal. But if you happen to take a tough tumble down a cold stairway in a prosperous society with an excellent health care system, well, then your chances of being well tended to and enjoying a speedy recovery are obviously quite good. My best friend's stabbing and my mother-in-law's fall made all of this readily observable.

Let me start with the stabbing. Ami (short for Amatzya) has been my best friend for some twenty years. We met at the University of Oregon, where we shared an office as graduate students in the sociology department. In addition to his love of Bob Dylan, hummus, and bike riding, Ami has always had a deep crush on Jamaica. He's worked and lived there on and off for several years in the northeastern part of the island, and the extensive friendships that he's established there are rich and true.

During one of his more recent trips to Jamaica, while visiting friends in Port Antonio, Ami went to a small bar after dinner. That's where he got stabbed. This is his version of what happened: A woman there, whom he didn't know, kept asking him to buy her a beer. He continually and politely refused, knowing full well that such an act in a rural Jamaican bar can come with strings. But she was persistent. She kept imploring. Finally, just to get her to stop, he bought her a Red Stripe. And that's exactly when her boyfriend entered the bar. When he saw Ami handing her the beer, he assumed that Ami was making moves on his woman. He rushed at Ami from behind and stabbed him in the lower back, aiming for—but fortunately just missing—his left kidney. Blood was quick to spurt, and the entire bar exploded in rage at Ami's assailant, whom they instantly attacked, beating him with their fists and feet and pounding him with metal folding chairs. Although lightheaded and in a state of shock from his profuse bleeding, Ami was of sound enough mind to know that he didn't want to witness a murder; it was actually his pleading and imploring on behalf of his own attacker that got the angry crowd to let up.

Once the mini-riot was quelled, attention turned to Ami's wound. It looked serious. Normally one would call 911 in such a situation, but this is Jamaica. Someone tried to call for an ambulance, but they had no luck; they couldn't get through, and when they finally did, they were told that there were no ambulances available. A friend of a friend said he knew someone with access to a car, so after about an hour, Ami was driven to the closest hospital. After waiting in the over-crowded and less than pleasant waiting room for some time, he was finally able to see a doctor. The doctor examined the wound and said, "You're going to be fine, but you're going to need stitches."

"Okay," Ami replied, relieved.

"But you're going to need stitches," the doctor repeated.

"Yes, okay," Ami again replied. "Go right ahead."

"You don't understand," the doctor continued. "I am telling you that you will need stitches because we don't have stitches at this hospital. We're all out of suture supplies. My deepest apologies."

Ami ended up just covering the wound with some duct tape. Fortunately, no infection ensued, and he recovered without any serious complications. But he was certainly left with a nasty scar.

Now here's what happened to my mother-in-law, who took quite a tumble. It was the same year as Ami's stabbing, although it happened in Denmark, where my family and I were living for the year. I was doing research on secularity in Scandinavia and teaching a couple of classes at Aarhus University, my wife was working on a screenplay, and our kids were in school, learning about Danish kings and queens. We were living in a small IKEA-smitten third-floor apartment on the campus of the university. My mother-in-law came to stay with us for ten days. One afternoon in the middle of her visit, she was playing a game on the outside stairway with my daughter Ruby. Somehow she lost her footing, slipped, and thudded down the stairs. Fortunately, she didn't break anything, but she was bloodied here and quite badly bruised there, and in a lot of pain.

We quickly got her to the local hospital, where she received immediate, excellent care. They took X-rays, treated her cuts and bruises, gave her medication for the swelling, gave her some pain pills, and then double-checked to make sure that nothing serious had unknowingly occurred. And all of this medical attention was totally free, of course— Denmark not only has one of the best health care systems in the world, but it is universal health care; it's free to everyone (including visiting in-laws), provided by the state, and subsidized by progressive taxation.

What these two anecdotes illustrate is just how different Jamaica and Denmark are, at least in terms of what we might refer to as standard measures of societal goodness and well-being. For starters, Jamaica is one of the most violent societies in the world, while Denmark happens to be one of the least violent; the current murder rate in Jamaica is 52 per 100,000, while in Denmark it is less than 1 per 100,000. Just to be clear: that means that there are fifty times more murders, per year, per capita, in Jamaica than in Denmark. And while health care is sadly substandard in Jamaica, Danes enjoy one of the best-developed, best-functioning health care systems on earth, which helps explain why Denmark consistently scores very high on the United Nations Human Development Index.

There are many additional differences between these two small countries—economic, cultural, geographic, demographic, political, and culinary. The history of Jamaica as a brutal, bloody link in the transatlantic slave trade bears significant stressing. And while Jamaica was on the losing end of colonialism, Denmark was certainly on the benefiting end. So yes, the differences between these two societies are many.

But the one key difference I want to highlight here is the matter of religiosity/secularity. Simply put: Most Jamaicans are a very religious lot. Most Danes are not. Most Jamaicans pray a lot. Most Danes don't. Most Jamaicans go to church regularly. Most Danes don't. Most Jamaicans place a lot of importance on faith in God. Most Danes don't.

Most Jamaicans believe that the Bible is the word of God. Most Danes don't. Most Jamaicans believe in heaven and hell. Most Danes don't. Most Jamaicans love Jesus a lot. Most Danes certainly like Jesus, but *love* him? Well, that's a bit much for your typical Dane. In sum, on just about every single indicator one can think of in an effort to measure religiosity or secularity, most Jamaicans lean very strongly toward the religious side, while most Danes lean very strongly toward the secular side.

I am focusing on Jamaica and Denmark—their differences in societal well-being as well as religiosity/secularity—because of what these two small nations represent globally. Jamaica can readily serve as a stand-in for the many nations of the developing world in similar sociological straits: poor, struggling, vulnerable, violent—nations like Haiti, El Salvador, Colombia, Liberia, Zimbabwe, or the Philippines. And Denmark can readily serve as a stand-in for many of the developed nations out there enjoying high levels of prosperity and peacefulness—nations like Norway, New Zealand, Japan, South Korea, Canada, or Australia. And when we compare these types of nations, we see that the religiosity/secularity correlation holds true the world over: the poorer, more chaotic, more troubled countries tend to be among the most religious, while the wealthier, more stable, more well-functioning countries tend to be among the most secular.

And yet this state of the world is not how things are supposed to be—well, at least according to conservative Christians and many other like-minded Americans, who deeply believe and routinely assert that religion is supposed to be good and beneficial for society, while the absence of religion is supposed to be harmful and bad. That is, strongly pious nations (like Jamaica) should be faring the best, while relatively secular nations (like Denmark) should be faring the worst.

But when we actually look around, we find just the opposite state of affairs. As University of London professor Stephen Law has observed,

"If declining levels of religiosity were the main cause of . . . social ills, we should expect those countries that are now the least religious to have the greatest problems. The reverse is true."

The Well-Being of Secular Societies

"No God, no moral society." So declared syndicated radio talk show host Dennis Prager recently in an op-ed in the *Jewish Journal* of Los Angeles. In today's American body politic, Prager's declaration garners much assent. For many Americans—usually the more conservative, but not always—there is a deep and long-standing distrust of atheism and secularism, two growing elements of modern life that many people fear are intrinsically dangerous or detrimental to societal well-being.

Consider former Republican congressional leader, presidential candidate, and best-selling author Newt Gingrich. He is one of our more outspoken religious conservatives, and he repeatedly makes the claim that religion is good and necessary for societal well-being, while the absence of religion is bad. *Really* bad. Indeed, according to Gingrich, a secular society would be hell on earth. As he said during a live television broadcast back in 2011, any country that ignores God or attempts to "drive God out of public life" will surely face all kinds of social problems, and a secular country would be "frankly, a nightmare." A few years earlier, in his 2006 book *Rediscovering God in America*, Gingrich characterized secularism as the most ruthless, destructive force threatening to ruin this country; indeed, if the United States ignores God or fails to worship God, the results will be hellish. In a more recent book, from 2010, Gingrich argued that secularism was as dangerous to society as Nazism. And in the aftermath of the wanton massacre of schoolchildren in Newtown, Connecticut, Gingrich publicly proclaimed that such violence was the obvious result— and inevitable consequence of—secularism in our society.

Newt Gingrich's position is not without its many historical predecessors. For example, in his 1790 classic *Reflections on the French Revolution*, Edmund Burke argued that religion was the underlying basis of civil social order. Voltaire, the celebrated Enlightenment philosopher, argued that without theism society could not function; it is necessary for people to have "profoundly engraved on their minds the idea of a Supreme being and creator" in order to maintain a moral social order. Alexis de Tocqueville, in his 1835 classic *Democracy in America*, argued that religious faith is "indispensable" for a well-functioning society, that irreligion is a "dangerous" and "pernicious" threat to societal well-being, and that nonbelievers are to be regarded as "natural enemies" of social harmony.

Such brazen assertions continue to abound. In addition to the likes of Prager and Gingrich, consider Fox pundit Bill O'Reilly. Back in 2011, during a televised debate with British atheist Richard Dawkins, O'Reilly made the traditional argument that an absence of religion results in societal depravity. "My hypothesis," he declared, "is that religion is a constraint on society." Religious beliefs, according to O'Reilly, hinder "bad behavior." And he's written similar sentiments, declaring in his best-selling books that a society without religion would be anarchic, chaotic, weak, and lawless. Pundit Tammy Bruce concurs; she has argued that Christianity is the "last bastion of morality, values, and decency" and that without it society will be "vague, empty, and lost." Or consider the perspective put forth by Larry Alex Taunton, the executive director of Fixed Point Foundation and the author of *The Grace Effect*. In a prominently placed op-ed on CNN.com in December 2011, Taunton declared that a nation lacking Christian faith is a nation in ruin, a nation in decay. Directly referencing the classic American film *It's a Wonderful Life*, starring Jimmy Stewart,

Taunton argued that societies strong in religious faith will resemble "Bedford Falls" (content, humane, peaceful, and moral), while societies without such religious faith will resemble "Pottersville" (corrupt, harsh, degraded, and immoral).

But the current state of the world reveals a very different picture. Indeed, it is actually among the more secular societies on earth that we find the greatest levels of social harmony, civility, freedom, equality, peacefulness, and prosperity, while it is among the more religious societies that we find the greatest levels of destitution, chaos, insecurity, inequality, oppression, immorality, and poverty. Truth is, the highly secularized "Denmarks" of the world are much closer to resembling the goodness of Bedford Falls, while the highly religious "Jamaicas" of the world come closer to resembling the destitution of Pottersville.

NOW, BEFORE PROCEEDING any further, let me be clear: I don't think that the Denmarks of the world are doing so well *solely* because they are highly secular, and I don't think that the Jamaicas of the world are struggling so much *solely* because they are highly religious. Thus I am certainly not blaming the Jamaicas of the world's problems on their high rates of religiosity, nor am I attributing the Denmarks of the world's success solely to their secularity. Such a view would be horribly simplistic and reductionist. And furthermore, the obvious case could be made that certain countries around the world are highly secular *because* they are doing so well economically, politically, and socially, while other countries are highly religious because they aren't.

Regardless, these results fly in the face of those who say that we need faith in God in order to have a well-functioning society, or that secularism is intrinsically bad for society. Both of these claims are demonstrably false.

To prove it, let's begin by considering which countries today are the most and least God-believing. Drawing on numerous international surveys that reveal what percentage of the population in various countries believes in God, has faith in God, prays to God, and so on, we are able to get a fairly good, reasonably accurate, and widely agreed-upon list of the most and least God-worshipping nations in the world. The most faithful nations on earth—those highest in theism—include Nigeria, Uganda, the Philippines, Pakistan, Morocco, Egypt, Zimbabwe, Bangladesh, El Salvador, Colombia, Senegal, Malawi, Indonesia, Brazil, Peru, Jordan, Algeria, Ghana, Venezuela, Mexico, and Sierra Leone. And as for the least faithful, most secular nations on earth—those with the highest rates of atheism, agnosticism, or theological indifference—we can include Sweden, Denmark, the Czech Republic, Japan, Canada, Norway, Finland, China, New Zealand, South Korea, Estonia, France, Vietnam, Russia, Bulgaria, the Netherlands, Slovenia, Germany, Hungary, Great Britain, Australia, and Belgium.

Okay, so which set of countries is faring the best, on average? According to the claims of many Americans, it should be the most God-loving nations. But such is not the case. Far from it. Rather, it is those countries with the lowest rates of God belief that tend to be the "healthiest" in terms of prosperity, equality, freedom, democracy, women's rights, human rights, educational attainment, crime rates, life expectancy, and so forth (though not all, to be sure, such as Vietnam or China), and it is those nations with the highest rates of God belief that tend to be relatively unsuccessful in terms of any standard sociological measurements of societal health—from having high infant mortality rates to high poverty rates, from entrenched inequality to a stubborn degree of corruption, from lack of clean water to absence of democracy.

Let's consider some specific examples. Take motherhood, something that just about everyone can agree on as being supremely important, if not deeply good. Which countries are the best for mothers? The

Save the Children Foundation, a nonprofit organization, publishes an annual "Mother's Index," wherein they rank the best and worst places on earth in which to be a mother. They take into account a host of factors, such as the percentage of births attended to by skilled personnel, maternity leave benefits, infant mortality rates, and other measures. And according to their most recent annual reports, of the top ten best nations on earth in which to be a mother, *all* are highly secularized nations, with most being among the *least* theistic nations on earth. Of the bottom ten worst nations in which to be a mother, *all* are highly religious, such as Yemen, Mali, and Niger. Not a single one of the most theistic nations ranks among the best nations on earth in which to be a mother, and many, like Bangladesh, Uganda, Sierra Leone, Senegal, and Nigeria, rank among the very bottom.

Consider peacefulness, yet another phenomenon that almost everyone can agree is a societal good. Which countries today are the most peaceful? Not the very religious ones. Rather, it is the least God-fearing nations that enjoy the greatest levels of peace. Just ask the nonprofit organization called Vision of Humanity, which publishes an annual "Global Peace Index." They calculate numerous variables, such as levels of safety and security in a given society, levels of violent crime, warfare, and ease of access to dangerous weapons, when compiling their index. And according to their most recent rankings, among the top ten most peaceful nations on earth, *all* are among the least God-believing—in fact, eight of the ten are specifically among the least theistic nations on earth. Conversely, of the bottom ten—the least peaceful nations—most of them are extremely religious. For example, Mexico ranks number 121, the Philippines number 136, Colombia number 139, Zimbabwe number 140, and Pakistan number 146.

One final variable: murder. If there is any one single, widely agreed-upon pathological element in a society, it is murder. So which countries have the highest murder rates? Which have the lowest? According to the United Nations 2011 *Global Study on Homicide*, of the nations with the highest intentional homicide rates, all are very religious/ theistic, and many—such as Colombia, Mexico, El Salvador, and Brazil—are among the most theistic nations in the world. But of those at the bottom of the list—the nations with the lowest homicide rates— nearly all are very secular, with seven being among the least theistic nations, such as Sweden, Japan, Norway, and the Netherlands. Additional research by sociologists and criminologists such as James Fox, Jack Levin, and Pablo Fajnzylber shows that murder rates are significantly lower in the more secular nations on earth, where atheism and agnosticism are more common, and higher in the more religious nations, where faith in God is widespread. Indeed, Robert Brenneman is a sociologist who studies gangs in Central America, and based on his extensive fieldwork, he notes that among the most violent, brutal barrios of El Salvador, Honduras, and Guatemala, atheism and agnosticism are virtually nonexistent.

The best countries in which to be a mother, the most peaceful countries, those countries with the lowest murder rates—their populations generally tend to be quite secular. And this correlation holds true for nearly every measure of societal well-being imaginable, such as levels of corruption in business and government, sexually transmitted disease rates, teen pregnancy rates, literacy rates, quality of hospital care, quality of roads and highways, rates of aggravated assault, degree of freedom of speech and freedom of the press, environmental degradation, pollution, sanitation, access to clean drinking water, voter turnout, and so on. We can even look at various studies that measure subjective happiness. Year after year, nations like Denmark, Norway, and Sweden, the least religious countries in the Western world, report the highest levels of happiness among their populations, while countries like Benin, Togo, and Burundi, which are among the most religious nations on earth, are the least happy.

One scholar who has researched this matter extensively is Gregory S. Paul, and he has created a "Successful Societies Scale," in which he tries to objectively measure a whole array of variables that are indicative of societal goodness and well-being. When he measures such factors as life satisfaction, incarceration rates, fertility rates, alcohol consumption rates, per capita income, inequality, and employment rates, and correlates them with religiosity/secularity, his findings are unambiguously clear: aside from the important but exceedingly outlying exception of suicide—religious societies have significantly lower suicide rates than more secular societies—on just about every other measure of societal goodness, the less-religious nations fare markedly better than the more-religious nations.

SO THE PATTERN is indisputable when comparing and contrasting countries from around the world. But let's bring this discussion closer to home and see if the same pattern also emerges when we look within our country. It does, unmistakably. The correlation of high rates of secularity with societal well-being remains evident and robust when looking at our fifty states. For when we compare the most religious states in terms of faith/belief in God with the least religious states, we find that yet again the least theistic states tend to fare better, on average, than the most theistic.

The ten states that report the highest levels of belief in God are Louisiana, Arkansas, Alabama, Mississippi, Georgia, South Carolina, North Carolina, Kentucky, Tennessee, and Oklahoma (tied with Utah). The ten states with the lowest levels of belief in God are Maine, Vermont, Connecticut, New Hampshire, Rhode Island, Massachusetts, New York, Alaska, Oregon, and California. It is important to remember, of course, that the populations of the last ten states listed are not wholly secular—far from it. In all of them, a majority of residents still believe in God. But the rates of theism are simply much lower in the latter ten than in the former ten. So, for example, 91 percent of people in Mississippi and 86 percent of people in South Carolina claim to believe in God "with absolute certainty," but only 54 percent of people in Vermont and 59 percent of people in Maine do so. And only 1 percent of people in Kentucky explicitly claim to not believe in God, compared to 9 percent in Oregon.

As expected, when it comes to nearly all standard measures of societal health, such as homicide rates, violent crime rates, poverty rates, domestic abuse rates, obesity rates, educational attainment, funding for schools and hospitals, teen pregnancy rates, rates of sexually transmitted diseases, unemployment rates, domestic violence, the correlation is robust: the least theistic states in America tend to fare much, much better than the most theistic. In fact, *Forbes* magazine recently ranked all fifty states in terms of the overall best and worst places to live, taking into account various national indexes and calculating numerous variables, such as self-reported levels of life satisfaction, physical health, job opportunities, economic opportunity, and basic access to food and shelter, and the expected correlation is there again: the most theistic of states clustered toward the bottom of the rankings, being among the worst places to live, while the more secular states clustered toward the top, being among the better places to live overall.

Heck, we can simply look at which states have higher rates of child abuse fatalities—perhaps the most heinous, tragic form of violence imaginable. On average, the rates of kids being beaten to death by their own parents are markedly higher among the most God-fearing states, and significantly lower among the most God-indifferent. For example, the child-abuse fatality rate in Mississippi is twice that of New Hampshire, and Kentucky's is four times higher than Oregon's.

As the data above reveals, high rates of secularity or nonbelief do not result in communal decay or contribute to societal degradation. And conversely, high levels of faith or religiosity don't seem to produce impressive levels of societal well-being. Gingrich and his ilk are simply wrong.

Common Critiques Considered

Whenever I bring this matter up—be it in some op-ed on *Huffington Post*, or while attending an academic conference with esteemed scholars, or while riding on an airplane next to some businessman from Wichita who wants to know what kind of work I do—I am met with the same standard critiques. Here they are:

First, people will insist that correlation is not causation. This is all too true. Just because secularity is correlated with societal well-being doesn't mean it is actually *causing* it. There are many, many factors— economic, demographic, historical, cultural, political, geographical— that are responsible for creating and causing societal goodness, and they may be much more important or significant than mere rates of secularity in a given population. And as alluded to earlier, it is quite likely that when societies become wealthy, peaceful, egalitarian, and democratic, secularity ensues. In other words, secularity does not necessarily cause societal goodness and well-being, but rather it may be the other way around. Independent researcher R. Georges Delamontagne's studies reveal just that: it is not a lack of secularity that causes societal dysfunction, but rather it is societal dysfunction that causes a lack of secularity.

Admitting all of the above, however, I would still argue that in many instances, and in the historical development of many societies, secularism—being a conscious, nonspiritual, rational ideology for social betterment in the here and now—has definitely been a key causal ingredient instigating and promoting various forms of societal goodness and contributing to beneficial social progress. For merely one significant example, consider the major historical-political improvement in the West that successfully moved us away from divine-right monarchies to modern-day democracies—this beneficial shift was largely spearheaded by secular philosophies and humanistic ideologies. The essential, progressive divorcing of religious authorities from the halls of government is truly one of secularism's greatest gifts to modern society. Women's rights is another obvious societal improvement that has been specifically spurred on by secularism; just about wherever secularism has become a strong force in society, the status, health, and wealth of women have dramatically improved. Secularism has also played a powerful role in the fight against caste in India. And it has been essential in the development of sane, effective sex education. And the creation of the enviably successful welfare state in Scandinavia was envisioned and enacted by decidedly secular social democrats.

A second criticism that often arises when discussing the correlation between secularity and societal goodness is the unavoidable matter of all those horrible atheist regimes of the twentieth century, like the former Soviet Union under Stalin or Cambodia under Pol Pot. We can hardly call such antireligious, ardently secularist societies models of societal goodness. There is no question that totalitarianism plus atheism makes for an ugly, repressive combination. But atheism isn't the main problem here; totalitarianism is. After all, some of the world's most tyrannical, corrupt regimes of the past century have also been explicitly religious: Uganda under Idi Amin, Zimbabwe under Robert Mugabe, Haiti under "Baby Doc" Duvalier, Chile under Augusto Pinochet, Iran under the ayatollahs, Spain under Francisco Franco, the Philippines under Ferdinand Marcos, the apartheid regime in South Africa—heck, the Third Reich under Adolf Hitler, a Catholic who was perpetually in good standing with the Vatican.

But rather than get into a meandering, macabre, and possibly point-less tallying of religious dictators versus atheist dictators, it is better to simply acknowledge that when state power is held undemocratically, the result will always be deleterious. That is, *all* non–democratically elected regimes of the past century have been corrupt. Fascism, totali-tarianism, communism—all such modern forms of political domi-nance have been based on might and repression, rather than freedom and liberty. They have all squelched societal progress and severely lim-ited societal well-being, be they religious or secular in form or façade.

Just as religion comes in all shapes and sizes—some vicious, others benevolent—so it goes with secularism. It is thus essential to always differentiate between secularity that emerges organically in a free culture versus secularism that is forcefully imposed upon a nation by totalitarian regimes. These are two very different vegetables alto-gether. In the totalitarian situation, religion is demonized and often outlawed, believers are vilified or worse, and the whole situation is not only repressive and inhumane, but generally quite untenable. But in the other, more organic situation—and this is the situation we're now witnessing in the United States and elsewhere in much of the world today—many people living in open, democratic societies simply stop finding religious beliefs sustainable or compelling, they lose interest in participating in religious organizations, and they maintain values, exhibit virtues, find meaning, and develop a sense of identity outside the canopy of religious faith. And as the data presented in this chapter shows, this cultural, organic manifestation of secularism is not a det-rimental threat to society, but if anything is correlated with positive societal outcomes.

So even if we admit that correlation is not causation, and even when we acknowledge that some of the worst societies of the past century have been led by atheist tyrants (as well as religious tyrants), we are still left with the undeniable reality that today, when we compare nations, as well as states within nations, the more secular are faring qualitatively and quantitatively better than the more religious, which are faring worse on just about every indicator of societal goodness imaginable. It may not be *because* they are religious, but their religiosity is clearly no panacea, to be sure.

I'VE ARGUED IN this chapter that a loss or weakening of religion is not detrimental or dangerous to society. But I've gone further than that by showing that those countries around the world—and those states within our own nation—that have undergone a process of organic secularization are actually faring much better than the religious on just about every measure that one can imagine. Societal well-being and secular living thus seem to go hand in hand. Not always, to be sure— throw a maniacal atheist dictator into the mix and things can get very ugly very fast. But when you've got a more democratic situation in which millions of individuals simply happen to live their lives without faith in God or much concomitant participation in religious rituals or religious organizations, and when such organically secular societies and cultures emerge freely and nonaggressively, the result is glowingly positive.

And this is good news. For as I mentioned in the introduction, there are more secular men and women alive today than ever before. And their numbers continue to increase. Why this is happening is the subject of the next chapter.

Chapter 3

Irreligion Rising

Secularity is not completely new. There have always been people who doubted religious teachings, were suspicious of priests, rabbis, gurus, and imams, and felt uncomfortable in pews. There have always been men and women, even thousands of years ago, who were—in the gracious of words of Max Weber—religiously unmusical. And thus before accounting for the recent wave of secularization currently surging in our country—and in so many other countries today—a brief acknowledgment of the rich history and quite prominent existence of secularity throughout the ages is warranted.

Consider, for example, a group of philosophers known as the Carvaka, who lived in India during the seventh century BCE. We're talking some twenty-eight hundred years ago, and in one of the most religious regions on earth. And yet even so long ago, and even in such a location, we find clear evidence of secularity in the doggedly naturalistic philosophy of these skeptical men. The views and teachings of the Carvaka—adherents of a school of philosophy known as Lokayata—constitute some of the earliest examples of consciously, purposively articulated secularism. The Carvaka were materialist thinkers who rejected the supernaturalism of ancient Hindu religion and were vociferous in their mockery of religious authorities. They were essentially atheists who saw no evidence for the existence of god or karma or any afterlife whatsoever. "Only the perceived exists," they argued, and "there is no world other than this."

Beyond the Carvaka of ancient India, we can find additional evidence of early irreligion in the philosophy of Xunzi, who lived in China in the third century BCE. Xunzi taught that there is no heaven other than the natural world and that morality is not divinely established but humanly constructed. Also from China, we find the proto-secular, naturalistic skepticism of Wang Ch'ung, from two thousand years ago, who argued that there is nothing spiritual or supernatural behind the wonders of the world, that fortune and misfortune are the mere result of chance alone, and that immortality is impossible.

Existential angst and earnest doubt are also abundant within the writings of the Jewish philosopher known as Kohelet of ancient Israel, third century BCE. Kohelet, the presumed author of the book of Ecclesiastes, suggested that all life is ultimately meaningless and that there is no life after death—facts that may be disheartening, and yet should not keep us from enjoying what we can, loving those around us, and seeking to do good. And the unknown author of the book of Job gave clear voice to ancient Jewish doubt and skepticism, an orientation that emerged even more prominently in Central Asia in the ninth century with the overt skepticism of Jewish philosopher Hiwi al-Balkhi, who blatantly questioned the divinity of the Torah, reportedly causing many people to lose their faith.

Emergent agnosticism, antireligiosity, and an all-around debunking orientation are also well represented among the ancient Greeks and Romans of the classical age. For example, Lucretius argued that the gods did not exist, that there was no life after death, and that everything we experience, even the most wondrous, is essentially natural. Epicurus taught that death is a nothingness that no one need fear and yet its unavoidable eventuality renders our efforts to enjoy this life all the more pressing, and that this life is, or most certainly can be, pleasurable and good. Democritus rejected the existence of anything divine, and argued that an individual's morality must stem from his or her own sense of self-respect. Protagoras articulated a proto-agnosticism, believing that it was simply impossible to know, one way or the other, whether gods existed or not. Carneades, a true skeptic, debunked standard arguments for theism and theories of divine creation. Anaximander sought to understand the workings of the universe scientifically, and was an early proponent of a naturalistic orientation. These individuals are but a handful among many other voices from ancient Greece and Rome who criticized the truth claims of religion and articulated a very secular this-worldly ethos.

But wait—there's more. We can also turn to early Islamic civilization for evidence of secular thought weaving throughout the past. There is the critical rationalism of Muhammad al-Warraq of the ninth century, who doubted the existence of Allah and was skeptical of religious prophets; there are the freethinking, antireligious assertions of Muhammad al-Razi of the early tenth century, who was overt in his criticisms of religion and worked hard to advance the sciences of physics, chemistry, and medicine; and then there are the soothing, inspirational affirmations of Omar Khayyám of eleventh-century Persia, who waxed poetic about the all too natural, all too mysterious, and yet compelling beauty of existence. "Men talk of heaven," he noted, yet "there is no heaven but here." And then we have the towering intellectual figure of Averroes of twelfth-century Córdoba, considered a founding father of nascent secular philosophy; Averroes's skepticism was so pronounced that the poet Dante included him by name in his *Divine Comedy* as one of those prominent heretics who dwells in hell.

In short, the evidence of various nascent forms of what we today would refer to as agnosticism, skepticism, atheism, naturalism, secularism, and humanism throughout history, going back even thousands of years, is quite rich.

It must be granted, however, that such secular expressions and articulations from long ago represented a tiny minority of humanity. Secular men and women were undeniably few and far between in the past, especially a thousand years ago. Or even a hundred years ago.

But today, they are rare no more.

In the beginning of the twenty-first century, secularity abounds. There are now literally hundreds of millions of people who eschew religious faith and religious involvement in favor of other forms of association and a decidedly naturalistic worldview. And in their recent research, demographers Vegard Skirbekk, Eric Kaufmann, and Anne Goujon have documented what may very well be a historic first: there are now more people leaving religion than embracing it.

So while the existence of secularity is nothing new, what *is* new is the sheer scope and magnitude of that secularity in our world today. Secularity has never been so widespread, open, or overt.

What the Numbers Reveal

Secularization is the historical process whereby religious faith, religious involvement, religious identification, and religious institutions weaken, fade, or become less significant in society. And while secularization is in no way inevitable or irreversible—what social phenomenon is?—when we look at the world today, the evidence for dramatic trajectories of secularization, occurring in many countries all over the world, is simply staggering.

Consider, for example, that in Canada one hundred years ago, only 2 percent of the population claimed to have no religion. But today nearly 30 percent of Canadians claim as much, and approximately one in five Canadians does not believe in God. Or consider Australia, where a hundred years ago less than 1 percent of the population claimed no religious identity, but today approximately 20 percent of Australians claim as much—and the country's recent prime minister Julia Gillard is an open atheist. Exploding rates of secularity are even more dramatic in Europe. A century ago in Holland, around 10 percent of the population claimed to be religiously unaffiliated; today, it is more than 40 percent. In contemporary Great Britain, nearly half of the people now claim no religious identity at all, and British historian Callum Brown has documented the degree to which "a formerly religious people have entirely forsaken organized Christianity in a sudden plunge into a truly secular condition." We find a similar situation in Sweden, where religion has become exceedingly marginal, and approximately half the population self-identifies as secular. Furthermore, 61 percent of Czechs, 49 percent of Estonians, 45 percent of Slovenians, 34 percent of Bulgarians, and 31 percent of Norwegians do not believe in God. Thirty-three percent of the French, 27 percent of Belgians, and 25 percent of Germans do not believe in God *or* any sort of universal spiritual life force. And the most recent survey information from Japan illustrates extensive secularization over the course of the last century: sixty years ago, about 70 percent of the Japanese claimed to hold personal religious beliefs, but today that figure is down to only about 20 percent. Such levels of atheism, agnosticism, and overall irreligion are simply remarkable—not to mention historically unprecedented. And beyond those nations mentioned above, there are also significant chunks of nonreligious people in regions all around the globe—including Uruguay, Chile, South Korea, Israel, and Azerbaijan—to name several disparate examples.

What about us?

For many years, the United States—"God's country"—has been held up as a glaring exception to this widely observable wave of secularization. Rates of religious belief and church attendance have persistently been much stronger here than in other industrialized democracies, especially Europe. And while this certainly still holds true—Americans, on average, continue to be a relatively religious lot—secularity has nonetheless increased significantly in the United States over the past twenty-five years. As Harvard professor Robert Putnam has recently acknowledged, there is now a truly burgeoning "secular swath" in this country.

Consider the following:

- The percentage of Americans who claim "none" when asked their religion has grown from less than 10 percent in 1990 up to somewhere between 20 and 30 percent today. This means that the number of "nones" in America has increased by well over 200 percent over the last twenty-five years, making it the fastest-growing "religious" orientation in the country.
- In absolute numbers, during the last decade approximately 660,000 Americans every year have joined the ranks of those claiming no religion, and there are now between 38 and 45 million nonreligious adult Americans. So nonreligious Americans are now the second largest "religious" group in the country, and Americans without a religious affiliation now comprise the only "religious" group growing in all fifty states.
- Between one-third and one-half of all "nones" are atheist or agnostic in orientation, and about a quarter believe in a "higher power," while only about 20 percent believe in a "personal God." So the rise of irreligion also means a simultaneous rise of atheism and agnosticism as well, something the Harris Poll has been documenting in recent years. Indeed, somewhere between 9 per-

cent and 21 percent of Americans are now atheist or agnostic—
the highest rates of nonbelief ever seen in U.S. history.

- Twenty-seven percent of Americans currently claim not to practice any religion, with 22 percent specifically stating that that
religion is "not a factor" in their lives.

- Rates of secularity are markedly stronger among younger Americans: 32 percent of Americans under age thirty are religiously
unaffiliated. This is a significant change from a few decades ago.
In the 1980s there were twice as many evangelical Americans in
their twenties than there were "nones," but today we find just the
opposite: twenty-something "nones" now outnumber twenty-
something evangelicals by a ratio of two to one.

- The vast majority of nonreligious Americans are content with
their current identity; among those men and women today who
now claim "none" as their religion, nearly 90 percent say they
have no interest in looking for a religion that might be right for
them.

Sally: Religious, Secular, or Neither?

While the numbers, percentages, and statistics above certainly indicate a significant growth of secularity in many parts of the world, as
well as here in America, they don't properly illustrate, accurately designate, or successfully capture the undeniably pervasive reality that
is Sally.

Sally LaConte is in her mid-forties. She enjoys ceramics, jewelry
making, and Chowhound.com. Sally is from Ohio. Her husband, Dale,
is an unapologetic atheist; he doesn't believe in God, he has no interest
in religion, and he is annoyed every time their son's Little League
baseball game begins with a group prayer. Sally is certainly secular,

but at the same time, she's definitely not an atheist—not like her husband, anyway. That is, while she doesn't identify with a religion per se, she's also not completely this-worldly in her outlook.

Sally was raised Catholic, but she rejected that tradition long ago, and she and her husband have raised their kids without any religious involvement whatsoever. Her kids are "nothings," as Sally likes to offhandedly joke. It is a joke, I sense, that evokes both pride and shame. On the one hand, Sally is proud that her kids are not shackled by beliefs she finds problematic. She is also proud that they haven't had a label of some religion or denomination foisted upon them; they are just themselves, their own individuals. But there is also a hint of worry or self-doubt in Sally's laugh as she describes her kids as "nothings." Similar to Jill, whom we met in the introduction, Sally worries that maybe she is being negligent as a parent by not raising them within an established religious tradition, like so many of the other kids in the neighborhood.

In responding to this worry, I said to Sally, "Why not just say that they are 'secular humanists'?" Her reply: "Then I'd have to explain to people what the heck that even is. I'm not even so sure myself." Fair enough.

Although Sally is nonreligious and doesn't raise her kids with religion, her secularity is not absolute. It is not clear-cut. For in her heart of hearts, Sally does believe. In God? Well, that depends on what you mean by "God." The term itself is not without its difficulties for her. She definitely does not believe in the God of Catholicism. Rather, she will say that she believes in *something*. What she associates with this *something* are concepts like love, hope, infinity, transcendence. And although religion is not at all a part of her daily life, she does have a small stash of assorted angels that she adores, which she displays with pride as part of her household decorations every Christmas. The point here is that Sally is like millions of Americans: not religious, but not totally secular either.

CLEARLY, NOT EVERYONE fits into a perfect little box labeled "atheist" or "Christian" or "secular" or "religious." Such categories are seldom, if ever, airtight. More often than not, they blend and bleed into one another. It is messy. Most religious people are secular in certain respects, and most secular people are religious in certain respects. Many scholars recognize this complexity, and they have concocted a plethora of terms to try to capture the messiness.

For example, sociologist David Voas speaks of "fuzzy fidelists"—people who are not adherents of a given religious tradition and yet do maintain a variety of supernatural beliefs. These might be people who eschew the Christianity of their parents but believe in ghosts or reincarnation. They might be people who were raised secular, and still consider themselves secular, and yet believe in karma as an actual spiritual, cosmic reality pervading the universe. In other words, they aren't religious in any traditional sense, and yet they also aren't absolute rationalist, empiricist, skeptical atheists either. And Robert Putnam talks about "liminals"—people who are "betwixt and between" a religious and secular identity, standing halfway in and halfway out of a given religious/irreligious identity. They occupy that "gray" space, not feeling religious or self-identifying as a believer, and yet simultaneously not feeling wholly secular or identifying as a bona fide agnostic or convinced atheist.

To add yet another type into the mix, Grace Davie has recognized the existence of people whom we could classify as "believing without belonging"—that is, folks who maintain personal religious beliefs but eschew religious involvement. These are men and women who, if asked in a survey, "Are you religious?" will most likely say, "No." And if asked, "What is your religion?" they'll probably say, "None." And yet if asked, "Do you believe in God?" they will say, "Yes." There are quite a lot of just such believers who don't belong to any church, synagogue, or mosque. And yet, conversely, there are just as many people out there, and maybe even more, who actually "belong without believing"; that is, folks who are active in religious congregational life, identify with a given religious tradition, and yet don't actually believe in God— or anything supernatural—at all. As my father likes to joke, "Shlomo goes to synagogue to talk to God. I go to synagogue to talk to Shlomo." I even personally know some actual pastors of religious congregations who, when pushed during a private conversation over a beer, will admit that they don't actually believe in God, or Jesus, or heaven, or hell. Yet they preach these things to their flocks nonetheless. So what are we to make of such belongers who don't believe? Are they religious or secular? Hard to say.

And closely related to this last type of people who belong but do not believe are the many men and women out there who could accurately be described as "culturally religious"—people who readily identify as being "Lutheran" or "Catholic" or "Muslim" in a sort of ethnic or heritage sense, but don't actually believe in any of the supernatural tenets or articles of faith of their religious tradition. They don't belong to a religious congregation, they don't believe in (or even necessarily know) the specific tenets, creeds, or dogmas of their religion, and yet if asked, "What are you?" will still identify as "Episcopalian" or "Christian" or "Sunni."

And then there are also those whom the philosopher John Shook has characterized as "apatheists"—people who, when it comes to the God question, just don't really care. They are usually apathetic, indifferent. Got other things on their mind.

And finally, there are various types of apostates—people who were once religious but are no longer, having rejected the religion they once adhered to.

Thus the simple binary of religious/secular won't do—at least not in the real world. So one useful way to conceive of the complexity of actual lived religiosity and secularity—and this schema has been developed by anthropologist Frank Pasquale—is to consider religiosity and secularity as existing on an imagined continuum, such as a ten-point scale. At one end of the spectrum (at number 1), are people who are totally, thoroughly, and completely religious in all aspects we might think of—from belief to behavior to self-identification. Think of a Buddhist monk who meditates eighteen hours a day in seclusion. Or a deeply pious nun who does little else other than pray, fast, study the Bible, and tend to the tasks of the cloister. They might be a 1. At the other end of the spectrum (at number 10), are people who are totally, thoroughly, and completely secular in all conceivable aspects. It is harder to come up with an obvious, readily familiar example of a completely secular existence. But perhaps you can think of a kindergarten teacher who loves dogs, collects old records, and has never felt a religious impulse or experienced a religious ritual or pondered a religious thought in his lifetime. He might be a 10. But the key thing to remember is that precious few people are complete 1s or 10s. Most are somewhere in between, perhaps leaning more toward one end of the spectrum than the other, and even veering in different directions at different times throughout the course of their lives.

And yet what is apparent today, and what largely underlies the very writing of this book, is that—as the statistics presented earlier reveal—more and more people are now veering more closely toward the secular end of the continuum than ever before. As social psychologists Bruce Hunsberger and Bob Altemeyer have succinctly put it, "The 'unreligious' are swelling in number faster than any religious group."

Sally is actually a perfect illustration of this recent societal process of secularization. Sally's great-grandparents, immigrants from Italy, were utterly devout in all respects, with nary a secular bone in their bodies. Her grandparents were also religious, but much less so; less church-attending, less sin-confessing, less Mary-loving. Her parents were even less religious than they were. And now we get to Sally, who is no longer Catholic, never attends church, didn't baptize her babies, and doesn't even believe in the concept of "sin." Although definitely not an atheist, she is still far less religiously involved and much less faithful than either her grandparents or parents were. In terms of her overall worldview, she has more in common with her nonbelieving husband than her local priest. And we can only surmise how Sally's kids will turn out—her "nothings," who have been raised with virtually no religion at all, save for their mom's angel collection that decorates the house at Christmastime.

Causes

What is going on? How do we explain this recent wave of secularization that is washing over not only Sally LaConte's family but so much of America as well?

The answer to these questions is actually much less theological or philosophical than one might think. It is simply not the case that in recent years tens of millions of Americans have suddenly started doubting the cosmological or ontological arguments for the existence of God, or that hundreds of thousands of other Americans have miraculously embraced the atheistic naturalism of Denis Diderot. Sure, this may be happening here and there, in this or that dorm room or on this or that Tumblr page. The best-sellers written by Richard Dawkins, Christopher Hitchens, and Sam Harris—as well as the irreverent impiety and flagrant mockery of religion by the likes of Jon Stewart, Stephen Colbert, Bill Maher, *House*, *South Park*, and *Family Guy*—have had some impact on American culture. As we have seen, a steady, incremental uptick of philosophical atheism and agnosticism is discernible in America in recent years. But the larger reality is that for the many millions of Americans who have joined the ranks of the nonreligious, the causes are most likely to be political and sociological in nature.

For starters, we can begin with the presence of the religious right, and the backlash it has engendered. Beginning in the 1980s, with the rise of such groups as the Moral Majority and the Christian Coalition, the closeness of conservative Republicanism with evangelical Christianity has been increasingly tight and publicly overt. Throughout the 1990s and 2000s, more and more politicians on the right embraced the conservative Christian agenda, and more and more outspoken conservative Christians allied themselves with the Republican Party. Examples abound, from Michele Bachmann to Ann Coulter, from Mike Huckabee to Pat Robertson, and from Rick Santorum to James Dobson. With an emphasis on seeking to make abortion illegal, fighting against gay rights (particularly gay marriage), supporting prayer in schools, advocating "abstinence only" sex education, opposing stem cell research, curtailing welfare spending, supporting Israel, opposing gun control, and celebrating the war on terrorism, conservative Christians have found a warm welcome within the Republican Party, which has been clear about its openness to the conservative Christian agenda. This was most pronounced during the eight years that George W. Bush was in the White House.

What all of this this has done is alienate a lot of left-leaning or politically moderate Americans from Christianity. Sociologists Michael Hout and Claude Fischer have published compelling research indicating that much of the growth of "nones" in America is largely attributable to a reaction against this increased, overt mixing of Christianity and conservative politics. The rise of irreligion has been partially related to the fact that lots of people who had weak or limited attachments to religion and were either moderate or liberal politically found themselves at odds with the conservative political agenda of the Christian right and thus reacted by severing their already somewhat weak attachment to religion. Or as sociologist Mark Chaves puts it, "After 1990 more people thought that saying you were religious was tantamount to saying you were a conservative Republican. So people who are not Republicans now are more likely to say that they have no religion."

A second factor that helps account for the recent rise of secularity in America is the devastation of, and reaction against, the Catholic Church's pedophile priest scandal. For decades the higher-ups in the Catholic Church were reassigning known sexual predators to remote parishes rather than having them arrested and prosecuted. Those men in authority thus engaged in willful cover-ups, brash lawbreaking, and the aggressive slandering of accusers—and all with utter impunity. The extent of this criminality is hard to exaggerate: over six thousand priests have now been credibly implicated in some form of sex abuse, five hundred have been jailed, and more victims have been made known than one can imagine. After the extent of the crimes—the rapes and molestations as well as the cover-ups—became widely publicized, many Americans, and many Catholics specifically, were disgusted. Not only were the actual sexual crimes themselves morally abhorrent, but the degree to which those in positions of power sought to cover up these crimes and allow them to continue was truly shocking. The result has been clear: a lot of Catholics have become ex-Catholics. For example, consider the situation in New England. Between 2000 and 2010, the Catholic Church lost 28 percent of its members in New Hampshire and 33 percent of its members in Maine, and closed nearly seventy parishes—a quarter of the total number—throughout the Boston area. In 1990, 54 percent of Massachusetts residents identified as Catholic, but it was down to 39 percent in 2008. And according to an "American Values" survey from 2012, although nearly one-third of Americans report being raised Catholic, only 22 percent currently identify as such—a precipitous nationwide decline indeed.

Of course, the negative reaction against the religious right and the Catholic pedophile scandal both have to do explicitly with religion. But a very important third possible factor that may also account for the recent rise of secularity has nothing to do with religion. It is something utterly sociological: the dramatic increase of women in the paid labor force. British historian Callum Brown was the first to recognize this interesting correlation: when more and more women work outside the home, their religious involvement—as well as that of their families—tends to diminish. Brown rightly argues that it has been women who have historically kept their children and husbands interested and involved in religion. Then, starting in the 1960s, when more and more British women starting earning an income through work outside the home, their interest in—or time and energy for—religious involvement waned. And as women grew less religious, their husbands and children followed suit. We've seen a similar pattern in many other European nations, especially in Scandinavia: Denmark and Sweden have the lowest levels of church attendance in the world, and simultaneously, Danish and Swedish women have among the highest rates of outside-the-home employment of any women in the world. And the data shows a similar trajectory here in America. Back in the 1960s, only 11 percent of American households relied on a mother as their biggest or sole source of income. Today, more than 40 percent of American families are in such a situation. Thus it may very well be that as a significantly higher percentage of American moms earn a living in the paid labor force, their enthusiasm for and engagement with religion is being sapped, and that's playing a role in the broader secularization of our country.

Additional Factors

In addition to the above factors—the reaction against the overt min-
gling of religion and conservative/right-wing politics, the reaction
against the Catholic priest pedophile scandal, and the increase of
women in the paid labor force—I would add two more possibilities concerning what might also be at least partial contributors to the recent
rise of irreligion in America: the greater acceptance of homosexuality
in American culture and the ubiquity of the Internet.

Since the days of Stonewall and Harvey Milk, more and more Americans have come to accept homosexuality as a normal, legitimate form
of love and pairing. For many, acceptance of homosexuals simply boils
down to a matter of fairness, civil rights, and equality before the law.
The overall stigmatization of homosexuality has weakened significantly in recent decades. We see that those Americans who continue to
malign homosexuality as sinful or immoral, and who continue to fight
against gay rights, do so *exclusively* from a religious vantage point.
And it is turning some people off religion. In my previous book, *Faith
No More: Why People Reject Religion*, which was based on in-depth
interviews with Americans who were once religious but are no longer,
I found that many of those who have walked away from their religion
in recent years have done so as a direct consequence of and reaction
against their respective religious tradition's continued condemnation
and stigmatization of gays and lesbians. The fact that Americans today between the ages of eighteen and thirty are the generation most
accepting of homosexuality in the nation's history, and are simultaneously those least interested in being religious—and the fact that
the states that have legalized gay marriage tend to be among the most
secular—might be coincidental, but I highly doubt it.

Next, the Internet has had a secularizing effect on society in recent decades. This happens on various levels. First, religious people can look up their own religion on the Web and suddenly, even unwittingly, be exposed to an array of critiques or blatant attacks on their tradition that they otherwise would never have come across. Debunking on the Internet abounds, and whether one is a Mormon, a Scientologist, a Catholic, a Jehovah's Witness—whatever—the Web exposes the adherents of every and any religious tradition to skeptical views that can potentially undermine personal certainty, rattling an otherwise insulated, confident conviction in one's religion.

We see direct evidence of this happening more and more. For example, in her ongoing research on nonbelieving clergy, Linda LaScola has found that many pastors and ministers who have lost their faith in God cite their time spent on the Internet as a factor in their emergent atheism. In another study of an extremely segregated, close-knit, almost secretive Satmar Hasidic Jewish community in Brooklyn, New York, sociologist Hella Winston also found evidence of the Web's secularizing potential. Many of her informants went online, often secretively, and what they found there helped to erode their religious provincialism, sometimes directly prodding their emergent questioning and even abetting their eventual rejection of their religion.

Second, the Internet allows people who may be privately harboring doubts about their religion to immediately connect with others who also share such doubts. In other words, the Internet fosters and spurs secular community. Nascent atheists, skeptics, humanists, agnostics— even those in the most remote or fundamentalist of communities—can reach out to others online, instantly finding comfort and information, which encourages or strengthens their secularity.

Third, and perhaps most subtle, the Web may be partly responsible for the rise of irreligion simply by what it is, what it can do, what it can provide, how it functions, and how it interfaces with us and our minds and our desires and our lives. The Internet may be supplying something psychological, or feeding something neurological, or establishing something cultural via its individual-computer-screen nexus, something dynamic that is edging out religion, replacing religion, or weakening religion. The entertainment available on the Internet, the barrage of imagery, the simultaneity, the mental stimulation, the looking and clicking, the hunting and finding, the time-wasting, the consumerism, the constant social networking, the virtual communication—all of it may be undermining religion's ability to hold our interest, draw our attention, tap our soul.

DR. BARRY KOSMIN is the founding director of the Institute for the Study of Secularism in Society and Culture, housed (none too ironically) at Trinity College, in Hartford, Connecticut. This institute, founded in 2005, is the first of its kind in America—or the world, for that matter. Its goal is "to advance understanding of the role of secular values and the process of secularization in contemporary society and culture." Dr. Kosmin is emphatic about the need to understand the rise of irreligion. As he argues, "We need to study secular people because they're a growing proportion of the population. This has political, social, intellectual, and moral implications. While the salience of religion has been duly studied, we also need to see what is happening on the other side. We need to examine the nonreligious portion of humanity. If we only study religious people, and we ignore secular people, we are not getting the whole spectrum, the whole picture."

I couldn't agree more.

There is an important, durable line that links the ancient Carvaka, Kohelet, Lucretius, Wang Ch'ung, and Muhammad al-Razi to Sally, the American mom of the twenty-first century. It is a fascinating, compelling line—part philosophical, part practical, part political, part personal—and it courses through history and winds ever strongly through our contemporary society. But it is a line of human culture that hasn't been adequately recognized, scrutinized, or appreciated. The Sallys of the world simply haven't been studied much. And this is not only strange but unfortunate, as it skews our understanding not only of what it means to be secular or religious, or what it means to be American, but what it means to simply be human.

It's Only Natural

Given that secular people are now more abundant than ever before, and that social scientists such as Barry Kosmin are finally beginning to study secular people with real deliberate rigor, hopefully our ability to counter some of the gross mischaracterizations out there concerning secular people will mature and strengthen. And the mischaracterizations out there concerning secular people—people like Sally—are quite troublesome. For example, many people characterize atheists or nonreligious men and women as some sort of aberrant, anomalous, or unnatural species of human being. And I'm not talking about Roman Catholic Inquisitors of the sixteenth century making such assertions but contemporary academics.

Consider Christian Smith, who is the William R. Kenan Jr. Professor of Sociology and director of the Center for the Study of Religion and Society at the University of Notre Dame. At a 2012 roundtable conference held at the Berkley Center for Religion, Peace, and World Affairs at Georgetown University, Professor Smith—who is one of the most prolific and erudite sociologists of religion in the country, as well as a really affable guy—put forth the thesis that religion is *natural* to the human condition, while secularity is not. By way of analogy, he characterized being religious as akin to walking forward and upright on two legs and being secular as akin to crabwalking backward on all fours; the latter can be done, but it goes against our true human nature.

And Professor Smith is far from alone in espousing this viewpoint; it is a fairly widespread notion, held by academics and nonacademics alike, that religiosity is the sort of natural, innate default position of humankind, while being secular is some sort of oddity, corruption, or aberration. Sociologist Paul Froese characterizes religiosity as "essential," "universal," and "fundamental" to the human condition, thereby rendering the secular condition as ultimately unnatural and untenable. Psychology professor Justin Barrett further argues that humans are literally "born believers," and thus atheism is a problematic, indoctrinated retardation of an otherwise natural, normal human predilection. Theism, such individuals tell us, is simply in our wiring, in our human nature—while atheism is decidedly not.

I HEAR VARIOUS permutations of this position all the time, and it basically goes like this: "Religion has existed in every human society and culture, right? Religion is basically a universal, isn't it? So doesn't that mean that religion is an essential and intrinsic component of the human condition?"

Not quite.

First off, one can readily agree that religion is pervasive the world over. And one can also happily acknowledge that religion has existed, in some form or another, in every society and culture for which we have data. Good enough. But that does not mean that *every member* of any given society or culture is religious, nor even necessarily a majority of any given society or culture. For example, 42 percent of the Dutch today describe themselves as being nonreligious, and another 14 percent describe themselves as being convinced atheists—meaning that being religious in the Netherlands today is actually to be in the minority. Same thing in the Czech Republic. And Japan. And anthropologists such as Daniel L. Everett have even lived among indigenous tribes deep in the Amazon rain forest whose members don't believe in anything supernatural—no gods, no ghosts. So just because religion is culturally and historically widespread does not mean that it is embraced by everyone.

By way of analogy, consider dance. Dance is just as universal as religion: it has existed, in one form or another, in every culture and society, past and present. And yet we know that many individuals don't care much for dancing. Many find it awkward. Many find it embarrassing. Many more are simply uninterested in it, or are downright oblivious to it. And still others are actively opposed to it, finding it to be immoral or wicked. So while dance may be "universal," that does not automatically mean that all humans are dancers. Millions are not.

For yet one more analogy, consider violent crime. It is just as widespread as religion and dance. It exists in all societies and cultures, past and present. And yet we know that not all people are violent criminals. Most aren't. So just because a phenomenon exists in all human enclaves does not make it innate or natural to all people. And I would argue that this is exactly the case with religion: not all humans are religious. As nineteenth-century abolitionist and feminist Ernestine Rose argued over a hundred years ago, "We are told that Religion is natural; the belief in a God universal. Were it natural, then it would indeed be universal; but it is not."

Which leads to my second point: as the earlier part of this chapter revealed, there are a hell of a lot of secular people out there in the world—according to recent analyses, approximately 450 to 700 million nonbelievers worldwide. Given those numbers, it is problematic to consider something so widespread as an unnatural aberration. As sociologists Marta Trzebiatowska and Steve Bruce have recently argued, "The proposition that all people are innately religious might have been plausible in 1800, but there are now so many people . . . who do not hold supernatural beliefs, who have no involvement with religious organizations, and who describe themselves as 'non-religious' that . . . we have enough non-religious people to defeat the universal claim."

Third, even if we can recognize that there are certain innate neurological, psychological, and/or cognitive predispositions that might tend to make humans religious (for example, the proclivity to see patterns, the tendency to assume some sort of agency behind certain phenomena, the desire to feel a sense of connection, to be part of a like-minded group)—as the work of such scholars as Pascal Boyer reveals—that does not mean that there aren't other similar, simultaneous, competing, or complementary innate predispositions that tend to make some humans skeptical, agnostic, atheist, religiously indifferent, or affirmatively secular.

So while the author Nicholas Wade writes of a "faith instinct," we can certainly argue that there is also a "doubt instinct" or a "reason instinct" that is just as persistent and inherent to our nature. As cognitive psychologists Armin Geertz and Guðmundur Ingi Markússon so astutely argue, "Atheism . . . draws on the same natural cognitive capacities that theism draws on," and both "religiosity and atheism represent entrenched cognitive-cultural habits where the conclusions drawn from sensory input and the output of cognitive systems bifurcate in supernatural and naturalistic directions. The habit of atheism *may* need more scaffolding to be acquired, and its religious counterpart may need more effort to kick, but even so, that does not, ipso facto, make the latter more natural than the former." Amen to that.

THE TRUTH IS that many societies today, as discussed in chapter 2, are highly religious, such as El Salvador, Zimbabwe, and Bangladesh, but many others are highly secular, such as Scotland, Slovenia, and Estonia. Some ethnic groups today are highly secular, such as American Jews, while others are highly religious, such as African Americans. Some societies are very religious for centuries, and then religion dramatically fades in a matter of two or three generations. Some societies are relatively secular for a spell, and then religion suddenly erupts with vigor. Many individuals are strongly religious for decades, and then they suddenly lose their faith, becoming convinced atheists, while many other individuals are secular for many years, and then suddenly find religious faith, becoming extremely pious. And just to add to the complexity, we know that many people are neither totally religious nor totally secular, but exhibit both orientations simultaneously throughout the course of their lives. Some people find themselves feeling or behaving particularly religious at certain times, and notably secular at others.

Simply put, faith and doubt, credulity and skepticism, theism and atheism, religious fervor and utter religious indifference—these are all *natural* components of the human condition. In some cultures or eras, one is stronger or more pervasive than the other. In other cultures or eras, vice versa. For some individuals, one is more dominant, and in other individuals, it is just the opposite. Some men and women live a happy life permeated by religion, while others get on just fine without it.

And it is to the actual details and contours of the secular life—its joys and challenges, promises and struggles—that we now turn.

Chapter 4

Raising Kids

t was the whole grace thing. I had never dealt with it in such an intimate way, and I must admit that I found it difficult to navigate, at least for a while. We'd sit around that big wooden table at my in-laws' three-story house, high in the Colorado Rockies, and it would be dinnertime, and my father-in-law would tell us to all join hands. I just wasn't sure what to do, how to be. Not the holding hands part—that I liked. Still do. But the prayer that would follow?

Stacy, my wife of more than twenty years, is not religious. But Stacy's mother and her husband are—very much so. For quite some time they've been born-again, church-involved, Bible-believing Christians. Their faith in God and their love of Jesus are sustaining, nurturing, and deeply important aspects of their lives. And they always say grace before their meals. And during those earlier years, when the kids were younger and being a father was newer, I found it particularly awkward.

Here's how the whole grace thing would basically go:

Having arrived at our in-laws' house late the night before, after a thirteen-hour drive from California, we spend our first full day mostly taking it easy. Perhaps we saunter around the nearby golf course in the morning, looking for golf balls. Maybe my father-in-law takes the kids out for lunch, or for an ice cream in the afternoon. I unload the car and unpack the bags and then lie around and watch cable TV, or perhaps a Disney movie with the kids, while nursing a large mug of black tea, trying to get used to the altitude. Stacy and her mom go for a walk to the creek, then go marketing, and then get to work in the kitchen.

Then it is dinnertime. And there we all are, assembled in the Protestantly perfect dining room: my secular self, my secular wife, our three kids, and my very generous, very loved, and very Christian in-laws. Our son fidgets and complains a bit in his big wooden chair, but his older sisters successfully settle him down. Then my mother-in-law nods to my father-in-law, and we know to quiet ourselves and grab one another's hands, and then my in-laws close their eyes and tilt their heads downward. My father-in-law begins:

"We thank you, Heavenly Father, for bringing Stacy and Phil and our wonderful grandchildren safely to us, for protecting them on their journey out here . . ."

Okay. That's it. I've entered the awkward zone.

The fact is, I've never believed in God—and my kids know this about me, especially my older daughter, Ruby. She knows that I love and appreciate my in-laws and that I'm happy to be in their beautiful home again. But she also knows that I'm not a believer, and that I'm not into praying.

My father-in-law continues: "We also thank you, God, for the beautiful nature that you have created for us . . ."

I can feel my children's eyes on me. I'm uncomfortable.

Here are my options:

I can just close my eyes and tilt my head, going along with the ritual. But it would be a decidedly feigned gesture. Dishonest. Tilting my head in prayer, with my eyes closed, has always felt strange and unpleasant to me. And if I did do that, then what message might such a choice be giving my kids? Perhaps it would simply be interpreted as a "when in Rome" kind of thing. Maybe they would think, "Hey, look at Pop, he's going along with the prayer with his head downward and eyes closed—how nice." But maybe not. Maybe it will look like I am hiding my secularity, or that I am ashamed to be nonreligious, or that I am comfortable being disingenuous and that disingenuousness is okay. I don't want to convey such things.

Another option is that I can just sort of sit there placidly with my eyes open. My children might interpret this as a benevolent, benign stance. I'm simply there, going along, not praying, but sitting pleasantly. But they might interpret such a choice as my being openly disrespectful to their grandparents. Inappropriately indifferent. I don't want them to think that either. I'm not trying to be impolite or rude.

Another option is to just stare blankly down at the table. But what might my kids think then? Am I mad? Annoyed? Shut down?

And as my father-in-law finishes—"In Jesus's name, amen"—do I say "amen" as well?

This indecisiveness of mine went on for several years. There were some times when I went ahead and closed my eyes and tilted my head downward, other times when I just sat there placidly, still other times when I would stare at the table, and also times when I would exchange a knowing look with Stacy or one of the kids—and occasionally I would do all of these things, one after the other in rapid succession, during the same prayer, in a sort of awkward-atheist-at-grace combopalooza.

There is no question that for most secular Americans, navigating one's relationships with religious family members is one of the stickiest of situations; it is difficult to be honest while at the same time seeking not to offend, to be respectful while simultaneously not obsequious, to be genuine and open even in the face of that which mystifies or even offends, to be loving while strongly disagreeing about very important, personal, political, and existential matters.

In those first few years, Stacy and I tried to set clear boundaries, establishing clear do's and don'ts for the grandparents. Or to be more accurate, clear don'ts. I think that my in-laws were somewhat hurt by our rulemaking, our rigidity, our resistance to their religion. Perhaps they felt like we were judging them, not respecting them. But as new parents, we were simply trying to do what we felt was best for our children. And there were times when we also felt judged and disrespected by them in turn. After all, didn't they think that we were going to hell for not believing in Jesus? Didn't they think our children were going to hell? And furthermore, they just didn't seem to get our secular orientation. I sometimes felt like they looked down on Stacy and me for not believing in God. We sometimes felt like they didn't respect our secularity, which we feel is a legitimate, respectable, noble life stance—not something to be condemned or pitied.

Eventually, however, over the course of the last several years, things have mellowed out. A respectful truce has emerged between us. Basically, we have just decided to try our best to not talk about religion with them. We know where they stand, and they know where we stand. And so we simply try not to get into it. Stacy likens it to a "don't ask, don't tell" family policy. As she explains, "We just don't go there. We want to be able to love and respect them, so why delve into these things that we feel so uncomfortable about? My mom's religious views do not stop me from loving her."

Also, both Stacy and I have lowered our defenses quite a bit in terms of feeling like we have to "protect" our kids. And as we have grown more comfortable and secure as parents, we have stopped policing the grandparents. Again from Stacy: "We came to see that our children will understand that this is Nana and Grandpa—that is who they are.

And we are still their parents. We will always be the dominant forces in their lives, making the deepest impressions. So we really pulled back and thought, 'Hey, if Nana and Grandpa want to talk to the kids about the blood of Christ and hell, then our kids will grow to learn that that is what they believe.' That's okay. That's life. They have a right to know what their grandparents believe, to know who they are. And it is Nana and Grandpa's prerogative to let their grandchildren know what it is they believe. It has actually been a relief and a revelation to come to that secure place."

For my wife and myself, the challenges of being secular parents have generally only arisen when we are interacting with my in-laws, especially when we're at their house in Colorado. That's when we have to contend with religion intimately, and when we feel our secularity most acutely. But back home in Southern California it is pretty much smooth sailing. Because we live in a small college town on the West Coast, we are rarely confronted with much religiosity. There are a lot of secular people here, a lot of lapsed Catholics, liberal Episcopalians, cultural Jews, Unitarians, atheists, agnostics, academics. People like us. Nearly all the people we know are nonchurchgoers. Our children have many friends who come from secular homes of varying degrees. Religion is not part of their public school life. City council meetings do not begin with a prayer, nor do local sporting events. Nearly everyone we know is suspicious of politicians who wear their religion on their sleeve. In short, we live in a very irreligious nook of America. And thus being secular parents is fairly normal and not something most of us spend too much time dwelling on or mulling over.

But many secular parents in America have a markedly different experience. Those moms and dads who live in extremely religious parts of the country experience a whole different reality when it comes to raising their kids. Those lingering moments of awkwardness that I used to experience around the dinner table at my in-laws' home are nothing compared to what some secular parents in America's Bible Belt are forced to contend with on an almost daily basis—mothers like Tonya Hinkle, who lives in a small town just outside of Meridian, Mississippi. In Tonya's world, religious leaders are widely respected, religious traditions are faithfully upheld, religious congregations undergird community, and religious beliefs run deep—and they are not withheld from the public square. In such rural southern communities, being a secular parent can be really, really tough.

A Secular Mom in the South

Tonya Hinkle, age fifty, has lived in her one-stoplight town in eastern Mississippi for over twenty years. She used to work as a childcare provider, then as a school cafeteria worker, but she's been a stay-at-home mom for the last decade. Her husband works for a local communications company. She describes herself as a "nonreligious person who *never* goes to church," which isn't a typical or common orientation among people in her little town. "When we first moved out here, the neighbors were friendly and charming, and then as soon as they discovered that we were nonreligious and had no intention of going to their churches, they became distant—or persistent. Others were just like, 'Oh, you're strange people. We don't want to know you.' . . . There's just a real strong Christian presence in this area. It seems like everything in this town, every event—I don't care what it is—always starts and ends with a prayer. And if you don't belong to a church, you don't exist. Everything revolves around the churches. And if you're not part of them, you're 'agin' 'em,' you know what I mean?"

Tonya initially enrolled her three kids—a boy and twin girls—in the local public school. She desperately wanted them to be and feel a part of their community. Being the child of a military father (air force),

Tonya had always moved around while growing up, and she most definitely didn't want that for her own children. She wanted them to have a sense of belonging, a sense of place. And she also wanted to be involved with their education. "I tried to help out, to assist in the classrooms, to be friends with the teachers." But the invitations to church started right away—from other parents, from teachers, from the secretary in the principal's office. It seemed like every time Tonya was at school with her kids, someone brought up the topic of religion and inquired about Tonya's religious affiliation. And every time Tonya said that she and her family were not religious, awkwardness arose. Or sometimes a smidgen of scorn.

Then the teasing started. Taunts in the schoolyard. Nasty notes being passed. Tonya went to speak with various teachers. Every single one was strongly Christian, and while they were sorry about the troubles that Tonya's kids were facing, they each suggested sending them to church as the solution. The principal—a very active member of the largest Methodist church in town—offered up the same sentiments.

Tonya felt isolated and frustrated. And soon the isolation and frustration were accompanied by real worry. One specific episode she recalls involved an instance of verbal harassment that her twins experienced on the school bus. As she recounts, "I think they were in first grade. I always waited for them when the bus would drop them off at the front of the house. I would go out there. And the girls got off and, you know, you could tell that they had been crying for quite a while. I mean, they just had tears running down their faces and they were hiccuping and crying. I calmed them down and asked them what had happened, and eventually I managed to get it out of them: this one girl had stood up on the bus and screamed—right in their faces—that they were going to HELL. That they were going to burn in all eternity because they didn't go to church! I later found out that it was this girl's parents that had talked to her about my children. You know—just vicious."

As on previous occasions, Tonya went to the teachers and the principal to complain. She met the same resistance. And she was forced to endure a fair bit of pious scolding from the principal's secretary, who more and more frequently exuded a growing air of disapproval every time they happened to interact.

But the worst was yet to come. And when it did, Tonya was left reeling. It was toward the end of the school year, in May, when her son was in fourth grade and her daughters were in second. She explained, often choking up with emotion, "When my mother got ill, she was put into a nursing home. Now, this is important—my mother was the only grandparent my kids had. My husband's parents were out of the picture, and my father had died before the kids were born. So Grandma was all they had. We would visit her regularly. Then one day things took a turn for the worse and she was, you know, moments away from death, and the nursing home gives me a call and says, 'You better get down here if you want to say goodbye. Now's the time.' And I was going to take my children with me there so they could say goodbye to their grandmother, whom they loved dearly. And I was told by the school secretary, in the principal's office, who I had had dealings with before—she knew my point of view—she said that they were not allowed to be taken out of school. My children. I could not take them out. She said, 'You need to have a signed doctor's note' or something. You know, she gave me a bunch of crap. That's the nicest way I can put it. When I explained the situation to her—that my mom was literally about to die and I wanted the kids to be able to say goodbye to their grandmother—she looked me in the eye and said that I could tell my children that they could see their grandmother in heaven."

Tonya felt as if she had been kicked in the gut with a bluntly sanctimonious, malevolently pious boot. She stood there shaking. She couldn't believe this was happening. Her mother was dying and her children were being held captive. She was at a loss. The secretary had made it sound like Tonya would be breaking the law if she forcibly removed her children from the school premises. As she laments, "You know, at the time I really didn't have the tools to defend myself." She wasn't able to get her kids out of school that day, and her mother died early that afternoon. Her kids hadn't been able to say goodbye.

Tonya never let her kids go back to that school. She was done.

Did she consider moving somewhere else, perhaps to a city, where things might be different? No. As she explained, "My husband's work is here. What can I say? A good-paying job is nothing to sneeze at in this country! But I guess it also boils down to stubbornness. I feel like I have as a much a right to live here as anyone else. Why should I have to move?"

So she began homeschooling her children. The beginning was actually really rough. She had no preparation for such an undertaking. She found it difficult to navigate the paperwork, the planning, the scheduling. There were some subjects that she needed to heavily brush up on. It took her quite some time to learn how to be a good teacher, to adequately foster their educational development, to give the proper level of feedback, and so on. And all the other homeschoolers in the county were extremely religious; they made it unmistakably clear that they did not want any secular folk in their midst.

But then, into this rather lonely and difficult situation, emerged some light. It came in the form of the late-night glow of the computer screen. Through the help of the Internet, Tonya found and got in touch with another secular mom in another small town about fifteen miles away. This was the best thing to happen to her in a long, long time. She and this mom became fast friends, their children clicked, and they've been homeschooling their kids together for over ten years now. It has been wonderful to have that support, that connection, that camaraderie. And in the past two years, two other families from a neighboring county have joined their "secular homeschooling" group. So now there's a small core.

Tonya's experience as a secular parent in rural America is far from unique. One nationally representative study found that 41 percent of atheists have experienced discrimination within the last five years due to their lack of religious identification. And in my research into secular life in America, I have spoken with and heard from many other mothers out there with stories strikingly similar to Tonya's. Mothers like Pat Cole, the wife of a truck driver, who lives in rural Arkansas, and also eventually chose to pull her only son out of public school because of the harassment he endured there, the constant proselytizing from teachers and school administrators, and the specific things that he was being taught on a regular basis: that abortion is murder, that evolution is "just a theory" that is inferior to the biblically supported notion of intelligent design, that homosexuality is a sin, and that "abstinence" is the only option for those teenagers who wish to practice safe sex. Or Becky Eaves, the wife of a military man, who lives in a small town in rural Texas, and knows all too well the isolation and alienation that can come from being secular in such deeply religious communities, isolation and alienation that are dramatically sharpened when children come into the mix, and one of those children is gay.

Tonya insists that although she is raising her kids without religion, she doesn't want them to uncritically accept her own spin on religious matters. She tries as much as possible to let them make up their own minds, or at least develop the capacity to do so. "I let them go to church things. If they want to go to this or that church activity, I let them. I try to give them a balanced view." But how? "I give them the facts. And then I show them what other people's beliefs are. And then I try to explain the difference between a fact and a belief. And let them choose for themselves."

In addition to talking with Tonya about the many struggles that she has endured while raising her kids without church or faith, I asked her about some of the good things that come with secular parenting. "Gosh, there are so many. Just really relating to them—as people. You know, they understand that the choices that they make have consequences. And I love to watch their minds grow. You can just see their minds opening up to all the different possibilities. You know—they are not limited. A lot of religious people are very limited in their way of looking at the world. Their religion tells them this and that, you can't do this and you can't do that. Religion is a way to control people, to tell them what to think, what to believe. And I want my children to make their own decisions. That's been my focus. What I want for my kids is to let them be their own voice."

Cultivating Morality in Children

Not all secular parents in America experience the extreme levels of alienation, isolation, and harassment that Tonya describes above. Those nonreligious mothers and fathers out there who, like myself, live in those parts of the country where religion isn't so strong and there is a greater diversity of cultures, worldviews, and social milieus do not experience the raising of their children as an embattled struggle fraught with what can sometimes be painful challenges. For those who live in places where there are a lot of other nonreligious folk, being a secular parent is not such a herculean enterprise. It is just something you more or less muddle through with relative ease, only grappling with certain choices or confronting particular conflicts now and then.

There can thus be no doubt that raising secular kids is a much softer and smoother ball of wax when you are living in San Francisco, Eugene, or Burlington than in Montgomery, Knoxville, or Sioux Falls.

Just ask Dr. Deborah Kaufman. Debbie grew up in a comfortably wealthy part of New York City and she currently lives in a comfortably wealthy suburb of Los Angeles, near the beach. For Debbie, who is forty-five and the mother of two boys, raising her children without God is easy, pleasant, and even slightly mundane. Nary a struggle has come her way.

Debbie is a psychiatrist and works as a head administrative supervisor at a large mental health facility. Her husband, a blue-eyed, blond-haired, chisel-cheeked Minnesotan, is a professor of political philosophy. Neither of their parents are believers, so unlike my wife and me, Debbie and her husband have experienced no conflicts with the grandparents. And none of the members of their rather large circle of friends are religious. Their boys, who are twelve and eight, have never met any kids who are strongly devout. They have never been invited to a church nor told that they should go to one. They have never heard anyone speak of hell, they've never met a Bible thumper, and they've never had religion pushed on them from teachers or administrators at school.

Sure, the God question has come up on occasion. Not a problem for Debbie. She has had no difficulty answering her sons' questions about God. "I always start by just saying that I think life is really wonderful, really beautiful, and that we are so lucky to be here, so lucky to be alive, so lucky that we can appreciate the beauty of the world. But I tell them that I don't feel the need to put God in there somewhere in order to appreciate all those things. So we tell them that. And then we say that some people do believe in God, but we don't."

And what about when the kids ask about what happens when we die? Again, Debbie handles this topic with relative ease. "I have just told them that it is a time of peace. You're not alive anymore. You're part of the world. You just go back to being part of the world, and your body becomes a part of everything. I always try to be positive, to put it in positive terms—that you will become part of the world and return to the earth."

What I admire most about the way Debbie handles such questions is her ability to be clear and honest about her lack of supernatural beliefs while at the same time not putting down religion, not condemning it or mocking it. It is important that her kids know where Debbie stands on these topics, while at the same time healthy and good that she doesn't sour them on the bulk of humanity—those billions of people who *do* believe in God or life after death. Debbie's answers exude confidence rather than defensiveness, ease rather than stress, and openness rather than closed-mindedness. This may simply be the result of her own personality. But it may also be a result of the sociological fact that her daily life is devoid of religious bullying, zealous proselytizing, or fervent faith, and so, unlike Tonya Hinkle, she simply doesn't ever feel embattled or condemned.

How about morals and values? How does Debbie provide a moral foundation for her kids without belief in God? On this front, she is certain that theism is not necessary for a viable moral framework. "I don't see how believing in God gives you morality. The way we teach them what is right and what is wrong is by trying to instill a sense of empathy—how other people feel. You know, just trying to give them that sense of what it's like to be on the other end of their actions. And I don't see *any* need for God in that."

In fact, Debbie is convinced that the secular morality she strives to instill in her children is actually much better, more mature, and ultimately more *durable* than a morality based on faith in God. "If your morality is tied to a religious belief system, well, that can come and go—because, who knows? I mean, if your morality is all tied in with

God, what if you at some point start to question the existence of God? Does that mean your moral sense suddenly crumbles? The way we are teaching our children about wrong and right and empathy and how to treat other people, no matter what they choose to believe later in life, even if they become religious or whatever, they are still going to have that system. Their morality does not depend on Adam and Eve being in a garden or anything like that. It just works on its own."

Debbie's discussion here relates directly to Sonja's "eye in the ceiling" hypothetical that we described earlier. If the morality we seek to foster in our children is totally or even partially dependent upon faith in a supernatural entity, such as the Eye of God watching us, or in ancient tales about talking snakes and original sin, then it is intrinsically less stable than a morality that is built upon rational explanations for why we should or shouldn't do this or that, or appealing to empathy and the feelings of others.

DEBORAH'S REFLECTIONS ON the moral instruction of her children also link nicely to the foundational work of Lawrence Kohlberg, the eminent professor of psychology who worked at both the University of Chicago and Harvard. Dr. Kohlberg is well known for his studies concerning moral reasoning and development. After years of probing how children, teenagers, and adults understand, think about, and explain morality, Kohlberg argued that nearly all humans pass through various stages of moral development as they grow and mature.

At first, when very young, children tend to understand wrong and right simply in terms of punishment. Thus at age three morality basically boils down to this: if you can be punished for it, it is wrong; if not, then it is okay. But as we grow older, this conceptualization of morality fades and other factors and considerations come into play. For example, social approval and disapproval become more significant.

And then, as we further progress and develop, we begin to see that something may be wrong not merely because there is a rule against it or because others condemn it, but because it may have negative consequences for others or for oneself.

Kohlberg outlined six stages of observable human moral development, and the final stage, usually not attained until late adolescence, involves moral reasoning that is based on universal ethical principles, such as justice, equality, respect for all human beings, and the Golden Rule.

And what many people think—including philosophers like Bertrand Russell, authors like Salman Rushdie, and mothers like Debbie Kaufman—is that religions, especially the more conservative or fundamentalist, seem to be trapped in the earliest, least developed stage of human moral progression, basing notions of wrong and right merely upon whether or not they warrant God's punishment. Furthermore, some studies indicate that religious parents who employ the threat of God's punishment can be at risk of developing in their children debilitating personality traits such as excessive self-blaming. So Debbie deliberately avoids emphasizing punishment in the moral upbringing of her sons. For her, talking about empathy, treating people the way one would want to be treated, and acting in this world in a way that one would want others to act, à la Immanuel Kant's categorical imperative, is not only a more humane form of ethical instruction, but also more sound.

What We Know About Secular Parenting

The experiences of parents like Tonya Hinkle of rural Mississippi and Debbie Kaufman of urban Los Angeles couldn't be more different. When it comes to secular parenting and feeling isolated or integrated, alienated or enmeshed, suspected or understood, defensive or easygoing, aware or oblivious, there is a broad range. A lot will depend on where in the country one lives, one's own personal upbringing, one's educational and occupational status, one's neighbors, and then some.

But what else do we know about secular parenting? Despite the fact that millions of people raise their children without religious faith, the phenomenon of secular parenting has been almost totally ignored by psychologists, sociologists, anthropologists, and historians. There is, remarkably, no established body of research on the raising of nonreligious kids.

However, it does look like a zygote of research is just now starting to gestate. In recent years there have been a few studies shedding some rays of light on secular parenting. One key finding is that when kids are raised without religion, they tend to remain irreligious as they grow older. The data backs this up nicely; in his recent longitudinal analysis of various generational cohorts in the United States, Stephen Merino found that "those with religiously unaffiliated parents as children are significantly less likely to express a religious preference as adults." Back in the 1980s, Hart Nelsen, a professor of sociology at Pennsylvania State University, documented the clear influence that the secularity of parents has on their children. He showed that just as kids of religious parents almost always tend to become religious themselves, the same holds true for the kids of secular parents—they too nearly all grow up to become secular. According to Professor Nelsen's analysis, among American families back in the 1980s, if the father was secular but the mother was religious, then about one-sixth of the children of such unions grew up to become secular. If the mother was secular but the father was religious, about half of such children grew up to be secular. And if *both* parents were secular, about 85 percent of their children grew up to be secular. This research was confirmed some years later—and quite glaringly so—by two sociologists in Scotland, Steve Bruce and Tony Glendinning, who found that children raised without religion rarely grow up to become religious themselves. As their survey results showed, "If someone was not raised in a particular faith, the chances of acquiring one later in life are small." How small? "About 5 percent."

In addition to the demographic information above, one can find a smattering of other interesting studies that contain at least a little bit of relevant information about secular parenting. These are studies that focus on religious family life but happen to include some nonreligious folk in their sample. For example, in his impressive study of sex and religion in the lives of American teens, Mark Regnerus, a professor of sociology and religion at the University of Texas, found that secular parents are generally more comfortable talking about sex with their teenage children, and end up providing them with better information about sex and safe sex practices than religious parents.

Vern Bengtson, a professor of gerontology and sociology at the University of Southern California, has been studying religion and family life for thirty-five years. He has included secular families in his latest investigations, and he reports that most secular families exhibit high levels of solidarity and emotional closeness, and that secular parents are quite articulate about their values, with many being "more coherent and passionate about their ethical principles than some of the 'religious' parents in our study." And what are some of their values? Sociologists Brian Starks and Robert Robinson found that nonreligious parents are more likely to value and seek to cultivate autonomy in their children, rather than obedience. The latter tends to be of greater value to religious parents, especially conservative Protestants. Indeed, according to various national surveys, when asked what characteristics they'd like their children to exhibit, secular parents are far less like to list "obey parents" and more likely to list "think for one-self" than religious parents.

The secular emphasis on cultivating autonomy in children bears impressive fruit; one recent study found that atheist teenagers were far more likely to agree that "it is not important to fit in with what teens think is cool" than their religious peers. And sociologists Christopher Ellison and Darren Sherkat found that compared to their Christian counterparts, secular parents were more likely to stress the importance of rational problem solving, not harming others, and pursuing truth.

Another study, by social psychologists Bruce Hunsberger and Bob Altemeyer, found that atheist parents were reluctant to impose their atheism on their children. Indeed, atheist parents were much more likely to want their children to make up their own minds about what they believed. This was in stark contrast to believing Christian parents, who were far more likely to consciously and deliberately attempt to pass their religious beliefs on to their children.

Professor Manning

If there is an expert on secular parenting out there, it would be Christel Manning, a professor of religious studies at Sacred Heart University in Connecticut, and the author of various articles and books on how secular parents raise their children.

Christel's academic trajectory has been quite similar to my own: she had been studying religious life her entire career, but then about ten years ago she too realized that very few scholars were looking at secular life. And nobody was looking at that most central aspect of secular life: raising kids. Recognizing just what a gaping lacuna this was, she took on the task herself, becoming the first person within academia to make secular parenting the main focus of her research. For more than a decade, Professor Manning has interviewed secular parents from all over the country, seeking to understand just how they do it and what goes on between them and their kids.

Professor Manning's research contains much that is insightful. For example, she has shown that there is a discernibly wide variety of types of secular parents—a spectrum including convinced atheists who are quite antireligious, agnostic types who aren't sure just what they believe, and those who are simply indifferent; they don't so much reject religion as ignore it. She also studied quite a few quasi-secular parents—those who are somewhat involved with religious life but don't really believe the specific creeds and tenets of the religion they affiliate with, and only participate out of habit or tradition. Professor Manning's research also confirms what I already broached above: that social location is key. Those parents, like Tonya, who live in highly religious enclaves are much more protective of their children, and as they raise their kids, they truly feel like a despised and rejected minority, while other parents, like Debbie, who live in nonreligious parts of the country don't develop anything akin to such a defensive posture.

Finally, confirming Professor Bengtson's research noted above, Christel Manning has shown that secular parents are far from amoral. They may not raise their children religiously, but that does not mean that they raise them without values or ethical precepts. Some common, consistent moral principles secular parents impart to their children include valuing and obeying the Golden Rule, being environmentally conscious, developing empathy, cultivating independent thinking, and relying upon rational problem solving.

FOR MANY NONRELIGIOUS PARENTS, raising children entails a lot of cobbling, guessing, experimenting, and muddling. Sure, all parenting can be characterized this way. But for those who are raising their kids as freethinkers, there simply aren't any set structures, long-standing traditions, or even clear guidelines. And yet despite this reality, millions are doing it nonetheless: raising their kids without religion. For instance, of Americans born between the years 1925 to 1943, fewer than 4 percent were raised with no religion; of those born between the years 1956 to 1970, 7 percent were raised with no religion; and of those Americans born between 1971 and 1992, almost 11 percent were raised that way.

I asked Professor Manning to describe in her own words some of the more significant things that she has learned from all of her conversations with secular parents over the years. Is there anything that secular parents have in common?

"A key pattern that I uncovered in my research—and this applies to parents from all over the country, and it held, overall, in all of my interviews—is that secular parents value the idea of *having choices*. This emphasis on having choices just really stands out. Secular parents want their children to have a choice about what to believe in and what to practice. And this makes them quite different from religious parents. You know, your typical Catholic parent will send their kids to CCD—catechism class—and Jewish parents will send their kids to Hebrew school, and what they want is to pass on their own worldview. But secular parents do not necessarily want their kids to turn out secular. Rather, what they talk about, what they emphasize is, 'I want my son or daughter to be able to freely choose his or her own worldview.' So many secular parents will even try to expose them to religion because they think it would help them make their own choices."

This last sentiment reminds me of a secular man from San Francisco I once interviewed. Once a month over the course of a year he took his ten-year-old son to a different church, as well as some synagogues and mosques, so that he would learn a bit about the various religious traditions out there in the world. After each service they'd go out for lunch and talk about the experience, reflecting on what they liked, what they didn't like, and what they wanted to learn more about.

As Professor Manning rightly notes above, for religious parents, passing on their own beliefs and values is generally an uncomplicated, straightforward endeavor. Religious parents typically find it a joy and duty to simply pass on their own religious beliefs and traditions. They don't worry about unduly influencing their children's belief system. Quite the opposite—you actively seek to influence your children's beliefs in accordance with your religious faith. But many secular parents see this very process of passing on one's religion to one's kids as a form of indoctrination. They see religious faith as something that is directly and unfairly *imposed* on kids. They view young children as intellectually vulnerable, willing and perhaps even evolutionarily designed to believe almost anything their parents teach them about the nature of the world.

The paradoxical situation many secular parents thus find themselves in is this: they don't want to influence their children's beliefs too much, and they want to provide an upbringing that allows for them to make their own choices, to develop their own ideas, beliefs, worldview. But they simultaneously know that this is not quite possible. Despite the best of intentions, parents simply can't avoid shaping and influencing how their kids see the world. Socialization happens. Even if we don't directly tell our children this or that, they observe us. They hear what we say on the telephone to friends or colleagues. They listen to what is said around the dinner table. They notice the books we read, the television shows we watch. They overhear the occasional arguments we have with our in-laws. Their worldviews will be influenced by us, no matter how hard we might try otherwise. It is inevitable.

Beyond the fact of this inevitability, don't all parents, as parents, actually *want* to influence their children's worldview—even those secular parents who say that they don't? No matter what some may contend, influencing our children is at the very heart of the parenting enterprise. It is a large part of what parenting is all about—to nurture and produce children whom we hope will eventually go on to exhibit the best in human potential. And not what someone *else* thinks is the best in human potential, but what *we* consider to be the best in human potential. And for most secular parents, when it comes to the best in human potential, freedom of thought is of unparalleled value. So how does one cultivate freethinking in one's children, when the very process of that cultivation entails an unavoidable amount of parental influence?

Being honest and discussing these matters openly and maturely with your kids seems to be the right place to start. As Professor Manning advises, "The first thing is to just be honest with your kids about your own relationship to religion, including whatever doubts you may have, and including how your perspective may change over time. And try to let your children make their own choices based on good information and critical, rational thinking. The best way to prepare kids for that is to encourage them to have questions and to really talk them through. And it is great to share with your kids your own thoughts on these things, rather than worry that you have to have a ready-made answer. It is great to have authentic discussions about all of this."

For many secular parents, be they academics who live in Connecticut or stay-at-home moms who live in Mississippi, having honest, heart-to-heart, thoughtful discussions can be truly joyful: to share the reasons that cause one to doubt the existence of God, while simultaneously pondering why it is that others might actually find reasons to believe in God, and beyond that, to explore the very nature of credulity and skepticism, faith and reason, belief and doubt; to broach the possibility of there being no life after death, while simultaneously stressing that the most important thing is to focus on this life, this world, this time, for since this may be all that we have, it must be cherished; to grapple with the ultimate source of morals and ethics, and what it might mean to accept that these things do not fall down to us from the mysterious heavens but are cobbled together here on earth, over time, and with occasional stark disagreement. Such conversations are among the highlights of secular parenting.

Ryan, His Son, and the Boss

Heart-to-heart philosophical discussions are one thing, but what about actual rituals and traditions? How are these experienced or constructed by parents and children within secular culture? An obvious way that nonreligious people experience and enjoy rituals and traditions is simply by tapping into the plethora of nonreligious options out there.

For example, consider Ryan Gorski. For him, it is all about the Boss.

Ryan is forty-eight, married, with two sons. He grew up in Delaware but now lives in Philadelphia, where he is a successful civil attorney. Ryan has never believed in God. But ever since junior high, he's believed in the musical titan from New Jersey: Bruce Springsteen. For Ryan, Springsteen concerts are moving, personal, and deeply transformative experiences. He's been to over seventy of them.

Ryan's love of the Boss started back in the early 1980s. "I was lonely. I was at a new school. Didn't feel connected. Super insecure. You know, my parents' divorce—just feelings of loneliness and isolation. Like we all have. But I had more than my dose of it. So anyway, I was getting a ride to school with my older brother's friend and he'd play that music and it just hit me. I bought a few albums and I just used to sit alone in my room and turn out the lights and light a candle and put on *The River*. And I wasn't even smoking dope! I was just so touched by the music." Then he went to his first concert. "I went by myself. And it was just amazing. And I walked out of there feeling like I had just spent time with fifteen thousand of my best friends—and I didn't know any of them. It's like the sense of community was completely overwhelming. And the content of the songs, you know, it is all about loneliness, despair, isolation, and *hope*. There's just this emotional content to the music that we can all connect with. The songs tell stories about people, everyday people who are struggling, who are lonely, who are fighting to get to a better place."

Ryan describes the concert like a conversion experience—uplifting, comforting, cathartic. For Ryan, a Bruce Springsteen concert is a far more "religious" experience than anything he's ever encountered in any church.

"When I go to the shows, there is a huge sense of rejuvenation, there's a huge sense of happiness. A real emotional experience. When Springsteen comes to town, I go to his concerts. If he's playing for three nights, I'll go to every show. I'll go back time after time. That's how much I get out of it. My wife is a lapsed Catholic. She grew up in a very, very Catholic family. Three of her aunts are nuns. And when she walked out of her first Springsteen concert, she said, 'I want to be a better mom. I want to be a better person. I want to be a better wife. I want to be better in every measure of my life.' I mean, that's how inspiring she found his concert to be."

A couple of years ago, Ryan took his oldest son, Zander, to a concert. "Now, you have to understand, I've been singing Springsteen songs to him just about every night, when I put him to bed, since he was a baby. He's gone to sleep almost every night to me singing 'Promised Land.' This music has just been such a huge part of my life. So to take him to a concert—okay, maybe six years old is a bit young, but I wanted him to experience something that has been so meaningful to me. I was able to get amazing tickets so we were right in the front row. It was his birthday and we made a sign for him to hold up that said, TODAY I'M SIX, and Springsteen saw the sign and waved to Zander and sang to him and spent some time connecting to him. This is in front of sixty thousand people. It was almost like a moment that was meant to be."

Ryan's deep love for and personal devotion to the Boss is extremely similar to many religious people's feelings for their savior or prophet; in fact, Ryan's wife recently bought him a bumper sticker that reads MY BOSS IS A SINGER FROM NEW JERSEY—an obvious parallel of the popular Jesus-referring bumper sticker proclaiming MY BOSS IS A JEWISH CARPENTER. And as Ryan explains it, a Bruce Springsteen concert is quite akin to a religious revival; what Ryan gets from Springsteen's music and concerts is similar to what religious devotees get from their involvement in religion: inspiration, hope, connection. This is most likely why secular people will often say that music is their religion, or literature, or nature, or theater, or football—they want to indicate and stress that such this-worldly, nonsupernatural things can provide heightened levels of meaning and sacredness. And they provide equally powerful and enjoyable rituals, traditions, and experiences—rituals, traditions, and experiences that can be shared with one's children.

Ryan took his passion for Springsteen and imparted it to his son by making it ritualistic in nature and cementing it as a family tradition. Whenever the Boss is playing a concert in town, Ryan takes Zander. And Zander loves it.

The Heretical Habitus

For secular Americans such as Ryan Gorski, there are various additional possibilities for creating and enjoying rituals and traditions within the family context. The first is to participate in secular activities: a rock concert, a baseball game, a monthly neighborhood potluck, a motorcycle parade, a pig pickin', a kindergarten graduation, or the Fourth of July. A second possibility is to participate in religious holidays and ceremonies that have been secularized: a Jesusless Christmas morning, an Allah-absent end-of-Ramadan breaking of the fast, a ministerless wedding, or a godless Passover seder. A third option is to join up with other secular humanists for celebrations of such occasions as Darwin Day, Earth Day, the summer solstice, or the vernal equinox. A fourth is to actively create rituals and traditions on one's own. For example, when our children were younger, my wife and I liked to create a little bit of mayhem on the morning of Saint Patrick's Day: we'd buy some Lucky Charms and throw them messily around the kitchen, we'd put green dye in the drinking water in the refrigerator door, we'd scatter the kids' toys a bit—and blame it all on mischievous leprechauns that had been in the house the night before.

An obvious fifth option for nonreligious parents is simply to participate in rituals and traditions that are overtly religious, even when the spiritual or theological content is problematic, or even offensive. For example, my wife and I sometimes go with the kids to their grandparents' church at Christmastime. It makes my in-laws happy, it's nice to see their friends, the music is good, the vibe is festive, and as for the sermon about Christ the King, well, we just endure it. And we happily attend the annual Passover seder at my cousin Julie's house not because we particularly enjoy the retelling of the troubling biblical story from Exodus, but because we love seeing our extended family gather around a long table one night a year, we love to see how our nieces and nephews have grown, we relish the food, we enjoy my father singing in Yiddish, and it feels good to remember aunts, uncles, and grandparents who used to sit around the exact same table but do so no longer because they are dead.

It all boils down to choice. That is essentially the secular approach to rituals, traditions, ceremonies, and holidays: personal, individual choice. And it is both beautiful and baneful.

The beauty of being secular on this front is that you and your children are not bound to rituals. You are not enslaved by traditions. You do not have to engage in such activities because it is expected of you, or because your family urges you to, or because you feel obligated or guilty or forced to. Secular families perform rituals, celebrate holidays, and partake of traditions only if they want to. If they decide to. Thus being nonreligious means that you have much more freedom to pick and choose what you want to do or not do, participate in or avoid, join up with or walk away from. This approach offers a freedom that can be quite liberating; it leaves open the possibility of discovering new rituals and traditions from all kinds of sources. It allows for flagrant, bold, and personally satisfying reinterpretation, restructuring, and redefining of rituals and traditions. And it allows for the creation of completely new ones. And furthermore, the secular approach to rituals and traditions means that one must actively, genuinely, and sincerely think about and contemplate the various rites and ceremonies one chooses to be involved with, which means that when one does choose to be involved, there is a greater sense of the reasons, purposes, and benefits of doing so.

But there is also a downside to all of this. First, all this active picking and choosing and contemplating and creating can be a bit of a burden. It is a lot of work. For religious families, rituals and traditions come much easier. Everything is already established, conveniently prepackaged. There is already a familiar framework. When a person dies, the religious funeral service is already set. When a baby is born, the baptism ceremony is already set. When your kid wants a bar mitzvah, the whole thing is already set. When one wants some psychological comfort through prayer, the prayer is already written. The rosary is in hand. The icon is there. The rite is ready. In other words, religious parents can generally be much more relaxed and even quite passive in their involvement with rituals and traditions since these things have already been established, laid out, written, constructed. But secular parents must be much more conscious, aware, active, involved. And all of this awareness and reinterpreting and recreating and rewriting and active questioning—it can actually be quite a drag at times.

Additionally, secular approaches to ritual and tradition, by their very nature, lack intergenerational consistency. Burning Man may be an awesome, transformative experience for many—but it wasn't for their great-grandparents, grandparents, or parents, because it didn't exist back then. A Bruce Springsteen concert may move Ryan Gorski in very deep and personal ways, but one day the Boss will be dead, and Ryan's grandkids won't be able to partake of the magic. A personalized, uniquely constructed funeral may be wonderful for those present, but when the next generation starts to die, what will their funeral services be like? Totally original, uniquely constructed creations as well? And if so, that is all well and good—but it severs the consistency and predictability of the tradition, and actually undercuts the very notion and point of "tradition." There is something powerful about rituals and traditions that have been *as they are* over many generations. It can be comforting and even inspiring to do some act or state some words or perform some rite that one's parents, grandparents, and great-grandparents also did in just the same way—and to simultaneously know that one's children, grandchildren, and great-grandchildren will do it thus as well. As sociologist Lynn Davidman argues, many people crave such unchanging, fixed rituals and traditions in a world that often feels rootless and ever-morphing. Such transgenerational consistency in ritual and tradition has the power to place an individual in a loving, noble niche, attached to a "chain of memory"—to use Danièle Hervieu-Léger's apt phrase—which simultaneously links an individual to his or her ancestors as well as his or her descendants. This sort of thing is, if not totally absent from secular rituals and traditions, then certainly limited.

Ultimately, what contemporary secular culture thus lacks is *heritage*. By heritage I mean inherited customs, rites, symbols, and lifeways that are shared by people with a common past and common future, people linked by similar memories and future expectations, people enmeshed in similar experiences over generations. Such a heritage is hard to discern within secular culture, at least overtly.

However, there actually may be a secular heritage, albeit a subtle one, something that might be understood as a distinctly secular legacy: a legacy of personal freedom, of individual proclivity, of ongoing choice. When it comes to being secular, though we do not impart to future generations specific rituals or traditions that we expect them to uphold, what we do provide for them, as a legacy—or simply as a consequential by-product or inevitable outcome of our secularity—is this: the gift of allowing them to be unencumbered, unrestrained, and unfettered in choosing how they want to construct their lives and express their individual orientations. Perhaps this is what secular men and women most clearly, even if unconsciously, bequeath to their children: rituals of their own choosing and manufacturing, and, though paradoxical as it may sound, a tradition of no tradition. Call it the Heretical Legacy. For after all, the root meaning of "heresy," derived from the Greek *hairesis,* is "choice."

Chapter 5

Creating Community

Ever since she read *Just Plain Maggie*, our daughter Flora had wanted to go to sleep-away summer camp. When she turned eleven, Stacy and I felt that she was ready. But which camp? We had sent our older daughter, Ruby, to a Jewish camp for her first away-from-home summer experience. Ruby had liked it. But she didn't love it. So we didn't think that it would be a great choice for Flora. We considered sending her to a music camp (Flora plays the cello), and also to a nature-outdoorsy camp in the Sierras where her cousins go every summer.

But then one day I happened upon the Web site of Camp Quest, and I was tickled by their tag line: "Camp Quest: a place for fun, friends, and freethought for kids ages 8–17." In reading more, I learned that Camp Quest was founded in the 1990s, when a group of like-minded parents, some from Ohio and some from Kentucky, noticed that while there were a zillion religious summer camp options available for the children of Protestants, Catholics, Jews, Buddhists, Sikhs, Muslims, Baha'is, Mormons, and even Scientologists, there weren't any for the children of atheists, agnostics, and/or secular humanists.

They decided to make it happen. The first camp session took place in Boone County, Kentucky, in 1996, with twenty campers attending. The enterprise has enjoyed impressive growth ever since, as there are now Camp Quests in Arizona, Virginia, Michigan, Minnesota, Montana, Connecticut, Washington, Ohio, Oklahoma, Tennessee, South Carolina, Texas, Kansas, and two in California.

Stacy was open to Camp Quest as a possibility for Flora, but we both wondered: was it really the right camp? We asked ourselves: why send Flora to a camp that *emphasizes* being nonreligious? If we don't want her to go to a religious camp, fine—there are countless nonreligious options out there, camps that focus on hiking, or tennis, or cooking, or gymnastics, or learning Mandarin. But I was further enticed by what I read on the Camp Quest Web site, especially their definition of what "freethought" means: "it means cultivating curiosity, questioning and a certain disdain for just taking the word of authority; demanding evidence and knowing you can make your own observations even if they lead you to disagree." I liked that. Stacy did too. We also liked what they emphasized in the bullet points in their mission statement, such as their goal to "*cultivate reason and empathy* as foundations of an ethical, productive and fulfilling life" and to "*demonstrate* atheism and humanism as positive, family-friendly worldviews." And we also thought that it would be nice for Flora to hang out with kids who are growing up in homes like hers, whose parents hold opinions and worldviews similar to ours, allowing her to find a sense of connection and belonging with other secular kids.

But perhaps more important, we wanted Flora to go to a camp that was openly, proudly, and self-consciously secular, so that she would understand that being nonreligious isn't simply the absence of something; it isn't just a rejection of something. It is about much more than _____ positive embracing of a naturalistic worldview, and of eth-___ reason and empathy. It is about inquiry and skepticism, reason and science, and independence of thought. It is about affirmative, purposeful community united by a grounded orientation to the goodness of this world.

So off she went to Camp Quest. And by sending her there, Stacy and I were actively choosing to include Flora in the growing swell of something relatively new in American culture: the conscious creation of affirmatively secular communities. Such communities are springing up everywhere, from small towns and rural outposts to large cities and major urban centers. From Seattle Atheists, to the Downeast Humanists and Freethinkers of Ellsworth, Maine, from the local chapter of Citizens United for the Separation of Church and State in Sarasota, Florida, to the Utah Coalition of Reason, the river of secular community is swelling. Ten years ago, the American Humanist Association had about 4,000 members; today it has approximately 13,000, with an additional 250,000 likes on Facebook.

People are starting up, organizing, checking out, and joining various atheist, secular, humanist, and nonbeliever groups throughout America for all kinds of reasons. For some, it is about collectively fighting against religion's presence in the public square and seeking to protect the ever-threatened separation of church and state. For others, it is about replacing certain aspects of religion that they miss, especially the experience of being part of a morally minded, multiaged congregational environment that many people cherished as kids. For some, it is about seeking refuge from a social environment in which religion is all-pervasive. For others, it is about deepening their knowledge of secularism—its history, its philosophy, and its potential as a force for good in the world. For some, it is about critiquing and debunking religion, which they see as a malevolent, irrational force. And for a handful, it is about dancing naked under the stars on the summer solstice. But for most, it is simply about getting together with other like-minded people.

Atheist Soldier

Consider Scott Renfro. As he began losing more and more army buddies, he also began losing his faith. He went to Iraq a Christian, but left an atheist. And soon after, he started up a secular club.

Scott is from a small town in central Texas. His father was a fireman for many years but now works as a sheriff's deputy. Scott's mom is a school librarian. Scott was raised a Southern Baptist, going to church every week and Christian camp every summer. He loved the *Left Behind* book series when he was in middle school—those books scared him and further motivated his Christian faith. And when he first met a kid, in his high school chemistry class, who said that he didn't believe in God, Scott's condemnation was swift. "I told him right then and there that he was going to hell."

Today, however, Scott is utterly godless. "I'm an atheist. I don't have a problem with that term. I know that some people prefer to use the term 'agnostic' or 'humanist,' but for me, it's 'atheist.'"

What happened?

"Iraq."

I asked Scott to explain.

"We were assigned to escort fuel trucks from the city of Mosul up to the Turkish border and back. Convoy operations. The route we went out on was getting hit pretty hard, and a bunch of soldiers on that same route had recently gotten killed—it was pretty terrible. Anyway, before we went out on our missions, the chaplain would come in and say a prayer. And this one morning he said something that really put it into perspective for me. It made me say to myself, 'Okay, this doesn't make any sense.' This chaplain said that the reason my unit hadn't had any serious losses yet was because God was protecting us. And I couldn't think of a worse thing to say. I just sat there thinking, 'Well, what about those four guys in that other unit—and I knew two of them—who got killed just yesterday morning? Where was God then?' That's when it really just clicked for me. I was really bothered by it. I got onto Facebook that night and I contacted my youth minister back in Texas and I said, 'Hey, I am having doubts. I don't think I believe this anymore. What should I do?' He couldn't say anything that helped. We exchanged a few messages back and forth and nothing he said convinced me at all. I knew that was that. I didn't believe anymore."

When Scott came home from Iraq, he initially planned on pursuing a career as a police officer. But the new GI Bill paid for college, and at the behest of his wife, he decided to check it out. He enrolled at the local state college, and he loved it. He ended up majoring in anthropology. And he also decided to found a new student group, a chapter of the Secular Student Alliance. "We've got this big campus, and every day you have to walk across it, from building to building. And this one day, last February, I was walking along and I passed three different religious groups that had tables set up in the quad area. And I wondered if there was a secular organization for students like me. There wasn't. So that night I went online and found the Web site for the national Secular Student Alliance and I e-mailed them and I said that I wanted to start up a chapter here and they helped me out and so I did it."

That was last year, when Scott was a junior. Forty students signed up within a week of the group's founding. At the school year's end, they were up to a hundred. Now Scott's a senior—and the group's president—and membership is up to about 150. "To get that many people to willingly sign their name on to such an organization—here in the middle of Texas—I couldn't be happier."

What does the group actually do?

"We host events—you know, panels and things like that. We show movies. We bring guest speakers to campus. We have a table out on the quad with pamphlets and information. And we meet twice a month in a room in the student center. We hang out. Play games. And we're all involved for different reasons. There's one guy in the group who is an ex-Mormon. He was a Mormon but he quit the church and he was really missing the fellowship, the community aspect. So that's why he comes.

"I guess we're a community with the goal to just exist—to exist as a group—to have a group for people who aren't religious. And some people have a problem with that. They say, 'Why do you need a group? Just to sit around and say that you don't believe in anything?' Well, no. It's about more than that. We feel like a minority—most people on campus and in the surrounding area are just so religious here—so it is nice for us to be with people who aren't. To be with people who are like-minded and to be able to just talk about things.

"And there is also a little bit of activism in there, too. People want to feel like they are doing something. There are a lot of issues—in the last election there was Governor Rick Perry holding big prayer rallies here in Texas, and Rick Santorum being against contraception and homosexuality, and Newt Gingrich and all of those types. The whole separation of church and state is a biggie for us."

GROUPS LIKE SCOTT'S are sprouting up just about every other month these days. According to the Secular Student Alliance's national executive director, August Brunsman, while there were only forty-two affiliated campus chapters nationwide back in 2003, by 2008 that had grown to 128, and in 2010 it was up to 234. As of their latest count, there are over 365 such secular student groups on America's college campuses.

There's even one in America's only naval academy, in Annapolis, Maryland. The name of this particular group is NAAFA—Naval Academy Agnostics, Freethinkers, and Atheists. It was started in 2011 by

Ken Forsi, age twenty, from Bridgeport, Connecticut. "I was raised in a fairly liberal religious environment. My mom is a Unitarian and she's pretty involved in her church—my dad not so much. I've always had friends who weren't religious. And I never really put a finger on my own orientation until I went to the Naval Academy. I had never felt a need to label myself an atheist or be out there about not being religious. But when I got to the Naval Academy, there was definitely a heavy presence of Judeo-Christianity."

As Ken explained, during his first week at the academy, there was a huge assembly in the main auditorium, with all the new plebeians present, and at a certain point they were instructed to identify their religion and gather with their coreligionists in specific sections of the auditorium. "They said, 'Okay, all the Catholics go there, all the Baptists go there, if you're Jewish go there.'"

It was very uncomfortable for Ken, as he didn't affiliate with any religion, and yet didn't want to stick out like a sore thumb and feel different; he ended up just going over to the Baptist group because that's where his roommate went. The permeating presence of religion at the academy continued to make him uncomfortable, especially during the structured, chaplain-led prayers that were held several times a week at lunchtime in the cafeteria. And the ethics class Ken took his first year was extremely religious in orientation, as well as the leadership class he took as a sophomore. And then his roommate started pushing the Bible on him. It was all a bit of a culture shock. "It's not like my home back in Connecticut. A lot of people are really religious down here. Coming to the Naval Academy opened my eyes. I was like, 'Wow. People really *believe* this stuff. And there are a lot of them!'"

It was the sanctioned, structured lunchtime prayers that really bothered Ken the most, and he soon found out that he wasn't alone; there were several others who felt the same way. "We started talking about the constitutionality of the prayer thing at lunch and we got very enthused about it. We talked to legal officers and we talked to some of the chaplains. We didn't really get very far, but I did come up with the idea of starting up a group for nontheists. I just thought it would be healthy—especially in this environment. So we sent out an e-mail to the entire brigade just saying, 'Are you interested in joining this nontheist group?' and that was it. We thought we'd be lucky if we got twelve guys responding to our e-mail—but we ended up getting fifty."

The U.S. military has a reputation for being a bastion of religiosity, generally manifested in the form of evangelical Christianity, alongside a pervasive antipathy for atheists, agnostics, humanists, and assorted non-Christians. Several cases in recent years have bolstered this reputation. For example, it was revealed that the army has mandated that all soldiers fill out a survey called the "Soldier Fitness Tracker." One component of the survey is meant to measure soldiers' "spiritual fitness," and if soldiers' scores indicate that they aren't adequately spiritual/religious, they could be designated unfit for duty; this happened to several nonbelieving soldiers, including Sergeant Justin Griffith of Fort Bragg, North Carolina. A couple of years before that, former Air Force Academy officer Mikey Weinstein filed suit against the U.S. Air Force, claiming that those in charge failed to prevent persistent, ongoing Christian proselytizing. And while serving in Iraq, soldier Jeremy Hall was harassed for being an atheist and then subsequently threatened by officers for his part in organizing a group of nonbelieving soldiers; the situation got so bad that he eventually filed a lawsuit against Major Paul Welborne and Defense Secretary Robert Gates. And although there are hundreds of thousands of nonreligious men and women in the military, the government will not allow secular humanists to serve as chaplains.

So the fact that groups like NAAFA are forming in numerous military academies and bases is significant, signaling a trend of collective resistance to this religious hegemony. However, most of the plebeians from the Naval Academy that I spoke with didn't experience any overt harassment or aggressive proselytizing. Rather, there was just sort of an accepted, taken-for-granted Christian culture that made them feel ever so unwelcome, ever so alienated.

Recently, NAAFA has been meeting once a week. They talk about dealing with religious roommates and coping with religious family members, they look at constitutional issues concerning the separation of church and state, they discuss what they're learning in their classes and the books they're reading, they contemplate philosophy and science, ethics and values, and they recently managed to pull off a small party celebrating Darwin Day. They've also been in touch with the national coalition organization MAAF—the Military Association of Atheists and Freethinkers—which is helping them with various programing ideas for the future.

Their biggest accomplishment so far has been to link up with a local Unitarian Universalist church in Annapolis that runs a weeklong humanist summer day camp for kids, named Camp Beagle (the name is in homage to HMS *Beagle*, on which Charles Darwin sailed during his trip to the Galápagos Islands). The camp emphasizes secular humanist values, nature awareness, and scientific thinking, and Ken and several of his friends from the Naval Academy have volunteered as counselors at Camp Beagle for two summers now, something they find extremely enjoyable. As Ken said, "I love doing something positive in the community."

Humanists Doing Good

When it comes to doing something positive in the community, a newly formed group in Sandy Cliffs, Colorado, is definitely noteworthy. They call themselves Humanists Doing Good. Affiliated with the American

Humanist Association, this new manifestation of secular communal life was founded by June and Jim Webb, a couple in their late thirties. June, who works as a clerk at the county courthouse, was born into a very religious Lutheran family (Missouri Synod), and while she couldn't stand the doctrines and beliefs of her parents' religion, she did enjoy the strong sense of community that church provided. Once she had a family of her own, she felt a real lacuna. "I missed feeling like I had that strong social bond with other people. And I especially wanted the kids to have that."

So she and Jim decided to check out the single small atheist group in Sandy Cliffs that met once a month in a back room of a public library. But it just wasn't what Jim and June were looking for. As Jim explained, "The vibe was too negative. It was a lot of criticizing religion, and that's not what we we're about. There was a lot of 'rage against the nativity scene' stuff—there is a nativity scene in front of city hall, and they were against that. Or it was 'rage against the bumper sticker'—someone had seen a religious bumper sticker on a city vehicle and they wanted it removed. You know, that sort of thing. And that's just not what we were looking for. We wanted something positive. And it was also a lot of *talking*. But where was the *doing*? We wanted to be out doing things, being motivated by our humanist values. And we didn't want to be in a group that was solely defined by its opposition to something. That feels too negative. We wanted to be *for* something, to be our own thing, and to find opportunities to be doing good." After talking one night about what their "dream" group would look like, Humanists Doing Good was born. Flyers were printed up, ads were placed in the local paper, a Web site was created—and people joined.

This past year, Jim and June have been good-deed-doers, with a vengeance. Along with about fifty other freethinkers, they have raked the leaves and shoveled the snow off the front lawns and porches of elderly people, they have done trash cleanups at various parks and rivers, they have volunteered at homeless shelters, they have painted animal shelters, they have arranged for elderly and disabled people to get transportation to and from the grocery store or pharmacy, and they have even spread humanist cheer on Christmas Day. "A bunch of our members baked hundreds of goodie bags for Christmas, and we drove around the county on Christmas Day and took them to every person who was working in every business that was open on Christmas Day. Because if you celebrate Christmas and you have to work that day, that sucks. And since we don't celebrate Christmas—for us it is just a day that you sleep in, watch some football, eat some enchiladas—you know, it's not a big day for us. So we ended up with hundreds of bags of cookies and we split up into two groups and we spent the whole day delivering them and it was so much fun. And it meant so much to the people—one of the ladies at Rite Aid wanted to take a picture with us."

It isn't easy to create community from scratch. It isn't easy to get a group of disparate individuals to come together, especially when the larger goal is not to play competitive sports or collect stamps or hunt geese but simply to do good deeds. But June had wanted her daughters to be a part of something akin to a religious congregation, and now they are. In addition to all the positive work they do in their local neighborhoods, the members of Humanists Doing Good get together twice a month for various social events: picnics, movie nights, Ultimate Frisbee games, and "universi-tea" nights, where they sit around drinking tea and discuss a book together. Fostering fellowship has been achieved.

Black Nonbelievers, Inc.

Fostering fellowship is also the key reason that Mandisa Lateefah Thomas founded Black Nonbelievers, Inc. of Atlanta.

Mandisa is thirty-five years old and works as an events services manager at the Centers for Disease Control in Atlanta. She was raised by a single mom in the South Jamaica housing projects of Queens, New York. When Mandisa was twenty-one, she and her husband moved to Atlanta. "The first question we got when we moved down here was, 'What church do you go to?' That's just one of the first questions you get asked, especially if you are black in Atlanta." It was hard to be secular in such an environment. People didn't trust you if they found out that you weren't a Christian. Some people didn't want their kids playing with your kids. And on top of that, there wasn't much in the way of opportunity for purposeful community if it wasn't within a religious context. Feeling somewhat alone as an atheist, and simultaneously feeling the need to make friends and be a part of a group of like-minded people, Mandisa initially decided to check out an atheist meet-up event. It was okay. But it was almost all white people, and being one of the few persons of color was awkward. So she went online and started connecting with a few other black nonbelievers, and they shared similar stories. "The meet-ups and conferences and conventions were predominantly white, and you would feel singled out or just kind of isolated." Did she or any of her online friends endure actual instances of overt racism, or was it more just a feeling of being exoticized? "All of the above."

Mandisa realized that there was a real need out there—the need for black nonbelievers to find one another and create community. Black Nonbelievers, Inc. was born. Although she juggles her time between work, family, and her singing, Mandisa couldn't be happier with this new addition to her life. "It has just been an awesome experience. It has been great. We have general meetings the third Sunday of every month. We do different things—people read poems, we sing songs, we have discussions. We have a lot of food. Lots of socializing. Bowling nights. Holiday dinners. And we signed up for an adopt-a-highway program. We also offer lots of moral support to some of our members who have problems with their neighbors or families or friends—people who are ostracized for being atheists or nonreligious. And we have had some of our members who have had some financial problems, and we have tried to all pitch in and help them out."

While there have certainly been many prominent black atheists and agnostics throughout American history—such as W. E. B. Du Bois, Zora Neale Hurston, James Baldwin, Langston Hughes, Lorraine Hansberry, Richard Wright, Butterfly McQueen, and Morgan Freeman— most African Americans are very religious. Indeed, African Americans are arguably the most religious racial/ethnic group in the United States.

For example, according to recent findings from the Pew Research Center's U.S. Religious Landscape Survey, African Americans have the highest rate of weekly church attendance compared with any group. Nearly 80 percent of African Americans say that religion is very important in their lives, while nearly 90 percent say that they are absolutely certain that God exists. Both percentages are significantly higher than for any other racial/ethnic group in America. Furthermore, only 8 percent of blacks claim to be nonreligious.

Thus Black Nonbelievers, Inc. represents a real minority within a minority. So far the group has about twenty members who regularly show up each month, but special events throughout the year usually attract between thirty and forty people. And Mandisa is sure that there are many more secular men and women out there within the black community. "I've had so many black people say to me, 'I thought I was the only one who didn't believe. I thought I was the only one who questioned.'"

Secular Community Within Church

One more newly formed group to highlight is AAHS—pronounced "*Aaahs*," like the sound a group of thirsty people would make after taking a collective swig of cold lemonade. It stands for Agnostics, Atheists, Humanists, & Secularists, and it was recently founded by Ian Dodd in Santa Monica, California.

Ian is fifty-three, married, the father of two, and he works as a television cameraman. He's also been an active member of a Unitarian Universalist church for nearly ten years now—something he would have never seen coming. "A churchgoer? No, not me." Ian has always been an atheist, he was raised by atheist parents, and he never had any inclination to be involved with religion. However, despite all this, he has found himself becoming quite involved with church life; he's served on a ministerial search committee, he's taught a church youth class for three years, and he's there as a congregant every week. What happened? Why wouldn't an atheist like Ian just stay home on Sundays?

"To be honest, I would stay home. But I like my wife, and I like my wife's company, and my wife is much more of a joiner, she's much more of a people-oriented person. So she was the one who first made the bid to check out the Unitarian church. She had gone to a funeral at the Unitarian church and was very impressed by it. So she came home after that—and this was just before her birthday—and she says to me and the kids, 'Okay, here's what I want for my birthday: I want for us to go to the Unitarian church for four Sundays in a row." By the end of the second Sunday, Ian's wife was ready to join. She felt like "these are my people, these are my values." So Ian agreed to join too. In addition to making his wife happy, a big draw for him was the programs that the church had for the kids, especially a class for those in middle school that explored values, beliefs, identity, and "the big questions." Their daughter enrolled and got a lot out of it. Ian eventually became one of the teachers.

However, despite enjoying many aspects of being in the Unitarian church community, Ian wanted something more, something different, something that was a little more true to his secular worldview. He felt that if he was going to be a member of a church, so be it, but he also needed to be a member of a group that affirmed his atheism. When a couple of older members, also atheists, expressed similar sentiments, the idea to form the group arose. "A handful of us started meeting throughout the summer of 2010, and by the end of the summer there were ten or twelve regular members. So we began trying to think of events that we could put on to promote our naturalistic worldview."

Their first public event took place the following fall, held in the church sanctuary, and it included a lecture by Greg Epstein, the humanist chaplain at Harvard University and author of *Good Without God*. Ian worked hard to publicize the event, and it paid off, as there were nearly two hundred people in attendance. "That event really put us on the map within the congregation. Since then, we've put on a number of other talks, and just last week we did a big barbecue in the church courtyard with this group called Generation Atheist—a meetup group that caters to nonbelievers in their twenties and thirties—and we had over sixty people for that. We also just held a dinner party with the guest of honor being a woman who recently edited a new edition of the Jefferson Bible. Since Thomas Jefferson was ambassador to France, we cooked up a French meal, we got a bunch of Bordeaux wine, and we had this great discussion about Jefferson's views on religion, the separation of church and state, and the First Amendment."

This community within a community has been very rewarding for Ian. He gets the best of both worlds: he is part of the Unitarian Universalist church, which makes his wife happy and provides a nice community atmosphere for his family, and now he is also part of AAHS, which satisfies him intellectually and allows him to be part of something collective that is more closely aligned with his secular identity. And the fact that many other people out there seem interested in what he is doing is quite affirming. "I've been contacted by members of other Unitarian churches in the area saying, 'Hey, we've heard about your group. We'd like to start something like that here as well—can you give us a hand?'"

The last time I touched base with Ian, he was branching out; the new Sunday Assembly of Los Angeles was just starting up, and he was on the governing board. Dubbed by the media as an "Atheist Church," Sunday Assembly is drawing impressive crowds for once-a-month gatherings of people coming together who are seeking to experience the best of religion—community, music, fellowship, charitable opportunities, and inspiration—but without any reference to or invocation of the supernatural.

Secular Identity and Individualism

Whatever the disparate reasons for joining such groups as those profiled above, there is one thing that these individuals all share: a sense that being secular is an important, defining aspect of their identity. It is a big part of who they are. They may be lots of other things—a woman, an American, a motorcycle enthusiast, a probation officer, a vegetarian, a flight attendant, a father, an accordionist—but being secular is also high on their list.

This is certainly the case with me; being secular is an undeniably huge part of my identity. But it strikes me that while most of the kids I grew up with were secular and still are as they wade through middle age, and while many of my current friends and colleagues are secular, hardly any of them think, talk, or even seem to care much about being so.

Unlike most of these friends and colleagues, for me being secular has tremendous significance. My personal heroes include unabashed freethinkers like Thomas Paine, Robert Ingersoll, and Ayaan Hirsi Ali. I subscribe to magazines like *Free Inquiry*. I am a member of the American Humanist Association. I am regularly invited to speak to groups such as the Freedom from Religion Foundation. I teach courses on secular life, I read books about secularism and secularization, and I write books about secular culture. And so if I had to make a list of the interests or passions that most define who I am as an individual, they would certainly include (though not in ranked order): apples, all things Scandinavian, music made between 1966 and 1973, and secularity.

And all of this brings me back to Camp Quest, and why I wanted Flora to go there. After all, if being secular wasn't such a big deal for me, I probably would have not been so attracted to the Camp Quest Web site. But I was. It drew me in. It spoke to me. And since being secular is a big part of who I am, I didn't want Flora to go to just any old camp that didn't have a religious element. No—I wanted her to go to a camp that was affirmatively secular.

BUT OF COURSE most secular people are not like me in terms of having such a pronounced secular sense of self. For most nonreligious people, being secular is way down on the list of who they are and how they see themselves. It isn't at the forefront of their identity. It isn't something they think too much about. They don't read about it, they don't write about it, and they don't obsess about it. And they certainly wouldn't be attracted to something like Camp Quest. In fact, only a tiny minority of secular people would even bother to get involved in the sort of secular groups described in this chapter.

How small a minority? "I would estimate that only somewhere between 1 and 2 percent of secular people actually get involved with organized secular communal life." That sober assessment comes from Dr. Frank Pasquale, an anthropologist who lives in Portland, Oregon. Frank has been studying contemporary secular groups in America longer than anyone—about thirteen years now.

As an ethnographer, he has spent time among and carefully observed numerous secular groups of various types—atheist groups, humanist groups, Unitarian humanist groups, Jewish humanist groups, skeptical/rationalist groups, and many more—mostly in the Pacific Northwest, but also in the Northeast. He's attended their meetings, their potlucks, their lectures and discussions, their film festivals, and other activities. He's interviewed them and surveyed them. And one of the main things that he has noticed is what I have just broached above—that people who affiliate with secular groups are generally people who place being secular at the core of how they see themselves.

"There is a small percentage of secular people who focus on secularity itself as a central or core of their identity. And they then are the ones who tend to become actively involved with secularist groups—and by 'secularist' I mean that they maintain a focus on secularism or secularity in such a way that they turn it into an identity, almost analogous to a religious identity, and it becomes an ideological core of people's sense of self. But again, they are a very small percentage." According to Dr. Pasquale, the "natural resting state" of secularity for most people is thus not active atheism or passionate irreligion, nor is it one of secular advocacy or secular group affiliation. Rather, it is mere *indifference* concerning religion—and indifference or lack of interest concerning secularist groups as well.

While Dr. Pasquale readily acknowledges that secular groups are currently exploding across America and that more and more are being created, with increasing membership and activity, he nonetheless doubts that they will ever match—or even come close to—the level of communal engagement one finds among the religious. Why? Because the very nature of being secular is such that it does not lend itself to joining large groups of like-minded people specifically on the basis of their secularity. At the very heart or core of being secular, at least for many people, is a degree of suspicion toward communal dictates, group conformity, or social immersion, particularly when based on religion, nonreligion, or irreligion. Psychological studies back this up; recent research indicates that atheists and agnostics tend to value the autonomy of the individual rather than loyal bonds to a collective. And a recent Pew study found that while nearly half of all Americans say that belonging to a community of like-minded people is very important to them, only 28 percent of nonreligious Americans say as much.

As Dr. Pasquale explains, being secular is strongly linked to and is very much a manifestation or expression of individualization and individualism, which involve (1) an emphasis on increased personal autonomy, (2) reserving the right of individual choice in many aspects of one's life, (3) a rejection of traditional worldviews, and (4) a reluctance to join or be a part of traditional forms of association purely on the basis of metaphysical beliefs (or the lack thereof). "If religion, as Emile Durkheim suggested, is a kind of social glue, reinforcing a sense of connection and a sense of societal solidarity, then secularity is a reaction to that—an individualistic reaction. It is, in a sense, saying, 'I'm deliberately distancing myself from the unquestioned authority of tradition, particularly traditions associated with supernatural ideas, and I am detaching myself from that.'"

Rather than becoming a member of a large-scale group where a lot of the beliefs and activities are essentially laid out—like a prix fixe menu—most secular people prefer to take an à la carte approach to constructing their worldviews, their lives, their social networks, and their contributions to society. "So when people become secular they are not only distancing themselves from supernatural thinking or religious institutions, but they are reserving the right of personal choice and also taking on personal responsibility for many aspects of their lives. They are saying, 'I am an autonomous human being and that means I have the right and responsibility to evaluate all of the traditions that have been handed down to me and of deciding where I think they are right or wrong.' Again, secularity really is a species of individualism." Other scholars agree with this assessment, such as University of San Francisco professor John Nelson, who notes that increased personal agency in determining one's own individual life course—a hallmark of our modern world—is significantly correlated with secularity.

Professor Pasquale is emphatic, however, on one point: just because secular people tend to strongly value autonomy and be more individualistic, this does not mean that they are all a bunch of antisocial hermits. It does not mean that they do not enjoy meaningful social connections. It does not mean that they don't get involved in causes or clubs or corporations or volunteer groups. They do. But they tend to develop these meaningful social connections and contributions *by choice*—through their relationships with their family, their friends, their colleagues, or with people who share similar personal interests, ideals, and passions. They tend not to find it by affiliating with formal, structured groups or organizations specifically on the basis of their secularity.

As Georgetown University professor Jacques Berlinerblau has quipped, "Secularism has a 'we' problem. Secularists don't do 'we.'" And while I would argue that this may be a bit of an overstatement— the mere existence of organizations such as Camp Quest and groups like AAHS clearly counter his assertion—Dr. Berlinerblau is certainly on to something about secular people's less than impressive communal inclinations. Recent research within the realm of psychology is relevant here. Dr. Catherine Caldwell-Harris is a professor of psychology at Boston University, and she has published several important papers looking at what might distinguish nonreligious people from their religious peers—personality-wise, that is. Some of the key differences that she has found are predicated upon the fact that nonbelievers generally tend to be much less social, less conformist, and more individualistic than believers on average, and ultimately "less in need of social support."

If Professors Pasquale, Caldwell-Harris, and Berlinerblau are correct—that the very nature of being secular involves an inherent reluctance toward joining or associating with structured, cohesive, like-minded groups—then attempts to create explicitly secularist communities in America may be, if not necessarily doomed, then certainly limited. The ironic fact is that even though secular groups like Humanist Friendship Group of Central Indiana or the Hawaii Secular Society or Alaskan Atheists are ostensibly antireligious in content and mission, such secular groups may still be too "religious-like" in form, structure, and style to attract most secular people.

Humanist Community Centers

But don't tell any of this to Greg Epstein, the humanist chaplain at Harvard University. I mentioned him earlier—he is the author of *Good Without God,* and he spoke at the inaugural event of AAHS in Santa Monica. Greg has devoted his life to creating humanist community, and his work in Boston has been very successful: hundreds of students are involved with his Humanist Community Project, whose mission is "to develop opportunities for connection, ethical development, and the celebration of life based on human reason, compassion, and creativity, not religious dogma" and to "organize, facilitate, promote, and/or study a wide range of educational programs, social meetings, service projects, human rights work, counseling, ceremonies, and contemplative practices that contribute to the growth of diverse and interconnected groups of Humanists, atheists, agnostics and the nonreligious."

Greg takes all of this stuff very seriously. It is his life's work. He is passionate, energized, smart, charismatic, articulate, driven—in short, if ever there was a humanist man on a mission in America, it is undoubtedly Greg Epstein. And in flagrantly optimistic dismissal of what anthropologist Frank Pasquale or psychologist Catherine Caldwell-Harris may say about secular people not being open to or interested in such endeavors, Greg is moving forward with his goal: to establish dynamic, successful humanist community centers in every city in America. As he passionately preached while speaking to the members of AAHS in the Unitarian Universalist church sanctuary in Santa Monica (I happened to be there for his talk), "We *can* have a thriving ethical, moral community for this ever-growing population of secular Americans. We *can* unite as humanists. And humanism will do best when it expresses itself organizationally as a network of local, multigenerational, multicultural communities spread across the country."

In order for such humanist communities to become a reality throughout the land, much is required: more charismatic leaders like Greg, lots of money, and a lot more people interested in gathering with others like them—not under the banner of being antireligious, because being *against* something isn't the quality of communal glue needed here, but rather under the banner of humanism, which is an affirmative, positive, optimistic alternative orientation.

If secularism is to be understood as a political ideology or social-movement agenda that advocates (at least) the separation of church and state or (at most) the diminishment of religion in society, then humanism can be understood as a related and yet distinct phenomenon; it is more of an optimistic cultural expression or personal world-view, defined by what beliefs it eschews as well as what beliefs it affirms. Simply put, humanism rejects belief in heaven, hell, God, gods, and all things supernatural, while at the same time affirming belief in the positive potential for humans to do and be good, loving, and altruistic. Humanism rejects faith in favor of reason, it rejects superstition in favor of evidence-based thinking, and it replaces worship of a deity with an appreciation for and love of humankind and the natural world. According to the proclamation of the Ethical Culture movement, founded by Felix Adler in 1877, humanism is based on the ideal that "the supreme aim of human life is to create a more humane society." Humanism is thus deeply moral in its fervent commitment to improving and enhancing life, and Greg believes that Americans would do well to gather and congregate as humanists in much the same way religious people do. "If you join a moral community that asks you to be a better person, well—surprise, surprise—you might find that this community actually helps you in becoming just that: a better person."

Greg grew up in Flushing, Queens, New York. His parents were Jewish, but purely in the cultural, ethnic sense, not in the religious, believing sense. Despite their own lack of faith, religion was definitely a topic of interest, fascination, and debate in the Epstein household, and the bookshelves were full of volumes on religion, spirituality, and related philosophy. And in Greg's neighborhood, things like faith, belief, ritual, and the search for ultimate truth and meaning were everywhere. As he explained to me, "Flushing is the most religiously diverse neighborhood in the most religiously diverse city in the most religiously diverse country in the world. I had friends from every religious background imaginable. And I saw that there were all these different things that people ostensibly believe in, and it made me ask a lot of questions. Which ones were true? Which ones weren't?"

These questions were pressing for Greg, even when he was just a kid. They lingered throughout his teenage years, and by the time he got to college he decided to be a religious studies major. "I wanted to know: What is true? What is meaningful? What is the good life?" Although not a convinced believer himself, he was open to whatever insights religion could offer on these matters, and he was drawn to the glow of religious inquiry and philosophy. He double-majored in Chinese so that he could simultaneously immerse himself in Eastern approaches to these existential, spiritual questions. Not compelled or moved by what he found within Judaism, Christianity, or Islam, but intrigued by Eastern spirituality, Greg headed off to China after graduating from college. He saw himself eventually becoming an ordained Taoist priest.

But that wasn't to be. In the words of acerbic atheist Christopher Hitchens, "There is no Eastern solution"—and that's certainly what Greg was to personally find out. "I got to China and I met the people that I would ostensibly be studying with and learning from and just being around them and being in that world—there was this really intuitive sense that I got about them that *they were just people like anybody else*. I think I was expecting some kind of transcendence. I was expecting them to be fully self-realized spiritual masters. And they were just people. They were no more fully self-realized than anybody else. Suddenly I just saw that Buddhism and Taoism were very much humanly created, just like every other religion I had ever studied. I realized that people are people and all religions are created by human beings for human purposes."

Greg came back from China somewhat disillusioned, and so he switched gears, focusing for several years on rock music rather than the ultimate questions of existence and meaning. But his hiatus only lasted so long, and soon he was drawn back to the deep philosophical and existential questions he so passionately cared about—and this time, he found a home in humanism. "I just knew. Humanism was the thing that I had been waiting my whole life to hear about."

In the early 2000s, Greg got involved in Humanistic Judaism, which was founded in 1963 by Sherwin Wine. Humanistic Judaism is a non-theistic Jewish movement that bases Jewish identity in communal, cultural, and historical experiences, focusing on the celebration of holidays and life-cycle events rather than belief in God. Greg was ordained as a humanist rabbi in 2005, and he then went on to earn a master of theological studies degree from Harvard Divinity School. Shortly thereafter, he got his current job as the humanist chaplain at Harvard University. It was an unusual trajectory for an atheist, to say the least. But Greg openly admits that he is not your typical atheist. In fact, he happily describes himself as having "an intensely religious personality without a scintilla of religious belief." When I asked him what he meant by saying that he had an "intensely religious personality," he replied, "I am really interested in these questions of: Who am I? Why am I here? Why are any of us here? What is life supposed to be all about? What does it mean to connect with other people? These questions are really important to me. I think that there is more to life than just being rational and logical. Those modes are not enough to being completely human. I tend to feel things very deeply, and I wonder a lot." The only thing that Greg doesn't like about religion is the supernatural beliefs. But otherwise, he's down with the enterprise. Hence his personal commitment to creating and developing humanist community centers that provide all that religions do, minus the theologies, the faith, the deities.

When I asked Greg to describe his ultimate vision of a fully realized humanist community center of the near future, his dream came pouring out with enthusiasm and excitement: "There would be a physical building and it would be a beautiful space, decorated by all kinds of art. There will be great music happening there—definitely a performance space that innovative artists would want to come to in order to perform and collaborate. And there would be programs for people of different ages and different cultural backgrounds, different personal styles. There will be some kind of 'Sunday school' for kids, where they can learn how to discuss questions like, 'What is my identity?' and 'What does it mean to be a humanist?' and they would learn about humanism as a core philosophy of life—a core life stance that they can call upon for inspiration, so they can approach questions like, 'What does it mean to be ethical? How do I find a sense of equanimity amidst the stresses of life? When are meaningful times to celebrate in life? How can I cultivate mindfulness?' So, yeah, lots of stuff for kids.

"And we would have therapists and psychologists and scientists and historians and artists help us design the lesson plans and the curriculum. And there would also be adult education offerings, exploring various aspects of humanist values and what it means to live a good life as a humanist. And lots of small groups and peer education. And there would be space for a diversity of cultural groups, such as Humanistic Judaism or a group for cultural Catholics or African American humanists or Confucian humanism and Indian humanism. And lots of artists of every kind, so there would always be art being created and music being created and stories being told.

"And there would be ceremonies of various kinds—humanist confirmations, humanist weddings, humanist funerals, humanist naming ceremonies, and weekly gatherings of various types, involving music, storytelling, inspirational discussion, food, and people getting to know each other. And most importantly, there would be a ton of community service going on, so that humanists would become known for taking on meaningful projects within their cities and towns that make a difference in the world. It would become known as a place for people to come and do community service that benefits humanity."

I FIND GREG'S passion contagious. Whenever we get together and talk, it is always the case that afterward I remain high on the fumes of our conversation for quite some time, feeling excited and enthusiastic about the prospects for creating humanist communities throughout the land. And I want to get personally involved. I want to experience the humanist community center of Greg's dreams: I want to see my younger kids in the Sunday school, writing sonnets or creating mobiles and learning about Picasso and Martha Graham. I want to see my older daughter leading a discussion on the books of Philip Pullman or Haruki Murakami. I want to be a part of a community service project, along with my fellow humanists, helping those in our neighborhood who are in need, or planting trees, or fixing bikes. And I want to attend a humanist weekly gathering where we read poetry by Walt Whitman and sing songs by John Lennon, and then afterward I want to eat coffee cake in a shaded patio and stand around talking to someone about how unbelievable it is that we have the death penalty in America and how Lars von Trier's latest film really stunk and how there is this great hiking trail near Mount Baldy that is practically empty. I want this community to exist and I want to join it.

I'm not so sure, however, if my wife, Stacy, would be that interested. The fact is, Stacy is all too typically secular in this regard: she isn't much of a joiner. Being part of a community has never had much of an appeal to her. She is as rugged an individualist as they come. A perfect anecdote illustrates this well: Several years ago, I gave a talk at a Unitarian Universalist church in Orange County—I had attended the whole service before giving my talk, and I had enjoyed the songs and the readings and the people and the whole collective vibe. When I came home, I said to Stacy, "You know, I liked that service. I think I would consider joining such a congregation."

"Why?" she asked.

"Well, for the community."

"Ugh. Who needs community?" was her caustic reply, which she offered while gesticulating her dismissal of the idea with a wave of her hands.

The difference between Stacy and me on this matter is clear. I am a bit more like Greg Epstein; I too am quite "religious" in my secularity. As I said earlier, it is a big part of my identity, I think about it and read about it and talk about it a lot, and I would be very interested in joining a community group of similarly oriented individuals. Stacy, however, is perhaps more truly secular in her secularity than I am. She is so secular that being secular is of little personal significance—she doesn't obsess about it, doesn't fixate on it, and would much rather spend her time doing other things and pursuing other personal interests and enjoying her own individual connections with her close family and friends than joining a humanist community center. But of course, if there were such a humanist center nearby, and if I were to get involved, I am sure she'd agree to come along now and then. Just as she agreed to send Flora to Camp Quest.

Which, by the way, was a great success. Flora had a blast. When I went to pick her up at camp's end, I couldn't help but bring along my tape recorder. And once we had all her things together (sleeping bag, ceramic creations, clothes), and after she had said her tearful farewells to her newly made friends and hugged her cabin mates and counselors good-bye, we got in the car and I hit record. Here's what Flora said about her Camp Quest experience, nearly verbatim:

"There was this one point where we had 'weird and wacky science' with Ross where we made a *real* battery that works. Here's what you do:

you lay a nickel and then you get a small quarter of lemon-soaked tissue or something, and then you lay a penny, and you do that for a while, and we got a battery. And also we made silly putty. And also he knows 150 places of pi, and he said it to us. It was so crazy! Blah, blah, blah! And then it was really fun—we had to take a forty-five-minute bus ride to this lake and it was so much fun and when we got there it was huge and beautiful but it was kind of embarrassing because we all had to wear swim caps. But the water was so nice. And Wendy was so nice. At first it was kind of like new and stuff, but then we got to know each other better and then we formed a group—me, Wendy, and then Raven. And we would wake up early in the morning and we would go down and get hot chocolate and then we would get to ring the bell. The food was *so* good. One time it was grilled cheese and tomato soup. Another time it was lasagna. And I had a jalapeño! It was *very* hot! We would sit around the table and see who could eat a jalapeño without needing water, yeah . . . and every night we sat around the campfire and had s'mores and sang songs and did skits. Oh, but this was the worst: one time I was sleeping in my bed and I woke up and something was running down my nose a lot and I was like, 'Oh, no—it can't be a bloody nose!' and it was like gushing and I couldn't sit up because it was just gushing so much. So I said, 'Wendy, I have a bloody nose!' and she was so nice, she just jumped right out of her bunk and got me some tissue. And one time we saw raccoons . . . [*So what was the best thing about camp? What did you like the best?*] The best thing was—I liked free time. You could do whatever you wanted. I would do archery or go to the climbing wall or go to the pool or do arts and crafts. I would do it with Wendy and Raven. . . . [*Did you learn anything?*] Yeah, we learned stuff. We learned that a very, very, very good person who was born in like BC or something—he was a guy with a beard. He was teaching people to think for themselves so the king or something, or the people, they made him drink hemlock."

A very, very, very good person who lived in "BC" and had a beard and taught people to think for themselves? At Camp Quest, that would be Socrates.

CAMP QUEST IS such a laudable model for the creation of secular community in America because it is not solely or primarily about being against religion. After all, any community that is predicated principally upon *anti*-ness is ultimately doomed to toxic curmudgeondom. So it's a good thing that being antireligious has little place in the goings-on of Camp Quest. Rather, it is principally about fostering positive humanistic ideals. And these ideals are bolstered by the cultivation of a sense of support and solidarity for the children of freethinkers.

Flora did not have secularism shoved down her throat while at Camp Quest. Rather, she learned a little about the history of free thought, a little about science, a little about nature, and a whole lot about fun and friendship. And hopefully, she got a comforting sense that there are lots of other people out there like her and her family— people who can find sanctuary under a canopy of trees, communion amid campfires, and meaningfulness through arts and crafts; people who believe that faith in God may be perfectly fine for others, but it is certainly not necessary in order to live an ethical and engaging life. Nor is such faith necessary when helping a bunkmate with a bloody nose; empathy and Kleenex are more than sufficient.

Chapter 6

Trying Times

W e met in French class. Her name was Krissy. She was sixteen. She had large eyes, she got average grades, she liked
MTV, she drank Miller Genuine Draft, and she was my
first serious girlfriend. And her father happened to be an evangelical
preacher. Originally from Kansas, Krissy's dad had gotten the call in
the early 1980s to move out west with his family and start a new
church in Southern California. And one Sunday morning, I accepted
their invitation go with them to their church.

It was in a large, unremarkable building near a mall in Newport
Beach. I had never been to an evangelical, nondenominational church
service before. There were a lot of people—well over three hundred.
Mostly white. And there was a lot of energy. People were into it. I enjoyed seeing Krissy's dad up there at the helm, leading the whole thing.
He had an earnest, unsappy demeanor that I found respectable. There
were songs, prayers, sermons, and announcements. But the moment
I remember most vividly was when Krissy's father called a young couple and their small baby up to the pulpit. They came forward, this man
and his wife, both in their twenties, cradling their infant in their

arms. They somberly faced the congregation as Krissy's dad raised his arms up over them, palms open, fingers wide.

Krissy's dad explained to his flock that this young couple's new baby had a heart defect and was predicted to die within the month. As he spoke these words, the young couple began to cry. Krissy's dad asked the entire congregation to pray together for a miracle, to pray for this young couple's baby to be healed, for her little heart to be mended. Everyone closed their eyes and began praying fervently, while Krissy's father led them with heartfelt words, beseeching God to save this little child.

I remember that as I sat there, my initial reaction was: flummoxed. Pray to God to heal a baby's defective heart? Really? But doesn't God, being omniscient, already know that this baby's heart is defective? And doesn't God, being omnipotent, already have the ability to heal the baby's heart if he wants to? Isn't the defective heart thus part of God's plan? What good is prayer, then? Do these people really think that God will alter his will if they only pray hard enough? And if they don't pray hard enough, he'll let the baby die? What kind of a God is that? Such coldly skeptical thoughts percolated through my fifteen-year-old brain.

But they soon fizzled out. As I sat there looking at the crying couple, listening to the murmur of prayers all around me, my initial skepticism was soon supplanted by a sober appreciation and empathetic recognition of what I was witnessing and experiencing. Here was an entire body of people all expressing their love and sympathy for a young couple with a dying baby. Here were hundreds of people caringly, genuinely, warmly pouring out their hearts to this poor unfortunate man, woman, and child. The love and sadness in the gathering were palpable, and I "got" it. I could see the intangible benefit of such a communal act. There was that poor couple at the front of the church, crying, while everyone around them was showering them with support and hope. While I didn't buy the literal words of the pastor, I surely understood their deeper significance: they were making these suffering people feel a bit better. And while I didn't think the congregation's prayers would realistically count for a hill of beans toward actually curing that baby, I was still able to see that it was a serenely beneficial act nonetheless, for it offered hope and solace to these unlucky parents, as well as to everyone else present there in that church who was feeling sadness for them, or for themselves and their own personal misfortunes. So while I sat there, absolutely convinced that there exists no God who heals defective baby hearts, I also sat there equally convinced that this mass prayer session was a deeply good thing. Or if not a deeply good thing, then at least a deeply understandable thing. I felt so sad for that young couple that day. I could not, and still cannot, fathom the pain of having a new baby who, after only a few months of life, begins to die.

Since that day, I have acknowledged and appreciated the benefits of religion for people enduring trying times. When people experience pain or suffering, illness or death, hardship or devastation, fear or loss, religion can be a unique balm. It works on two fronts, providing both communal support and personal psychological comfort. Those experiencing life's difficulties can rely on the care and camaraderie of their coreligionists, who will pray for them, bake for them, watch their kids for them, raise money for them, donate blood for them, and then some. And for the soul of the individual who is suffering, having faith in God can provide a sense of inner peace, love, or hope. Such a faithful person can know that they are not lost entirely, they are not alone, no matter how dire or painful their situation may be. God is up there, with outstretched arms.

Given these undeniably comforting aspects of religion, it comes as no surprise that extensive research over several decades has revealed the positive and beneficial ways in which religion helps people cope with life's trials and tribulations. For example, numerous studies have shown that religion can help people cope with various forms of stress, it can help parents cope with the death of their children, it can help people seeking to overcome alcohol addiction, it can help people deal with chronic illness and pain, it can help people cope with cancer, it can help comfort refugees fleeing persecution, it can help the victims of sexual assault, and in still more ways. Such extensive research allows leading psychologist of religion Ralph Hood to confidently declare the justified truism that "turning to one's faith in times of difficulty is helpful and constructive in dealing with both problems and emotions." What is common to all of the above research, however, is that it generally shows that people who are *already* religious are able to successfully draw from their faith or religious community in coping with difficult life circumstances. As the leading expert on religious coping Professor Kenneth Pargament readily acknowledges, it comes as no surprise that the people who find religion most helpful as a coping mechanism are those very people who already maintain higher levels of religiosity, and thus "those who invest more in their religion gain more from it in coping." This is to be expected.

But what about the nonreligious? What about those who don't believe in God and don't believe in the efficacy of prayer and aren't interested in joining a religious congregation? What do these millions of secular men and women in America do when they face hard times? How exactly do they cope without the benefit of religious faith or community?

In my research, I've sought out and interviewed many such nonreligious people who have experienced traumas, tragedies, and all-around tough times. I've interviewed those who are battling cancer, parents who have lost children, children who have lost parents, siblings who have lost siblings, spouses who have lost spouses, people who have gone through nasty divorces, endured prison, disease—and I've even talked to quite a few atheists who have spent a good amount of time in foxholes, from Normandy to Da Nang to Baghdad. I've spoken to atheists who have experienced spinal cord injuries, agnostics who survived the Holocaust, and nonbelievers who have battled severe drug addiction. Their experiences and insights reveal that while it may not be as easy to endure trying times without the comfort of religion, it still can be done. In fact, it *is* done—every day, all the time.

Overcoming Injury

On a rainless night in Seattle, at around 2:30 in the morning, Amber Olson was sitting on her idling moped at an intersection, waiting for the light to turn green. She had just bought some cigarettes and was heading over to a friend's apartment, which was about two blocks away. The light was still red. That's when a drunk driver plowed into her from behind and sped away into the darkness, leaving Amber mangled on the pavement—bleeding, alone, and unconscious. She woke up several days later in a hospital bed, heavily sedated. Her mother was at her side. The doctors informed Amber that she had had a T-6 complete spinal cord injury, which meant that she was permanently paralyzed from the mid-sternum down. "And I can't feel anything either," Amber explained to me. "From my chest all the way down to my toes."

Amber was twenty-six when the accident occurred. She is now thirty-two. She is pretty, smart, and exudes a calm demeanor as she sits in her wheelchair. You can see some pale scars scattered across her face—scars that I assume are from the accident, but I didn't directly ask about them.

Amber was born and raised in Provo, Utah. Both her parents were Mormon, as were her grandparents, great-grandparents, and so on.

"They go back to the beginning of the church. They came across the plains. They were pioneers."

By the time Amber was in the fifth grade, she realized that if she wanted to have any social life at all, she had to be religious. Everyone else was, literally—every single kid in her school and in her neighborhood was actively involved in the Mormon faith. So even though her folks actually were no longer very interested, Amber became religious. "I started going to church on my own. Involvement with the Mormon religion is like a daily thing. I went to church every Sunday, but there was also a young women's club with activities throughout the week. And service projects. And it was something we all did together—all of my friends. And then also camp in the summer." Amber was also a believer. Her enmeshment in the Mormon religion wasn't thus strictly a social matter. It was definitely very much about faith. "I believed. I prayed. I definitely did. I read the Book of Mormon. Later, I took two years of seminary classes. I got up every morning at six o'clock in the morning to learn and study and pray. I really did believe."

But then, when Amber was fifteen, she moved to Montana with her mother for a year. Upon their return to Utah, something had changed. Maybe it was simply getting away from Provo for a spell. Or maybe it was meeting other people and making new friends—friends who weren't Mormon and didn't know anything about Mormonism; some of them even smoked cigarettes and drank wine coolers. Or maybe it was just that she went through puberty. But whatever it was, during the year after Montana, when Amber was back in Utah and a junior in high school, her faith melted away. It happened fairly quickly, and absolutely. She no longer believed—at all.

As she explains, "I was sixteen or seventeen. At that point it was just like, 'This is *crazy*.' I just *knew*. It was like I just knew that I don't believe there's a God. I just *can't* believe there's a God. And not even just removing it from Mormon theology—but just in general. All of it—

God, religion. How can you die and go somewhere? I mean, you die and there's something that goes somewhere? *What?* I just don't believe that. So the whole thing, yeah, I just couldn't believe."

Amber found a few like-minded students and hung out with them for the remainder of her high school days. And she's been utterly secular ever since. Although she personally doesn't like or use the label, she's a convinced atheist. She thinks science is the only possible method for understanding any questions pertaining to the nature of the universe, and she knows that there's nothing mystical, spiritual, or magical out there. Just the natural world. "I simply cannot know the forces behind existence. I just don't think that there is any 'spiritual' element involved—but I still stand in awe at the physical forces that shape our universe."

After graduating from high school, Amber moved to Tacoma, Washington, where she lived with her aunt. She learned how to weld at the local community college. She then moved up to Seattle, where, in addition to her welding, she started working at an independent bookstore. Life was really, really good. She was in her twenties. She was making enough money to afford a small but nice apartment in a perfect part of town. She had health insurance through her work at the bookstore. She had great friends, cute boyfriends—a rich social life. She had her favorite coffeehouses, her favorite bands, her favorite nightclubs, and her favorite mode of transportation: a used Vespa moped.

It, too, was mangled that night, along with her spine.

In an instant, everything in Amber's life changed for the much, much worse. "The firemen who arrived on the scene saved my life. It was actually my friend that I was going to meet—he heard the ambulance sirens and came out to look and see what was going on and so he told me what happened. The firemen, the paramedics, they got there almost right away and they did everything right and they took me to a good hospital. When I eventually woke up, I was heavily drugged. My dad says that the first thing I said was, 'I can't fucking feel anything. What's going on?'"

Although she had health insurance from the bookstore, it wasn't comprehensive. It didn't cover the extensive costs of her dire medical situation, such as any outpatient physical therapy. "My mom shelled out so much money. You wouldn't believe how much. All her life savings. But still—the hospital where I could have gone for the best physical therapy and rehabilitative training, well, it was just too expensive. So I ended up just kind of having to do it on my own. It took a long time. It took a lot of effort. It was really humiliating, all of it. And it's still humiliating. It's not just that I can't walk. I can't feel anything. I have no feeling—so I can't tell if my bladder is full, you know? Instead of having a body that you can do things with, I have—it's like a sort of alien thing that I have to manage, stuck to my brain. It's just not very . . . I don't know . . . not fun."

Depression hit her hard. In the bleak year after the accident, Amber found adjusting to her new situation almost impossible. She didn't want to live. Suicide seemed like a viable option.

But it was the love she had for her mother, and her mother's love for her, that kept Amber going. "My mother forced me to live. That was what started out my recovery. I was thinking, 'I can't kill myself because my mom will be so sad. I can't do that to her.' My mother didn't leave my side for six months. She took a leave from her job and was just there. She did everything. She found me a wheelchair-accessible apartment and she lived there with me for months. She went and bought furniture—just everything. She's the saint in all of this. So I guess I was living for someone else at first—for her. But soon you think, 'Okay, it can be done. It's manageable. It could be so much worse.'"

From the first sedated hours in the hospital, through that first difficult year and beyond, Amber never once turned to God. "I didn't even think about God. I never did. I never really even thought about it. My nonbelief is so complete that, well, there you go." But wouldn't having had some faith in God have been advantageous during that time after the accident, at least psychologically?

Amber doesn't think so. "If you believe that 'God is in control'—I don't think that's helpful. And I don't think you learn from that. I don't think you can learn anything from that—just giving up or giving away your responsibility to God. There's potential to learn from these kinds of things, and you give it away when you give responsibility to something that you don't see and then believe in. . . . I prefer to affirm belief in life. *You* have the potential to change, to change it *yourself*, and you don't have to give it away to some 'higher power.' You have to be able to take responsibility for your own—for the next steps that you need to take after something traumatic. If I was a believer, I don't know . . . I can see that it is comforting to think that there is a 'reason,' that there is a 'plan,' and that there's somebody watching out for you, somebody that will provide the answer—like, someday you'll know why. 'When you die, you'll find out. So you should look forward to that, and just rest assured that it's for a good reason.' But it's like, I *know* there is no good reason for this to have happened. So what you do is you pick up and move on."

So how did she cope, if not with all that comes with religion?

Her mother was central, no doubt. And in addition to her mother, Amber benefited from having solid friends. "I had a lot of support from friends. Everyone was really great. People visited me in the hospital. Everyone was really helpful. I had a very small group of really supportive friends." In addition to her mother and her friends, Amber cites good old self-reliance as another key ingredient to her coping. "You focus on what you can control. I had completely lost control of everything that I had known before. Even—just—my body.

"So you have to really think about what you *can* control. What can I actually *do*, literally? It takes thought. It's not just something that you can 'give over to God.' Or give over to someone else or something else, something higher, you know? You can't just be like, 'Oh, everything will work out.' Because you physically have to *make* it work out. *You* do. I had to actively decide to—to want to live. *I* had to make that choice. And then I had to do what needed to be done. When I fall out of my wheelchair and am lying on the ground, alone, God isn't going to lift me up. *I* have to lift up myself. I have to figure out how to crawl to the corner of the room, find some leverage between the wall and the bed, and get back up again. It wasn't easy. It took me half a year to be able to figure out how to do that."

Although she can still weld, Amber can no longer work in the bookstore. Life is certainly much better today in many respects than it was five years ago, but it still isn't easy. "I am living on disability. It is very little money. It is barely enough to pay rent and food." To help make ends meet, a friend of Amber's is letting her live rent-free in the Airstream trailer in her backyard. It seems to be a good situation, for the time being. And Amber recently decided to go back to college, to pursue a bachelor's degree in history. She'd like to become an archivist.

Amber maintains a serenely fatalistic take on things now, and she feels perfectly at peace in her godless universe. "I take comfort in the fact that we're on a planet, spinning through space, with no reason. That's comforting to me. None of this matters. I think about that often. Nothing—the meaninglessness of everything is actually the biggest comfort of all. It doesn't matter that all of this has happened. So the only thing you can do is move on and not abdicate your responsibility to—to yourself. And although I embrace a certain existential meaninglessness, there is of course tremendous meaning to be found everywhere, if one wants to find it. There is meaning in not only being personally responsible, but in responding to others, in responding to the people in your life, to their needs and feelings, and their experiences."

Reading philosophy has become a hobby of Amber's this past year, and she carries around two quotes with her at all times, which she finds both comforting and instructional. The first comes from Friedrich Nietzsche, written in 1873, from an essay titled "On Truth and Lies in an Extra-Moral Sense." It is a quote that provides Amber with a great deal of existential solace:

> In some remote corner of the universe, poured out and glittering in innumerable solar systems, there once was a star on which clever animals invented knowledge. That was the highest and most mendacious minute of "world history"—yet only a minute. After nature had drawn a few breaths the star grew cold, and the clever animals had to die. One might invent such a fable and still not have illustrated sufficiently how wretched, how shadowy and flighty, how aimless and arbitrary, the human intellect appears in nature. There have been eternities when it did not exist; and when it is done for again, nothing will have happened.

The second quote comes from an essay titled "Transcendence Without God," written by contemporary philosopher Anthony Simon Laden. It kindles Amber's sense of meaning amid life in this remote, fleeting corner of the universe:

> In the absence of God, all there is left to human life is human action and interaction with ourselves and each other and other aspects of the natural world, and the only meaning any of it has is the meaning we manage to give it.

Surviving the Holocaust

Nazis. Roll call. Line up. *Schnell!* Growling German shepherds on taut leashes. Bleak courtyard. Zenon feels frail, weak. He's scared. But he tries to stand as stiff and as strong as he can. The Nazis are shouting orders, beating people at random. Suddenly, one of the Nazis points at Zenon. "You!" Zenon freezes in fear. The Nazi strides directly toward him. He yells again, "You!"—but it is actually the redheaded young man directly to Zenon's left that he is glaring at, not Zenon. The red-headed young man steps forward. Five other Jews in the assembly are also called out in a similar fashion. They form a small line at the front. Six men. The yelling Nazi takes out his pistol and shoots each one in the back of the head. Their thin bodies crumple to the ground, right in front of Zenon. Everyone is ordered back to work.

Just another day in the Tomaszów ghetto in Poland, April 1943.

Zenon Neumark was fifteen years old when the Germans invaded Poland in 1939. By the war's end, thirty members of his family would be dead, including his parents, grandparents, and nearly all of his aunts, uncles, and cousins, as well as almost all of his childhood friends and neighbors. Zenon's life as a teenager during the Holocaust was a constant nightmare of fear, persecution, and uncertainty. For years, daily life was fraught with peril and grief. From the time he was fifteen to the time he was twenty, his very existence was precarious.

Zenon's childhood was spent in Lódz, Poland. His was a middle-class, nonreligious Jewish family. Neither his father nor his mother believed in God. They did go to synagogue once a year, for Yom Kippur, but this was largely just to go along with the community tradition, not for any religious or spiritual reasons. "I think my father spent more time outside the synagogue, talking to friends, discussing politics or something. And we kids were running around with other kids, playing and whatnot. We never really participated much in the service." Although Jewish in heritage and ethnicity, Zenon's family was decidedly secular. Zenon himself never believed in God—not as a kid, and not at any time during his long life. He is now eighty-seven, and as he explains, "I would say that I am an agnostic. I graduated in physics—science. I have to have proof before I can accept something."

When the Germans came to Poland, Zenon's parents thought things might be easier by moving out of the large city of Lódz to the smaller, more rural town of Tomaszów, where some of Zenon's relatives lived. So three months after turning fifteen, Zenon headed to Tomaszów, with his parents and sister to follow shortly. But they never came. They kept postponing their departure, until it was suddenly too late and they were trapped in the Lódz ghetto.

Tomaszów, of course, turned out to be no safe haven after all; the Jews were quickly rounded up there as well, and Zenon, along with several other family members, was soon imprisoned in the Tomaszów ghetto. Conditions were cramped, cold, and hungry. There were typhus outbreaks, one of which killed his grandfather. There were gunshots. Bloodied bodies in the streets. Rumors soon seeped into the ghetto about mass exterminations of Jews in gas chambers. Most people rebuffed such harrowing rumors. Who could believe such insanity? Zenon could. "I knew. To some people it was just rumors. To me it was fact. They didn't believe it. I did. I knew that we are being exterminated." And sure enough, one day in October 1942, half of the Tomaszów ghetto was "liquidated." Over six thousand men, women, and children were forced at gunpoint onto cattle cars and sent to the Treblinka death camp, where they were summarily gassed to death. Zenon luckily missed that deportation—he and a few hundred other Jews had been assigned work duty in a labor camp just outside the ghetto walls that day. But his three aunts, Rena, Rachela, and Celina, as well as his eleven-year old cousin Olek and several other distant relatives and friends were not so lucky.

Now Zenon was completely alone. And he had no idea if his parents and sister, back in the Lódz ghetto, were alive or dead.

He continued to work in the labor camp adjacent to the Tomaszów ghetto, where he received rudimentary training as an electrician. He was fed a piece of black bread and watery soup twice a day. And that was considered a lot. Then one day he heard from his German supervisor that the entire ghetto was to be liquidated. All the remaining Jewish inhabitants would be shipped off to the Treblinka death camp. The "action" would take place the next day. "Tomorrow will be too late," he was warned. So at three in the morning that night, Zenon hid, crouching in a remote corner of the ghetto, behind a stack of lumber. He watched and waited. As soon as the armed Ukrainian guard turned his back to walk in the opposite direction, Zenon scurried over the six-foot wall of the ghetto.

Now he was a lone Jew in occupied Poland, and if anyone identified him as such, he would be arrested and most likely killed. His first place of refuge was the home of a distant friend of a relative who lived on the outskirts of Tomaszów. She reluctantly allowed him sleep in her toolshed for the night—an extremely dangerous thing for her to do. "There was a proclamation put out by the Germans. It said, number one: any Jew found outside the camp or ghetto will be shot. And number two: any Pole providing lodging, food, or any help to a Jew will be shot." Zenon knew that he couldn't stay in that shed for more than two nights. It was simply too risky. He decided to make his way to Warsaw, Poland's biggest city, figuring that it would be easier to survive there, with a possible degree of urban anonymity attainable. He also had some contacts there—Poles who were friends of friends, who might give him shelter, despite the risk.

He got to Warsaw without incident, and was able to stay in the seventh-floor apartment of one of his contacts, a young woman named Janina. But on the third day there, someone—perhaps a neighbor—betrayed him. Two uniformed men broke into the apartment, beat Zenon, and then locked him in a room while they went to get a car in order to take him to the Gestapo. But Zenon managed to pick the lock before they could return, and he fled. For the next year and a half, he survived many such close calls, and many homeless nights, and many hungry days. Yet he was able to stay alive in Nazi-occupied Warsaw. His survival was largely predicated upon pretending to be a Pole. He wore a crucifix around his neck. He started attending church regularly, fastidiously learning the Catholic prayers and hymns, as was necessary to make his cover convincing. And his ability to speak perfect Polish was extremely helpful; most Jews in Poland spoke Yiddish, or Polish with a Yiddish accent, both of which were dead giveaways. He also did not look stereotypically Jewish. He was thus able to pass as a Pole. He eventually got a decent job working as an electrician. He managed to procure false identification papers, with a fake Polish name. He rented a small room.

Though living a somewhat secure life—certainly much more secure a life than that of the captive Jews inside the Warsaw ghetto—every day was nerve-rackingly dangerous. Any person, at any time, could suspect that he was a Jew, denounce him, turn him in. And that would be the end of Zenon. It was not easy living this way. "There is a saying in Polish that best describes me at that time, '*Na zlodzieju czapka gore*,' and it literally translates as 'A thief's hat glows,' but we would translate it as 'A guilty person looks guilty.'" There were many times when a particular landlord might give him a strange look. Zenon would leave immediately, finding a new place to stay in a different part of town. He'd move yet again, just to be sure. And again. He was always on guard, always nervous. "I was haunted by fear and forever insecure about being recognized and betrayed. Each new interaction—with a German supervisor, a Polish coworker, someone at the cafeteria, a neighbor—all were a constant concern. I worried over how I would answer personal questions, how I would react to an offhanded anti-Semitic remark. Could they tell that I was not one of them? Could they tell that I was a Jew? I fretted over my demeanor, my facial expressions. This worried me to the point that my anxious look itself probably became a source of suspicion."

But he managed, month after month. He eventually began working for various underground resistance movements. He functioned mostly as a courier, distributing secret information, cash, and weapons to other resistance members and various underground fighters. This was extremely dangerous work. Sometimes he found himself on trains packed with Nazi officers. Other times, he was followed down alleyways, or eyed suspiciously at bus stations. Sometimes he was asked to do things by people he didn't know and wasn't sure about—were they allies? Were they really part of the resistance, or was he being set up? Occasionally he was stopped at random by police or soldiers, who asked him about his business, scrutinized his identification papers—and had they looked into whatever package or suitcase he was carrying, well, that would have been the end.

And yet he managed to get by, incident after incident. "I was filled with a passion and real sense of purpose. Life was full of danger at every corner, with every encounter, but it was also filled with an incredible sense of accomplishment and satisfaction. I gave of myself the most one could give, and I knew that, in a small way, I was helping people survive. I know of three people specifically who survived because of me, directly because of me and how I helped them." Zenon thus focused not solely on his own sole survival, but in helping others to survive as well. He helped get people false papers so they could find work or avoid arrest, he helped people who were in need of hiding find safe houses, he distributed weapons to other people so that they could defend themselves. What was his underlying motivation? Why not just focus on his own survival, rather than put himself at great risk for the sake of others? "I wanted to help. I wanted to help. Can there be any other reason? I wanted to help other people."

Zenon witnessed the uprising in Warsaw against the Nazis in 1944, and the brutal, devastating repression that followed. But when Germany's grip over Poland began to finally weaken, and as the Russians came closer to taking Warsaw, Zenon was arrested during a Gestapo sweep. He wasn't arrested as a Jew, but rather on suspicion of being part of the Polish resistance. He was sent to a concentration camp, whose inmates were slated for deportation to Auschwitz. But luck was with him yet again. A small group of Polish workers was being selected for work in Vienna, and when a German guard recognized him as an electrician, Zenon was saved. He was switched into this small group of Polish workers slated not for Auschwitz, but Vienna.

They were put into a cattle car, heading west. One day, the train stopped at the Kuloszki railroad junction—a busy intersection for trains from all over Poland. They were stuck there for hours. Late in the afternoon, another train pulled up right beside them. Zenon could see through the slats of his cattle car that it was full of emaciated Jews. He quietly began conversing with one of the men in the other train. The man said that their train was from the Lódz ghetto. Did he know Zenon's parents and sister? Yes. And in fact, he confirmed that they were on that very train—although in a different cattle car farther down. "I could hardly believe what he said to me. I felt sick. I felt a pain in my stomach. I felt as if my heart—it had stopped beating. I felt totally, utterly helpless. You can't imagine." Zenon crumpled to the floor, covering his face, holding in the sobs. He could not let the other Poles in his cattle car know of the pain he was going through. He pretended to be sick, and then to be asleep. Eventually, his train departed, as did the train from the Lódz ghetto, carrying his family; they were taken on to Auschwitz, where his parents were gassed. (Zenon's sister, however, did survive.)

The cattle car full of Polish workers took a full three weeks to get to Vienna. Zenon and his fellow travelers received food and water only sporadically, often going three days at a stretch without either. "We were hungry and thirsty all the time. And we were very, very dirty. We had not washed in weeks. The time passed very slowly. We just sat on the floor quietly, expressionless, half-dazed, half-numbed." When they reached a small town just outside of Vienna, they were quarantined. They were ordered to strip naked and to shower, while their clothes were disinfected. This is it, thought Zenon. His circumcision would give him away, and that would be that. But he was lucky yet again. The Polish workers were sent into showers together along with female prisoners from another transport; everyone was distracted by the naked women, and no one noticed that he was a Jew. When they reached Vienna, they were put to work in a labor camp. Zenon escaped. After several days of homeless scavenging, he managed to get work as an electrician with a small German firm (still pretending to be a Pole, of course).

When the war was finally over, the Russians came to Vienna, and they refused to believe that Zenon was a Jew. They accused him of being a Polish accomplice to the Nazis—a collaborator. They took him out into the nearby woods to be executed. "Here I had survived the damn Nazis. And now here are the Russians who are going to shoot me, and for nothing!" But the two soldiers assigned to do away with him in the woods—for reasons Zenon will never know—decided not to kill him. Instead, they marched him out to a small road between the trees and told him to start walking and not look back.

He had survived the Holocaust. He eventually found his sister in a displaced persons camp in Germany, as well as two aunts. One night, after a pleasant dinner with these relatives, he laughed. He can't remember what it was that made him laugh, exactly. But it was the first time he had laughed in nearly six years.

Zenon's survival was based on several key factors: being young and fit, being able to speak perfect Polish, not looking stereotypically Jewish, being able to get on well with people, having good instincts for when to take risks, and being very, very lucky. But what did not help him, in any way, was religious faith. Since he was thoroughly secular, God simply wasn't part of the picture.

But I wondered if, when things were particularly bad, had he ever prayed, even just for the immediate comfort such prayer might give him in the moment? "No. I did not. I did not." What about that very dangerous moment when he was about to climb over the wall to escape the Tomaszów ghetto? "No. I did not pray to God. All I was thinking was, how can I jump without the guard seeing me? That was the only thing. When should I make my move? How much risk it was—that was all I was thinking." What about when the Russians were taking him into the woods to be shot? "No. I didn't pray. I didn't even think to. Pray to what? I just felt anger that here I was—I had survived so much, only to have it end like this. That was all that was going through my head."

But what about all those lucky breaks? There were so many close calls: the tip from the German supervisor about the imminent liquidation of the Tomaszów ghetto, escaping from that seventh-floor apartment in Warsaw, getting sent to Vienna rather than Auschwitz, not being detected as a Jew during quarantine, and so on, and so on? Might one perhaps interpret all of this as some form of divine intervention? Maybe it wasn't just "luck" pure and simple that explains Zenon's amazing story, but perhaps it was God, looking out for him? Zenon does not accept such an interpretation. "Look, if I have to give credit to God for the good things that happened to me, then I would also have to blame him for the bad things that happened to me, and what I had to endure. If there was a God at that time, then he was not on my side. He was not protecting me. All that I went through? All that I suffered? The murder of my family, parents, relatives, friends? The beatings, the arrests? The endless fear? So much fear all the time. So much destruction. The entire ghetto liquidated—thousands of people killed. Millions killed. No, I cannot see how there is a God in all of this, looking out for anyone. I survived. But not because of God. No."

So how, then, did he cope through it all? If he didn't turn to God, what did he turn to?

"You know, I was just numbed. I don't know the right term. But I was somehow almost hypnotized. I just focused on surviving. And this state of mind somehow shielded me from pain, even from hunger, at times. I don't know. But I relied on myself. I did what I had to do to live. And I tried to do the little that I could to help others. That's all."

After the war, Zenon moved to Italy for several years, where he got a degree in electrical engineering. Then he moved to America, and after receiving a scholarship and BA from the University of Oklahoma, he received a master's degree from UCLA. He settled in Los Angeles with his wife, worked in the aerospace industry, helped to raise two daughters, and now, happily retired, occasionally gives talks to high school and college students about his experiences in the war. Framed pictures of his grandchildren maintain pride of place in the center of his living room.

As was the case with Amber and the facing of her spinal cord injury with determined tenacity, Zenon's successful survival during the Holocaust and post-Holocaust thriving were the result of numerous factors. But the tenacity that they share is clearly predicated upon and deeply embedded in the secular virtues of pragmatic problem solving, personal fortitude, and—as will be further illuminated below when considering Gail Stanton's story—steadfast self-reliance.

Surpassing Addiction

Secular people employ nearly all of the same coping strategies that religious people employ when life is rough: they rely on family and friends, or they seek counseling and professional guidance. But unlike the religious, who turn to the God they believe in, secular people lack that otherworldly option. Secular options are all of this world. Thus instead of turning upward to the heavens for help, the nonreligious must inevitably turn to themselves. That gets to the heart of secular coping: a greater degree of raw, resilient self-reliance. I have heard it expressed many times, in various ways. And Gail Stanton, who is forty-one years old and lives in Tucson, Arizona, embodies this rugged secular self-reliance as explicitly and as inspirationally as anyone.

As a result of her father's untreated bipolar disorder, Gail's family moved to a new state every year of her childhood. She dropped out of high school while in Vermont, and by the time she was in her late teens she was living in the streets of Austin, Texas, addicted to heroin, alcohol, pot, and just about everything else. She committed a variety of crimes to support her addiction, she was often arrested, and she was often in prison. Her boyfriend died of a drug overdose. Life as an addict in Austin was nasty and brutish. Finally, after a year's stint behind bars—an experience Gail describes as "heinous on so many levels"—she decided to change, to make a decent life for herself. She left Texas, got sober, got into a healthy relationship, got her GED, went to a community college, transferred to a four-year college, got her BA, got a scholarship for graduate school, earning an MSW and an MPA, and a license in clinical social work. She is currently married, the mother of two boys, and the director of a large outpatient facility that helps people overcome drug addiction and related substance abuse problems. "I'm highly motivated by beneficence and justice. I think a lot of people get the short end of the stick, and we as a society don't do much to help those that are less fortunate. And I'd like to leave this planet a better place than when I came. So if there is anyone I can touch, anyone I can help . . ."

For Gail, the transition from heroin addict in the streets of Texas to happily married mother of two and well-educated director of an outpatient clinic wasn't easy, and it took a long time. She enrolled in several drug treatment programs, she attended Narcotics Anonymous and Alcoholics Anonymous meetings. She found the traditional twelve-step program particularly helpful. But the twelve-step program is intrinsically spiritual, and at its core is a professed belief in a "higher power." So Gail just got into the habit of mentally plugging in her own secular substitutes anytime the words "higher power" or "God" were put forth. "Many people in the twelve-step community definitely look at that 'power greater than oneself' as God. But I could never buy into that. So I always just thought about it as being my connection to other human beings. Feeling a part of life. There's an emptiness at the heart of addiction. And they often talk about filling that void with God. So I would just think about filling that void with 'connectedness.' Being connected to other people. The group is my higher power. So that worked for me."

Gail found heaps of insight and wisdom in the writings of Viktor Frankl and Erich Fromm. Frankl taught that in order for life to be worth living, it must have personal meaning, and we all must actively create that meaning for ourselves, while Fromm taught that *connection* is one of the greatest sources of meaning, and thus our loving connections to others are of paramount importance for human thriving. Gail also took up meditation, which she sees as a good technique to simply quiet her mind, and nothing more. And she's even attended a few twelve-step programs specifically designated for atheists. "It was nice to go to a meeting now and then and not have to force myself to 'not hear' the word 'God' every time people say 'God.'"

Gail acknowledges that her godless way of overcoming addiction is extremely rare. In her many years of experience—as a user, as a recovering addict, and as someone who now works with other addicts—she is fairly certain that over 95 percent of the people that she has known and has worked with have been religious, have believed in God, and have found tremendous help in overcoming their addiction by turning to God. "Those that have a strong faith in God, it definitely helps them. Definitely."

And yet Gail did it without. How?

"I'm internally driven, I guess. In all the mess, you know, I had to look internally. And prison did help, I will admit. That one year in prison I did get clean. And so when I got out—the longer you are away from drugs, the weaker the pull is. I mean, I still wanted to get loaded when I got out, but the pull wasn't so overwhelming. So that helped me, in that regard.

"But I didn't pray or anything like that. I just had to draw from inner strength. I had to look internally to find that. To embrace my own resilience, to get through it all. I think that's what happened here. Just—getting into college, managing graduate school, it was very grueling. I had two little kids—the master's program was pretty intense! And quite a few people dropped out. And although it was bad—seriously—I just *did* it, I *got through* it. I worked so hard.

"If you can't find stuff outwardly, you're going to turn inward. If you can't find it out there in a God, you're going to find it inside—inside yourself. I couldn't turn to a God, so I turned to myself, because that's all that I had. That was the only choice left. I don't feel like I'm exceptional or anything, I'm just me. But I had a lot of challenges, and I managed it, and I did it."

Secular Coping

Such stories from people like Amber, Zenon, and Gail are quite illu-minating, and the similar themes that emerge from their accounts are obvious: the whole "let go, let God" sentiment just doesn't always work. Although it certainly has a Zen-like quality of acceptance that is admirable—sometimes we do just need to accept situations and not fight against or stress about circumstances beyond our control—the underlying assumption of accepting a higher power doesn't cut it, at least for the secular among us. Amber could not "let go" with the onset of her paralysis. She had to fight and strive and recover and find meaning and value all on her own, and with the love of her mother and the help of friends. In Zenon's eyes, no prayers were going to save him as a teenager in the Holocaust. He had to save himself. And while many people who deal with drug addiction find tremendous strength in believing in God, for Gail, belief in herself was more successful, more realistic, or rather simply more her way.

IN SEEKING TO gain a better understanding of how secular people cope with difficult life circumstances, I've spoken with various profession-als whose work involves helping and studying nonreligious people who must deal with physical or emotional challenges.

One such professional is Hilary Wells, the founder of Secular Thera-pists of Chicago, an association of counseling psychologists who offi-cially offer "nonreligious counseling and therapy." Hilary is in her late fifties, and she's been a practicing therapist for over twenty-five years. She explained the birth of her practice: "When I looked up secular therapists or secular therapy on the Internet, I couldn't find anything. All I could find were plenty of religious sites, and plenty of spiritual options. You can find Christian therapists that offer 'Bible-based' help, and Jewish therapy groups, or counseling specifically geared toward Catholics, and so on. But nothing came up for specifically secular people. So it seemed like a good idea for people to be able to find secular therapy if that was what they were specifically looking for." But what does secular therapy mean, actually? "It means that the therapist is coming from a position of not holding or teaching supernatural beliefs, and I generally I work with nonreligious clients."

For Hilary, religious beliefs are, at root, illusions. And while some illusions can sometimes be psychologically comforting, they are not the best building blocks for long-term emotional stability. "For people who are trapped in an unbearable situation that they can do nothing about, illusions such as that God is looking out for you and good will triumph in the end—these might offer some relief from the emotional and physical stress. But on the other hand, it is likely to hinder or even stop people from realistically figuring out what needs to be done in their life."

So what do secular people do when life gets hard and they are having difficulty coping? "It all boils down to our connections with other people. We are social animals. We derive comfort, meaning, and love from those around us, the people we are connected to in our social environment. That's where secular people look when life is hard, or when they are suffering. And when those social connections aren't there, then yes, secular people must look to themselves and become more self-reliant—which is actually easier to do when you have a secular outlook. When it comes to self-assurance and self-reliance, the nonreligious are definitely on more solid ground than the religious, who are much more dependent on their God or gods."

Another expert who can shed some light on secular coping is Karen Hwang, a professor of counseling psychology who has worked for several years with people who have suffered a spinal cord injury (SPI). As an employee in the Department of Physical Medicine and Rehabilitation at the University of Medicine and Dentistry of New Jersey and the New Jersey Medical School, Professor Hwang has looked at various aspects of the SPI experience, such as how women with SPI handle motherhood and marriage, how SPI affects sexual functioning, how certain drug therapies can help reduce spinal cord inflammation, and more. And she has also looked specifically at atheists with SPI—people like Amber, discussed earlier.

In her pioneering research, Professor Hwang has found that when comparing nonbelievers who have experienced SPI with believers, there are no significant differences in self-ratings of overall happiness, and that most atheists actually report that their nonbelief helped them cope with their injury.

"You might think that because secular people don't have religious beliefs to fall back on, that they might be kind of lost when such an injury occurs. But I actually found the opposite. Some of my interview subjects brought up the fact that because they never had the religious beliefs to begin with, that means they never went through any 'crisis of faith' or anything like that. So it was very easy for them to accept that these things happen. And it's not that God doesn't love you or you are being punished—there isn't a 'why did this happen to me?' crisis. There isn't that spiritual or existential disappointment. It is very easy for them to say, 'Well, it was an accident. What do I need to do now?'"

Rather than questioning the "meaning" or "purpose" of their disability, those secular individuals studied by Professor Hwang were markedly comfortable with the arbitrary nature of their injury. "A nontheistic outlook on life provided a logical and coherent basis for integrating disability within a larger life context." Other studies bolster Dr. Hwang's assertions that being religious can sometimes have its downside when people are faced with trauma. For example, researchers Martie Thompson and Paula Vardaman found that in the aftermath of the murder of a loved one, people from religious families can experience increased levels of distress when pleading with God during their grieving process. And Kenneth Pargament found that some religious believers can feel psychological discontent during times of war, when their prayers to God seem to go unheeded. And as Judith Herman argues in her book *Trauma and Recovery*, traumatic events can often "violate the victim's faith in a natural or divine order and cast the victim into a state of existential crisis."

While there is no question that for most people religious belief serves as a soothing balm in times of pain and suffering, what the counseling experience of Dr. Wells and the research of people like Dr. Hwang alerts us to is the fact that—at least sometimes, and for some people—religious beliefs can be counterproductive. And further-more, in certain situations, secular men and women might actually be on better footing during trying times.

Luke Galen is a professor of psychology at Grand Valley State University in Allendale, Michigan, and he is one of only a handful of academics in America who specifically study the psychology of secular folk. He's been at it for several years now, looking at atheists, agnostics, freethinkers, humanists, and various other such irreligious people, seeking to discover the ways in which they are psychologically distinct from—as well as similar to—religious people. In his research, he has studied local secular communities in Michigan, but he has drawn from national samples as well.

In comparing and contrasting nonreligious people who are involved with secular organizations to demographically similar religious people who are members of churches, he has found that the two groups aren't all that different emotionally or psychologically, with a few notable exceptions: those affiliated with secular organizations are more likely to be male and more highly educated (whereas churchgoers are more likely to be female and less educated), and when it comes to standard measures of personality, church members tend to score a bit higher in terms of agreeableness than their secular counterparts, but nonreligious people affiliated with secular groups tend to score a bit higher in terms of openness to new experiences, as well as being more intellectually oriented. And while both groups claim to be more or less equally satisfied with their lives, religiously affiliated people report having higher degrees of social support.

When I asked Professor Galen about the many studies which report that religious people seem to enjoy better levels of mental health than secular people, he explained that while this may certainly be due to the social support factor, it may also be a result of conformity—the positive outcome of simply being in line with one's broader social context.

In other words, people who are doing what most people are doing tend to report better states of mental health than people who are not. As he explains, "A lot has to do with the definition of 'normality' within your given culture. For example, when we look worldwide, it is true that, overall, religious people have a slight edge in terms of life satisfaction or lower depression. But that may be because they are engaging in what is considered to be normal, common behavior in their societies: participating in religion.

"But if we look at religiously active people in highly secular societies, where most people *aren't* religious, then suddenly the effect disappears—religious people aren't doing better psychologically, and may in some cases actually be doing worse than secular people. So, for example, when looking at the more secular countries of Europe, religious people there don't exhibit better mental health. And even within the United States, in the more religious parts of the country, religious people tend to report better mental health—but not religious people in the least religious parts of the country. So it looks like at least part of good mental health is just being embedded in the normative community."

In truth, when it comes to the specifics of secular coping—the range, contours, and efficacies—we don't know much. Secular coping has been an almost totally neglected area of research. However, we do know that people who are clearheaded problem solvers, people who can say, "Okay, here's what I need to do to make things better, here's step one, step two, and so on"—such people tend to do better in general when coping with problems in life. As Professor Galen explains, "Secular people don't believe in a God they can rely on or in the magical power of prayer—there are no 'spiritual' or 'mystical' solutions. So they've got to look at a sad or hard or difficult situation and think to themselves, 'Well, what do I need to do here?' So secular people use those basic, rational problem-solving mechanisms more often than religious people, and they probably do so more successfully when coping with trauma."

In Luke's own experience with loss, he didn't turn to God for comfort. Although a believer as a child, he had become an atheist by his mid-twenties. And it was then, just as his atheism was overshadowing his theism, that his beloved father unexpectedly died the day after Christmas. "So that was really a test of my atheism, when my dad died. I mean, I was like, 'If this is true that there isn't a God, then I'll never see my dad again. He's not in heaven. There is no afterlife.' I really had to seriously think about the implications of that. And I did—very deeply and very seriously. And I knew that I just couldn't believe any of it. My dad was gone, and that was that. But it was actually not as traumatic as you might expect, because I found that I didn't need to believe all that religious stuff from my childhood in order to feel better. I still had the memory of my father, and that was good enough. The things that I valued about my dad were still there, inside of me. He lives on in me, and in my brothers. Why did I need to think he was in heaven looking down at me? Why did I need to think I would someday meet him again? In all honesty, I think those things seem kind of weird to me now."

But how did he cope, exactly, when his dad died?

"Friends and family. Friends and family. That's it."

Comfort from the Religious

Secular people endure trying times by turning to friends, family, and, if nothing more, themselves. Social connectedness, rational problem solving, and perhaps a slightly higher dose of self-reliance. But it must be acknowledged, as I conclude this chapter, that for some these may not be enough. In the wake of tragedy, being secular can have its disadvantages—especially when family and friends falter.

I will never forget a conversation I had many years ago when I was working as a director of a summer day camp near Hollywood. There was a woman named Sarah, a mother of one of the campers, who would often linger at the camp long after the other parents had left. Sarah would hang out with me each morning and chitchat while we watched the kids play capture the flag or dodgeball. One day we happened to be talking about being secular, and she said to me, "You know, Joey is actually my second child. My first son died. He was hit by a car. He was eight. I've always been an atheist, but I really felt the emptiness of it then. After he died, all my friends—who are all nonreligious—they just didn't know how to handle it. They didn't know what to do or what to say. Same with most of my relatives. It was like people were just too freaked out, too scared. They avoided me. And I found myself incredibly alone and depressed.

"And then a neighbor—who I hardly knew—she came over to my

house one day and said that she was a Christian and that she was sorry for my loss and that she had been praying for me. And she invited me to her women's group at church. I went. The women there were so kind, so loving. They were so open to me and so open to the pain I was going through. I ended up going to that women's group for several months.

"I never did accept Jesus as my personal savior, and I never turned to God. I just can't believe all that stuff. But I'll never forget how those religious women took me in. They were so warm and sympathetic—and they didn't even know me. Let me tell you: there's nothing like that out there when you're secular."

SARAH'S EXPERIENCE IS illustrative of the fact that not all aspects of secular culture are admirable or ideal. As she expresses, secular coping when times are tough is not—at least not for everyone—all about staunch self-reliance, pragmatic problem solving, or sustaining support from family and friends. There are times when being secular can be isolating and alienating. There are times when a lack of a committed community of religious faith can be a real vacuum.

There are, in short, some aspects of secular life that don't measure up well when compared to their religious counterparts. In any assessment of secular life, this must be acknowledged. And hopefully, such honest acknowledgment can spur us to creatively and compassionately think about what needs to be done within secular culture as we seek to live life—and face life's troubles—without certain benefits that come with being religious.

Chapter 7

—

Don't Fear the Reaper

E verything dies. Everything. And that's just how it works."

"What's there to be afraid of? When I'm dead, I'll be dead."

"This is it. This life is all there is. Death is actually what gives life its meaning."

"If there's something more, then I'll find out after I die. But for now I'm here, and this life is good and is to be enjoyed."

"You have to live life to its fullest. Cherish life. Suck the marrow out of it, you know? And try to be as good a person you can be and try to make a positive difference. Because there's no other life. That's the heart of being agnostic—to me. If you think you are going to go to heaven after you die, well, then, this life is just sort of a staging area, isn't it? Then this life is just a precursor or transition to something better. I think that makes people apathetic—if that's what they truly believe. Or it can make you not do things—or not *feel* or *love* as strongly as you could or should. But if there is no heaven or reincarnation—and that's what I believe—then this is actually the whole thing. This is everything. *This* life is all we get, and that means we have to truly love it. And never, never, never take it for granted. Because it's precious."

These quotes are a mere sampling of some of the more common

shared sentiments that I've heard secular men and women express concerning the topic of mortality. Although every individual obviously has his or her own personal approach to, experiences of, and feelings about death, most secular men and women articulate certain basic themes: (1) this life—miraculous, rich, and fleeting—is the only life, (2) we must seize it, savor it, and be open to it, and (3) there is nothing to fear when it comes to the end.

First Death

"It was sort of like a whacking sound," Michele explained. "But more like a *smack* than a *whack*."

"What was it?" I asked.

We were in Michele's room. I was lying on the unkempt floor and she was sitting on her unkempt bed. It was a lazy Sunday afternoon in the mid-1980s. Bauhaus was playing in the background. We were teenagers. Michele was recounting the adventures of her previous night with Flea, the frenetic bass player of the Red Hot Chili Peppers. She had been in love with him for quite some time; I am fairly certain that she was his first groupie. She had been going to Chili Peppers shows from the get-go, when they were just a raggedy, goofy, unknown punk-funk band from Fairfax High School. And then she started sleeping with Flea a few months after the release of their second album. We were all very impressed—but not too surprised. Michele was like that: she loved things, she got way into them, and she went for them with gusto.

So Michele was recounting to me how, the night before, she and Flea had been lounging on this big couch at some random house in Echo Park where there were a bunch of other people and some of those people were messing around in the kitchen and then somebody had dropped something and it had made a huge mess—and a bizarre sound.

"It was sort of like this loud *swap*," she continued.

"More like a *thwap*?" I offered. "Like the sound of a steak *thwapping* against a Cyclops's eye?"

Michele paused.

"Huh?"

"You know," I explained, "like in that story of Agamemnon or Prometheus—that guy who fights the giant Cyclops and then throws a steak in his eye?"

Michele clutched a pillow against her belly and started laughing.

"That was Odysseus," she said. "And it wasn't a steak—it was a *stake*!"

For a moment I just didn't understand her, and then it struck me, embarrassingly. I had always thought it had been a steak—a thick piece of raw red meat—that had been thrown onto the Cyclops's eye, and as my mistake dawned on me, Michele just started laughing ever more hysterically and then she threw a pillow at me and I started laughing really hard and I kept trying to talk, to come up with some face-saving defense having to do with a reference to the steaks you always see in Tom and Jerry cartoons, but we both just laughed so hard that it hurt in the gut, and then we laughed some more and somehow started riffing on whether or not it would be a "rib-eye" steak or a "rib-*aye*" steak—was Odysseus a Scottish sailor?—and we laughed some more and then as we stopped to catch our breath we suddenly started up again and this went on for quite some time and I never did find out what the noise from the kitchen was.

Michele and I had been friends since the third grade. In elementary school, we shared a love for water fights, which we often organized in the neighborhood on hot summer days. We also shared a love for music; she gave me the LP of *Revolver* at my eleventh birthday party—

a surprise birthday party that she helped organize, and which inevitably devolved into a water fight. We also shared a love for the theater— in junior high, she was the star of *Auntie Mame* and I played her ward, Patrick Dennis. In *A Midsummer Night's Dream* we were both in the troupe of mechanicals—she played Tom Snout and I played Peter Quince. In high school, we comforted each other when too drunk or too stoned, we hiked in the local mountains when we felt too restless, and we went to see the movie *Brazil* six times, often donning high-heeled shoes tied upside down on top of our heads in homage to one of the characters in the film. And of course, we went to a lot of Red Hot Chili Peppers shows.

One of my favorite memories of Michele is when she knocked on my window one very early morning, just around dawn. It was raining hard. She had had a bad night with a troubled boyfriend. She was also having some problems at home. So she came into my room and we lay in my bed and listened to "The Castle" by Love, over and over, on my record player; I had to keep picking up the needle and replacing it back at the start of the song. Even now, every single time that I hear that song I remember that rainy morning.

After high school, Michele went up to Santa Barbara to attend college. I visited her twice during her first year there—I remember going with her to her "movement" class, where we stretched, twisted, and then learned how to relax and waggle our tongues. I so enjoyed hanging out with her and her friends in their funky house in the student ghetto of Isla Vista. Her boyfriend at the time was really into Donovan, and I remember her dancing on the sidewalk with undergraduate abandon, singing "Wear Your Love Like Heaven" for his and my amusement.

And then about a month later I got a call from another friend, Claudine. She was crying. She told me that the car Michele had been in had gone over a cliff. The first words out of my mouth were, "Which hospital is she at? Let's get going." No, that wasn't possible, Claudine explained, because Michele was dead. It was difficult for me to understand what Claudine was saying. I can remember my mind not functioning properly, not being able to fit Claudine's words into the proper filing cabinet in my brain's organizational system. The words that Claudine's voice pushed through the phone resembled something close to this: the night before, Michele and several of her friends from Santa Barbara had driven down to Los Angeles to see U2. After the concert, they had headed back home, taking Highway 1, the scenic Pacific Coast Highway. Midway between Los Angeles and Santa Barbara, their car careered off the road and landed in the dark sea below. They all died. No one knows if the driver fell asleep at the wheel, or if they were run off the road by a drunk driver, or what. Nobody knows. But the car was found by fishermen the next morning, bobbing upside down in the ocean, Michele's body still buckled in the backseat.

In the days and weeks after Michele's death, I was devastated. Not only was she an irreplaceable friend whom I loved and who I felt loved me, but she was just such an exuberant light—such a ball of creativity, energy, laughter. She emanated so much *life*. How could someone so full of existence and kindness and eccentricity and joy be extinguished like that, in her teens?

The constriction of sadness knotted in my throat took a long time to dissipate. Michele's boyfriend, the Donovan fan, was gutted. So too was Michele's family; her younger siblings were crushed. I can't fathom what her mother went through. Michele had so many friends, and the sorrow we all felt brought us very close together. Groups of us gathered at one another's homes, talking, crying, despairing.

One afternoon, I drove with Anna—one of Michele's other close friends—up the Pacific Coast Highway, to the spot where the car had careened off the road. We sat on some large rocks and stared out at the water. We tried to say things that were meaningful, poignant, or soulful—tried to hold our own little ceremony of sorts. But our senti-ments fell flat. We were simply sad and depressed. Later that night, while sitting around the dinner table with Anna's mother, we tried to find or construct some sort of silver lining. Maybe Michele is up in heaven right now, we mused, watching us with loving eyes. Maybe we will be able to contact her with a Ouija board. Maybe the instant she died, she was reincarnated into some different living thing, something even more beautiful, more sublime. Maybe we will meet her again someday, in another life, in another plane of existence. On and on we pondered, trying our hardest to at least invent some spiritual hope of sorts to ease the sorrow.

And that's when Anna's mom, a school psychologist by trade, chimed in. Her words were frank and sobering. She said to us, "Lis-ten. The possibilities you are wondering about may or may not be true. Maybe Michele has been reincarnated. Maybe not. Maybe she is up in heaven right now, looking down at us. Maybe not. Maybe you will be with her again one day in some spiritual realm. Maybe not. We don't know about these things. We have no evidence about such things. But what we *do* know, and what I can tell you with certainty, is this: Michele is gone to us now. She will *never* come traipsing into this house again, singing and laughing. She will never again try to balance an apple on her nose. She will never call you up on the phone again. She will never come knocking on your window late at night or early in the morning. She is dead. And it is so, so sad. This is the time to grieve, to mourn. But, hopefully, if you can try to live your lives as exuberantly and freely as she did, then she will live on, in a way, at least in the last-ing effect she has had on you both, as well as in the memories you have of her." When Anna's mom said these words, I knew that she was right. And that was my first personal experience with a secular approach to death.

Greatest Generation

Since Michele's death, I've gained an ever deeper understanding of the secular approach to death, not only because more of my own friends and family have died over the years, but because of the many people I have interviewed in my professional work, people from all different kinds of backgrounds, who have experienced death intimately, or who work with or near the dying, or are simply near death themselves.

Consider Walter Pines, age ninety-three. If anyone is contemplating, coping with, and unavoidably facing his own mortality, it is Walter. When I spoke with him, he looked downright wretched: much of his face had been eaten away by an aggressive form of skin cancer, and the deep crevices on his cheeks were full of rotting scabs. He's completely bald, and the splotchy skin on his head is in bad shape. He's hunched. His arthritis is advanced. His hearing is fading. And aside from the vigorous smile in his ice blue eyes, you'd think he wasn't going to last much more than a week or two. But it's hard to tell. On the one hand, his body is clearly ravaged. But then you start talking to him, and you look into those very vibrant eyes, and you come to realize that his mind is perfectly sharp, his wit intact, and his personality still very youthful. So you start to think, "Heck—maybe he's got another ten years?" But either way—whether he's got one day left or five thousand—he's not worried. He's not troubled by his impending end. He doesn't want to die, but he doesn't obsess about it either. Not in the least.

Walter doesn't consider himself an "atheist." He doesn't like that word. He's simply not interested in God. And he is quick to point out that he has nothing against religion. "But it just never really took, you know what I mean?"

Walter was born in 1919 in eastern Ohio. His father worked in the local steel mill and his mother stayed at home, tending to him and his seven siblings. Walter grew up working in coal mines and cornfields, and then he was drafted, serving as a rifleman in an infantry division during World War II. He saw a lot of action, especially at the battle of Caumont Hill, in the immediate wake of D-Day.

He can talk at length about those combat experiences. There was one day in particular when he and his unit were driving the Germans back through the countryside in France. A river had to be crossed. They found three rowboats, and his platoon got in. As they were crossing, a German machine gunner on the other side of the river opened fire—two of the American rowboats were "taken out." But not Walter's. He and his remaining men managed to reach the other side and subsequently "take out" the German machine gunner. However, the fighting was intense, and Walter took a bullet in his neck. Miraculously, it did little harm, missing his jugular vein by half a hair's breadth, according to the medic. He was back on the battlefield the next day, and for many days and weeks and months after that.

And throughout it all, he never turned to God. He never prayed for deliverance, even when under heavy fire. "So there are atheists in foxholes?" I asked. He laughs hard. "Oh, sure there are. Sure there are. You bet. Look—in those situations, you just have to do what you have to do. You rely on yourself and your friends and your fellow soldiers. That's all you've got. You're there. It is kill or be killed. That's that. I never even thought to pray in those times. I just did what I had to do."

After the war, Walter got married and earned a degree in accounting. He raised two children, eventually became a vice president of finance at a successful company, bought himself a very nice house in a very nice neighborhood, helped his wife cope with manic depression, and always kept in touch with his army buddies—most of whom are now dead. And now, at ninety-three, Walter is clearly near the end of his life. I asked him if he considered the possibility of there being a heaven or hell. "No, no. As I always say, heaven is here, right now. Heaven is my everyday life. Heaven and hell exist for people while they are here on earth. This is it."

Walter's approach to life, especially as its end draws ever nearer, can be summed up in one word: *appreciation*. He is simply grateful for every day. He enjoys his breakfast, especially the fresh fruit. He likes to sit in his backyard on summer days and watch the neighborhood kids splash in his pool. He still corresponds with an old friend in Guam. He loves his children and grandchildren dearly, and relishes hearing about their lives—what they are doing at school, how things are going at work. He is grateful for the help he gets from his live-in nurse. He likes watching the History Channel. Sure, the pains of his failing body are no fun. But they don't diminish his spirit of appreciation. As he repeated, "I just enjoy every day. I just enjoy every day."

Walter's appreciative attitude evidences a core secular virtue, what I would refer to as a profound embracing of the "here and now." Rather than looking forward to or pining for an imagined afterlife, Walter has always relished what is right before him, in the here and now. Life is to be appreciated and cherished. Walter's lifelong lack of belief in God or an afterlife has never resulted in despondency, depression, or apathy. Just the opposite: it has undergirded his valuing and loving of his days. Yes, they are numbered. But that makes them all the more precious.

I asked Walter if he was afraid to die. "No, no. I'm not afraid to die. I've seen so much death in my life—I know it is inevitable. I don't worry about it. Never have. And anyway, there's nothing you can do about it. So why worry? When it comes, it comes."

Resurrected Atheist

While Walter is facing his impending death without fear, Mildred Wilcox has already been there and done that. Her lack of fear couldn't be more pronounced—or more fully based in personal, firsthand experience. After all, Mildred died about a year before I interviewed her in her pleasantly nondescript hometown in Nebraska.

There aren't many atheists in this town of forty-six thousand inhabitants. But there is a handful. And about four years ago, thanks to the Internet, they got in touch with one another and decided to start a group. They began meeting one night a month in a small community room at a mall to talk about atheism, secularism, religion, and various issues pertaining to the separation of church and state. At one of these meetings, in March 2011, Mildred came early. She had baked a batch of oatmeal-raisin cookies and wanted to set them out before the meeting began. Once the cookies were in order, she started to make some coffee. Another member of the group arrived: Sheila. They said hello, and then, as Sheila was arranging the folding chairs into a circle, she saw that Mildred was in trouble. Mildred, who was eighty-six at the time, was dying.

As Sheila explained, "I saw Mildred kind of crumple—she had her head on her arms down on the counter. I said, 'Mildred, are you all right?' And I ran over to her and her eyes were starting to roll over and we laid her on the floor and she was starting to turn blue. Her eyes started to dilate. I knew that she was in serious trouble. So I started doing CPR. But there was no response. She had no pulse and no breath. So I called 911 and got them on the line and they gave me the rhythm to do the compressions—they sent the squad on the way—but we were in a sort of small, out-of-the-way corner room in the mall and the squad had a really hard time finding us. But I kept up the CPR until the squad finally got there and then they took over and they took her to the hospital. We were sure that she was dead. Or I was sure that she was going to die that night. In fact, she *did* die—her heart had completely stopped for fourteen minutes. We know because she had a pacemaker in from before, and the pacemaker recorded the data of what was going on during the heart attack and the doctor later told us that her heart had stopped for a full fourteen minutes. He also said that given her age and the location where it happened—he said that she had had a less than 1 percent chance of surviving this whole circumstance. And yet, here she is—alive and well! Same old Mildred—talking a mile a minute!"

A miracle? Not to Mildred. She is still as firm an atheist as they come—has been virtually all her long life—and her death and resurrection did nothing to change that orientation or alter her secular perspective on life and death.

Mildred, now eighty-seven, was born and grew up in Springfield, Missouri. Her mother, who was from "Oklahoma territory," was a housewife and writer of children's stories, and her father was a refrigerator engineer and bona fide "hillbilly"—he had been born in the Ozarks, to a fifteen-year-old girl, in a log cabin with a dirt floor. Although raised a churchgoing Christian, Mildred lost her faith by the time she was nineteen. What happened? "Simple. I went to college and got educated." And then she met her husband, a scientist and an atheist; his atheism only confirmed and deepened her own.

And if anything might have challenged her atheism—if ever she might have turned to the solace of religious faith—it certainly would have been when her second child, Billy, was diagnosed with leukemia at age three. He died at age four. It was the worst experience of Mildred's life, and yet her atheism remained intact. "I remember, just after Billy died, when the first person said to me something like, 'Well, you know, the Lord has called Billy home—it was just Billy's time.' I said to him, 'No—don't you tell me it was "Billy's time." I won't hear it.' That made me mad."

So how did she cope with the death of her son? "Shit happens. Well, we didn't know that phrase back then—but that's about it. That's life. There are no guarantees. That's what life is like. Children die. No god was making me suffer because it wanted me to suffer. No god was taking Billy away because he wanted to take him away. It just happened. Not that I wasn't unhappy. Because I was. But his death certainly didn't make me want to become religious. No. Instead, we had another child."

What about her own death—or near-death—experience? Did her heart attack of the previous year have any effect? "No." Did she have any sort of spiritual or mystical experience while her heart was no longer pumping? "No." Did she see any white light? "No." Did she experience any feelings of peace or tranquillity? "No." How about pain, regret, longing, or doom? "No. Look—I didn't feel anything and I don't remember a thing. Nothing. That's it."

Although the phenomenon is most likely explained as being the result of oxygen deprivation, much has been made of near-death experiences. Many people have spoken of and written about seeing white lights at the end of tunnels, or floating over their own bodies and observing themselves, or seeing previously deceased relatives, or of feeling the presence of God. Many people who have such experiences, or hear about them, find these accounts to be pretty good evidence for life after death. Not Mildred. She doesn't believe them to be scientifically verifiable, she thinks they certainly have naturalistic explanations (psychological or neurological), and she herself didn't experience any such stuff. Mildred's fourteen minutes without a heartbeat did not produce any spiritual visions or experiences, and the whole trauma didn't cause her to think about God, to question her atheism, or to seek religion.

And while her reluctance to embrace religion after experiencing a traumatic heart attack may strike some as unusual, it actually isn't. In a study of nearly 350 men who had recently had a heart attack, researchers Sydney Croog and Sol Levine found that the experience caused no changes in the men's worldviews, beliefs, or orientations: those who were religious before the heart attack stayed religious afterward, and those who were secular before the heart attack stayed secular. And related studies indicate that many seriously ill individuals—people similar to Mildred—as well as many doctors who come into direct contact with death on a regular basis, do not believe in life after death and maintain a secular orientation to their own mortality.

I wondered if the whole heart attack experience scared Mildred. "No. Not at all. I have always been totally and completely unafraid of dying. Still am. What's there to be afraid of?"

MANY PEOPLE ASSUME that a deep, existential fear of death is an unavoidable aspect of the human condition. No one wants to die, we are all afraid to die, and thus—voilà—you get religion. As psychologists Benjamin Beit-Hallahmi and Michael Argyle have observed, "Death is the most universal, and most negative, aspect of the human condition, and dealing with it is at the heart of all religions." There is no question that the vast majority of the world's religions construct some version of life going on after death in their cosmology, a promise of immortality or nirvana that many people find comforting.

But not everyone buys it. Walter and Mildred are but two examples of secular individuals who can and do accept their own mortality—and there are millions of others just like them. For example, according to data from the World Values Surveys, 67 percent of Hungarians, 64 percent of Armenians, 61 percent of Germans, 55 percent of the French, 53 percent of Norwegians, 49 percent of the Japanese, 42 percent of the British, 39 percent of the Taiwanese, 37 percent of Argentinians, 36 percent of Australians, and 27 percent of Canadians do not believe in life after death. That's just a handful of random countries—but already they include many millions of people on planet earth today who accept that death is the end. And although a majority of Americans claim to believe in life after death, tens of millions of us don't. In fact, approximately 25 percent of Americans don't. That's a heck of a lot of people—one-fourth of the nation—accepting their own finiteness and the inevitable, unavoidable finality of their very being. For such men and women, promises of or belief in an afterlife are empirically unsubstantiated and manifestly implausible.

But that doesn't mean that death doesn't have to be confronted or dealt with. It does. Not our own death, per se. But certainly the deaths of others.

Caring Daughter

The death of a family member, spouse, or friend is generally the most painful experience humans are forced to endure. And when it is the death of a close relative, such as a parent who requires our immediate care, it is not only draining emotionally, but it can be physically and financially taxing as well. This is one of the times when being a member of a religious community can really help. But secular people often must go it alone.

Lupita Portillo's father, Juan, was from New Mexico, and that's where Lupita was born. Lupita's mother left the family when Lupita was a baby. Subsequently, in an effort to make a clean start, Juan moved with Lupita and her two older half siblings from a previous relationship to San Jose, California. He never remarried, and thus did the best he could, raising his children as a single parent. He was a deeply religious man. "A true believer," Lupita recalls. He prayed every night, and he cherished the crucifixes and pictures of the Virgin Mother that adorned the walls of his bedroom. But despite the comfort of his faith, he was often depressed. The loss of his wife pained him, the burdens of being a single dad were plenty, and he thus turned to drinking, which hindered his ability to hold down a job; he made an on-and-off living as a part-time janitor and gardener.

Although Lupita could appreciate the piety of her father and older siblings, she was never religious herself. By the time she was a sophomore in college, she was a full-blown atheist. Shortly after she graduated with a degree in political science, Lupita's father was diagnosed with cancer. For the next several years, he endured surgery after surgery, struggling to hold the disease at bay. He was often tired, or unable to eat, or both. He became forgetful. Additional health problems began to accrue. In the meantime, Lupita started law school down in Los Angeles. So tending to her father became more difficult, given that she was now 350 miles away.

Her older siblings did not step up to help. "For some reason, my siblings—who were very religious—were never really active in the caretaking responsibilities. And even though they were more local than I was at this point—I tried so hard to get them involved in the caretaking—they just wouldn't. So I would literally drive up six hours, sometimes in the middle of the night, to be there to take care of him, or to take him to a doctor's appointment, or to the Social Security office, or whatever." His health declined further, and Lupita eventually put him into an assisted living facility and then a convalescent hospital.

She was continually driving back and forth between Los Angeles and San Jose, struggling to get through law school, cultivating a new romantic relationship, and yet always wanting to do right by her dad. She kept asking her siblings—who were financially stable, had homes of their own, and had spouses to help—if they could share some of the burden, but they would not. "They had time to go to church on a regular basis," she notes, "but not time to help me out or tend to their dying father."

After Juan died, Lupita carried out his wish to be buried in his small hometown back in New Mexico. His death was very sad for Lupita. She felt a real loss. And yet, given that she had been losing him slowly and steadily over the course of the past few years, and given that he had been so unwell for so long, she also felt some relief; he was finally at peace. So she actually coped with his death relatively well. Her siblings, however, were a different story. "They were a wreck. I was the pillar. I dealt with everything. All the arrangements. Okay, I was grieving, I was very sad—but I was also doing what needed to be done. But not them. For example, when we went out to New Mexico for the funeral, Miguel was having a major breakdown. He was literally freaking out. He thought he was talking to God and that God was telling him all this disturbing stuff. He came banging on my door at the hotel, claiming that he was having all these visions. He was really having a breakdown. They had a much harder time emotionally than I did."

Of course, as a sociologist, I fully understand the frailty of argument by anecdote. I know that it is impossible, from Lupita's story alone, to derive any grand conclusion about the benefits or demerits of secularity or religiosity in the face of a dying parent. Just because Lupita happened to deal with her father's death more actively than her religious siblings does not mean that this is always the case in every family. Of course not. And I am sure there are countless secular individuals out there who have failed to help out with a dying parent, while their religious siblings did everything. But Lupita's story struck me, and I have included it here, because it is a story that I think is rarely trumpeted: secular people can and do assist and aid in ways similar to the religious. And this underscores a broader point, namely, that secularity and/or religiosity often has nothing to do with how decent or moral a person is, especially during times of pain, loss, or death. Religious people, like Lupita's siblings, can believe in God and confess their sins and do all that their faith requires of them in terms of rituals, prayers, genuflections, and donations, and yet simultaneously fail to help or assist a dying father. And nonreligious people, like Lupita, may not pray or study the Bible or go to Mass, and yet they can clearly exhibit the best, most loving of human potential nonetheless. Clearly then, the impetus and ability to care for a dying loved one can have secular sources or motivations.

A second aspect about Lupita's story that merits emphasis is that she was able to cope with her father's death better emotionally than her siblings. She was in a much better frame of mind psychologically. This is quite counterintuitive, if you think about it. After all, if her religious siblings honestly believe in life after death, then for them there is the nearly certain expectation that their father is doing fine up in heaven, and they'll be with him again in the not too distant future. So what's there to freak out about? And Lupita, given her lack of belief in an afterlife and her strong conviction that she'll never see her father again—in this life or any imagined other—should be the one truly devastated. As an atheist, she doesn't believe that her father exists anymore, and she doesn't believe she'll ever be with him again. Shouldn't she be more emotionally devastated than her religious siblings? And yet, as we have seen, she handled his death with much calmer acceptance and maturity.

I wondered about this, and I asked her why she thought she was more emotionally okay with her father's death, even though she believes that she will never see him again, whereas her siblings, who believe in an afterlife and believe they will be with him in heaven, were so distraught. "Yeah," she says with a sigh, "I try to wrap my head around this all the time. I don't know. I did grieve, and I was sad, and I thought about my dad a lot after he passed away—but his death also made me just think about death a lot, in general, and what it made me think is: This is just it. This life—this is it. For me, when you are dead you are dead. And I think losing my dad, when he died, I think that was the first time that it made sense to me. This life is it. And I'm okay with that. This is life. There's death. There is an ebb and flow. Life and death. Happiness and sorrow. That's life."

Lupita's story, though hers and hers alone, is nevertheless illustrative of how many secular people confront mortality: with capable sobriety, levelheadedness, deep grief, and ultimately acceptance.

Secular Funeral Officiant

Lupita's father's funeral was traditionally Catholic. Indeed, most funerals today are religious in nature. And that's how most people want it to be. But not everyone. For example, Lupita doesn't anticipate a religious funeral for herself. And we are seeing that more and more Americans are also expecting to have nonreligious funerals; according to the American Religious Identification Survey, nearly 30 percent of Americans do not expect a religious funeral for themselves. What will they do instead? They'll probably have some sort of a secular memorial—a gathering of friends and family, perhaps at a funeral home, or maybe at the beach, or maybe in someone's backyard, where their loved ones will share memories, listen to music, perhaps watch a video presentation of old photos and home movies. If their loved ones want the service to have a more organized form and structure, they'll hire someone like Quincy Risskov, who specializes in officiating at secular memorials.

Quincy, age fifty-six, lives in Buffalo, New York. He is married and has two sons. His wife is a part-time writing teacher, and he is a part-time museum docent. As he says, "There are no more full-time jobs in Buffalo." Quincy also serves as a nonreligious wedding and funeral officiant. Since many states won't allow an atheist to officiate at certain life-cycle rituals, and since many states also require that ceremonial officiants be some sort of clergy, Quincy went ahead and got ordained online, via the Universal Life Church. Given his charisma, his talent at speaking thoughtfully in front of crowds, and his very pleasant Web site, he frequently gets asked to solemnize various rites of passage.

People—even the most ardently secular—still want, need, and enjoy structured moments of reflection, recognition, and consecration. At such times—births, weddings, funerals, and so forth—they want to stop and take in the moment, feel the significance, relish the beauty and poignancy. They want to hear words of inspiration, guidance, or comfort. But they don't want these to be religious in nature. For instance, most secular men and women don't want to hear at a wedding that "God has joined these two people together." But they do want to witness an exchange of heartfelt vows, or hear words of wisdom concerning commitment, or hear good poetry. And when it comes to funerals, most secular people don't want to hear that the deceased is now "in a better place" or is dwelling in the House of the Lord. They don't have a need for prayer. Or forgiveness of sins. But they still yearn for a meaningful, authentic ceremony that allows them to come together and be a part of a ritualized gathering that marks the occasion as special, set apart, sincere, heartfelt.

Such rituals and rites of passages usually need a leader—someone to officiate, to set the tone, designate roles, offer words, lead songs, be at the helm. Thus Quincy. The son of an agnostic father and a nonpracticing Christian mother, he first got into officiating at funerals when his brother died back in 2004. "My brother had a lawn business, and in the process he developed a lung disease that took his life when he was forty-nine years old. The pastor that had married my brother and his wife had passed away prior to my brother's death—and that pastor was literally the only religious clergy person they had ever known. Because they didn't go to church. My brother was agnostic and his wife is also a secular person. So I stepped up."

Since that first funeral, Quincy has officiated at many others. In such work, he first meets with the relatives of the departed—talks to them about their loss, asks them how they want their loved one to be remembered and honored, makes suggestions for the kinds of things they might want to include in or contribute to the ceremony, and so on. After such consultation—which involves a fair degree of counseling as well—he tries his best to respect and implement the wishes of those he has met and consulted with, weaving their words, memories, and reflections into the service. He seeks to make each memorial unique, tailored around the idiosyncrasies of the person who died, incorporating music or poetry loved by the deceased, and infused with any other special, personal components those attending the memorial want to have included. But at each service, he also stresses certain common themes, such as forgiveness and acceptance, and he talks a bit about how he thinks people should approach and understand death. "In death, we don't lose somebody—what we do is enter a new phase of our relationship with them. And that's the new phase of remembering. And I say during the service that in the days, weeks, months, and years ahead, we're going to touch or hear or see something that reminds us of the departed, and it is important that we embrace that moment, because those are the jewels of that person's life. Embrace those memories."

In his work, Quincy is clearly meeting the needs of the growing population of secular men and women out there who want a meaningful memorial service that does not invoke God, prayer, heaven, or an afterlife. And Quincy himself does not believe in such things. For him, death is final. So I asked him—if this life is all there is, then what is its ultimate meaning? And what does he say to grieving people who want to understand the meaning of life in the face of death? "Your life is as meaningful as you want it to be. If you feel your life is meaningless because you don't continue on after life, then that's the choice you make to live a meaningless life. Some Christians seem to have a deep need to think that this life is a preparation for some other life in the future. And if that helps them, then it is important that that need be satisfied with such a belief. But I don't have such a need. This life is, for me, full of meaning. I find meaning everywhere—in raising my two sons, in participating in community theater, and in working as an officiant, helping and comforting people during significant moments in their lives. There is so much in this life that I enjoy and love."

Funeral Director

Like Quincy, Audrey Fitzpatrick works with people who have recently experienced the death of a loved one. While she doesn't officiate at funerals herself, she does spend her days facilitating them. Audrey is the licensed funeral director of a large funeral home in downtown Los Angeles. And her observations of various types of funerals offer some interesting insight into the nature of how secular people celebrate and solemnize the loss of life. And make no mistake—in the fourteen years that Audrey's been a funeral director, she's seen all kinds of funerals. They are usually religious in nature. Within a five-mile radius of her funeral home there are communities of Ethiopians, Russians, Armenians, Guatemalans, Thais, Jews, Vietnamese, African Americans, and many more, all containing their own diverse religious traditions.

However, over the last decade, Audrey has seen a notable rise of people wanting to have funeral services without any religious components at all: secular funerals. "I love those," she declared. "As a director with lots of experience, I find that the nonreligious funeral ceremonies tend to be much more personalized and that a lot more thought has gone into it being specifically about that person. You get a lot more personal photos, videos, music, and people speaking more freely. There is definitely a qualitative difference between religious and nonreligious funerals. Generally, a religious service already has its own path that it follows, its set structure. Which I do think can be very helpful for a lot of families, especially if that is something they are very used to and have come to expect. They rely on that familiarity. They need it. But when you have a chance to work with a family that isn't going that route—that prestructured, religious service route—they're coming at it in an almost more organic way, literally asking themselves, 'How do I best honor and remember my dad, or my partner, or my friend?' So it opens up this whole other world of possibilities. I think a lot more thought goes into such nonreligious ceremonies. Sometimes people want specific music played, or poems read, or they want balloons, or they want to release doves—all kinds of ideas. But it just becomes more free, because you aren't obligated to do it this traditional way, or say this specific prayer. It becomes completely open territory to create from scratch something that is *all* about that person. Those memorials where it is just all about that person, and a lot of thought has gone into the details, and people speak so openly—I love that. I always walk away from those funerals with a much clearer sense of the person that has died—who they were, what they cared about, what had meaning for them—than I get from traditional religious ceremonies."

Death with Dignity

One last individual whose experience and perspective I'd like to explore—an individual whose work also involves dealing with death, but from a different angle—is Peg Sandeen, the executive director of the Death with Dignity National Center in Portland, Oregon. Peg has spent many years working passionately on end-of-life issues, devoting her time and energy to helping those who are dying, and actively assisting those who want to die on their own terms.

For Peg, educating the public about the right to die and legally fighting to help people end their lives as they themselves see fit, with as little pain and suffering as possible, is a personal passion grounded in her own values of empathy and seeking to help those in need. "I believe that everyone should die well. There should be personal choice about dying. I very much believe in personal choice—to the end. As a social worker, when I think about what helps people do well and what facilitates well-being, I know that people succeed and do well when they have choices. When they have options. And so I really believe in extending that to the end of life."

Back in 1994, a majority of the citizens of Oregon voted to pass the Death with Dignity Act, which made it legal for physicians to assist terminally ill patients to end their lives. Oregon was the first state in the country to pass such a law—but it wasn't easy. In 1997, opponents of the act sought to repeal it via Ballot Measure 51, but that attempt was rejected by 60 percent of Oregon voters. The act was then challenged yet again by certain members of Congress, as well as by the George W. Bush administration, but it was upheld by the Supreme Court in 2006. So the Death with Dignity Act still stands.

According to the law, an adult Oregon resident of sound mind who has been diagnosed (by two separate doctors) with a terminal illness that will result in death within six months may request a prescription for a lethal dose of medicine in order to end his or her life. The request must be made orally as well as in writing, confirmed by two witnesses (at least one of whom is not related to the patient and is not entitled to any portion of the patient's estate), and then, after a fifteen-day waiting period, the lethal dose may be prescribed. And no physician or pharmacist is forced to participate—they are free to recuse themselves from the process. Since its implementation, hundreds of Oregon residents have taken their own lives with the help and guidance of a doctor.

I am sure that America's first Death with Dignity law was passed in Oregon because Oregon is one of the nation's least religious states. For instance, in Oregon about 40 percent of the people seldom or never go to church, about 40 percent of the people consider the Bible merely a book written by humans and not the word of God, about 25 percent claim "none" as their religion, and almost 20 percent of the population could be considered atheist or agnostic in orientation—making Oregon of one of the top ten most irreligious states in America. And according to a recent census study conducted by the Association of Statisticians of American Religious Bodies, Portland is the least Christian city in America. Thus the fact that our nation's first successful Death with Dignity Act passed in this relatively secular part of the country makes perfect sense. Part of Peg's job is helping other states enact legislation similar to what passed in Oregon, and her efforts are bearing the most fruit in other relatively irreligious states like Washington, Massachusetts, and Vermont. "We have a saying in our office here, and that is, 'Not south of the Mason-Dixon Line.' Death with dignity is just not feasible in certain parts of the country, and yes, I think religion is a part of that." As Peg decisively declares, "The primary opponents to what we do have always been—and continue to be to this day—the religious."

The fact is, where there is strong religion, there is strong opposition to right-to-die initiatives—and where religion is weaker, there is greater acceptance. Indeed, according to the research of sociologists Jenifer Hamil-Luker and Christian Smith, "the odds of the nonreligious approving physician-assisted suicide are three times greater than the religious."

While both religious and secular Americans definitely agree that life is of eminent value and should be preserved and protected at all costs, it is secular Americans—in contrast to their religious peers—who are more actively concerned about prolonged end-of-life suffering, and are more willing to do what it takes to facilitate peaceful, less agonizing deaths.

That's certainly where Peg falls. She first got interested in the right-to-die movement when she was working with people suffering from AIDS. She saw many people in a lot of agony. She saw a lot of very sick people begging their partners to kill them—to have mercy and help end their suffering, as an act of love. And she saw a medical profession that wouldn't or couldn't deal with such requests appropriately, or legally. Given that Peg's attitude about death has always been one of comfort and pragmatism, she was motivated to make death-with-dignity legislation a reality. "My mom was a hospice nurse. So when I grew up, death was just a fact of life. It was very real. My mom would talk at the dinner table about people dying. It was her job. And I would go visit her at work, a place where people were dying. So I guess I do view death differently than some people. It's just more of a reality to me. I have much more of a practical notion of death than perhaps other people."

That "practical notion of death" guides Peg in her work. And it is a notion that transforms into an ethic, which manifests itself into social and political action of real consequence. Peg's desire to help empower others at a time when they are most powerless, to afford people the right to die in a way that they want to die, with as little suffering and as much dignity as possible, stems from the best of secular virtue.

Death Dread

Toward the end of our interview, I asked Peg if she was afraid of death. "No, I don't think I am afraid of it. I wouldn't be pleased to find out that I am terminally ill. But no, I don't feel afraid of it at all." I've found that most secular men and women—including the likes of Walter Pines, Mildred Wilcox, Lupita Portillo, and Quincy Risskov—seem to harbor an approach to their own mortality similar to that of Peg Sandeen: we don't want to die, but we aren't consumed with fear or dread concerning its eventuality.

But I guess I am one of the few nonbelievers out there—well, perhaps along with Woody Allen and Ingmar Bergman—who is actually scared of death. I don't sit well with it. I am not sure why. I mean, I have no problem with the idea of personally not existing anymore. After all, I didn't exist one hundred years ago—and that reality causes me no anguish—and so the idea that I won't exist one hundred years from now doesn't bother me at all either. And yet still, it must be admitted: I dread death.

Perhaps it started when I was in a car accident at the age of seven. I was driving with my mom and my brother, David. He was sitting in the front passenger seat and I was in the backseat. We were in a blue VW station wagon. None of us were wearing seat belts (it was 1976). A teenager was speeding on Sunset Boulevard, coming in the opposite direction. He lost control and plowed into us. In the immediate moments after impact, my mother and I sat up, looked at each other, and then saw that my brother was hunched over, motionless. My mom lifted him up by his shoulders and his head rolled back. His eyes were closed, he was unconscious, and there was a single streak of red blood running diagonally across his pale face. It was then that my mom let out a harrowing scream, which triggered my own scream. Some people carried David out onto a nearby lawn. Paramedics soon arrived. My brother soon came to. He was okay. We all were, although my mom's injuries were pretty bad. Later that evening, my mom mentioned the horrible scream I had let out when we first saw David's unconscious face. I said that I had screamed because she had screamed. But she said that she had never screamed at all—that it had only been me. To this day, I think that what I must have "heard" was some *internal* scream, some visceral horror at the sight of my unconscious brother. Or maybe my mom did scream before me, but she just doesn't remember. Either way, it was a traumatic moment for me. A deathly moment. And throughout my life I have now and then been plagued by fears of mortality.

My discomfort with death—its physical as well as existential reality—reared its disquieting head more recently, when Stacy and I happened to be in Berlin, at the home of Peter Pfefferkorn, age eighty-three. Peter is one of my father's oldest friends. They met in college in the 1950s. When I was eighteen, I went backpacking through Europe, and stayed in Peter's home in Berlin for a week. I went back to Europe again when I was nineteen, and this time I visited Peter for a week at his four-hundred-year-old peasant villa on a hilltop in Tuscany. At that time, he was there with his girlfriend, Heidi. The three of us went swimming in nearby lakes, we sampled the various tiramisus in numerous small restaurants, we discussed Günter Grass and Luca Signorelli, we took naps, and we enjoyed one another's company, despite our age difference. When I was in my late twenties, I returned yet again to that old villa in Tuscany, this time with Stacy—my then fiancée. The four of us—Peter, Heidi, Stacy, and I—spent night after pleasant night together, drinking bottles of local red wine, eating good bread and even better plums, talking, laughing, playing bridge, and enjoying the July air. It was so nice to sit around the old wooden table, our faces illuminated only by candlelight. Stacy and I were twenty-eight, Peter and Heidi were sixty-eight.

Then, a month ago, Stacy went with me to attend a conference in Finland (I didn't want to fly alone). On our way, we stopped in Berlin for three days to visit Peter. He had sold his Italian villa several years before and was now living in Berlin permanently. He was looking much older—he had difficulty walking, and he drooled a bit as he ate his breakfast. But his wit and charm and mind were all as intact as ever.

Unfortunately, such was not the case for Heidi. She had developed Alzheimer's disease, and was now living in an assisted care facility down the road from Peter's house. On our second day in Berlin, Heidi was found wandering aimlessly around Peter's backyard. She had somehow gotten out of the assisted care facility and made her way to Peter's. The maid brought her into the kitchen and sat her down at the table. She had no idea where she was. She had no idea who I was. She had no idea who Stacy was—although, interestingly, she spoke to both of us in English, so on some level, she knew something about us. But not much. When I asked Peter if he thought she knew who we were, he scoffed and said, "She doesn't even know who I am." We sat with her at the kitchen table, eating bread and honey, drinking coffee, trying to make pleasant conversation, but Heidi mostly just had a faraway look in her eyes and a sort of feeble smile. There were a few pleasant moments, like when she recognized the wooden table in the kitchen—the same table that used to be at the villa in Tuscany. But the overriding feeling of the gathering was one of acute loss, acute deterioration. Heidi's mind was nearly gone. She was old, soon to die, and she no longer remembered anything much.

After finishing my coffee, I got up from the table and went out onto the back porch and cried. I just felt such existential grief. How could Heidi not remember the wonderful times we had all spent together during those summers in Tuscany? Yes, yes, yes—I know: she has Alzheimer's and she is old and soon to die and that's what happens, that's how it goes. Peter is also very old and soon to die. Stacy and I will be there as well someday. Maybe I will lose my mind as well, and not remember anything—not remember how Stacy looked in Tuscany some twenty years ago, as she and Peter painted portraits of one another under a large olive tree in the late afternoon. I cried some more on that porch as I contended with mortality: Peter's, Heidi's, Stacy's, my own, everything. What the hell is it all about? What is the point? For some reason, seeing Heidi in that state, seeing Peter so old—it just made me feel a visceral sadness at the fleetingness of it all.

And yet I must say, that moment of existential despair did not last for very long. In fact, it evaporated rather quickly. And instead of ushering in a debilitating state of despair or depression or apathy, it made me feel all that much more alive. It made me feel the urgency of living all the more sharply. My tears were brief, and I left the back porch to return to those within. I held Stacy's hand a lot that afternoon, I savored my coffee, I made a renewed effort to tell Peter funny stories, I Skyped with the kids that evening, and I fell asleep that night thinking about how lucky I am to be alive, to be sleeping on the floor of an old house in Berlin, to know the people I know, and to have had the experiences that I have.

One day I'll be dead. And all that does is make me want to appreciate every aspect of life all the more deeply and passionately. And I know that I am not alone in this orientation—many millions of other men and women are out there in the world who also accept their own mortality and the fleetingness of life and they are not depressed by this, nor are they rendered apathetic or despondent. On the contrary. They are living rich, meaningful, and deeply appreciated lives.

Life Is Real

For years my parents kept a small book of poetry in their bathroom. It sat there on a small side table next to the toilet, often buried under copies of the *New Yorker*, *Jewish Currents*, and the *Jewish Daily Forward*. When I was growing up, I'd always open up that book of poetry and read all the various entries from the world's great poets. For some reason, despite all the poems I read while sitting there, and despite the fact that I read all those poems numerous times, I only retained one line from the entire collection, which has always stuck with me: "Life is real, life is earnest, and the grave is not its goal." The line comes from a poem titled "A Psalm of Life," written by Henry Wadsworth Longfellow, first published in 1838. Although the poem does contain a reference to "God O'erhead," I nonetheless have always considered it to be a fiercely secular poem—one that passionately celebrates this life and this existence. The poem calls us to live our lives as best we can, to strive, achieve, and pursue, despite the fact that, one day, we will die.

The poem affirms an orientation that is shared by nearly every secular person I have ever met: a firm belief in, or rather a serene acceptance of, the fact that this life is all there is, and that we thus must make the best of it. For secular people, the reality of mortality renders life all the more urgent, and all the more precious, and all the more wonderful. As Dan Barker, a onetime Christian preacher turned public atheist, has recently observed, secular people don't believe in life after death, but rather, they believe in life *before* death.

Such sentiments have been expressed by atheists, agnostics, and skeptics for centuries, going all the way back to the Greek philosopher Epicurus, born in the fourth century BCE, who argued that there is no life after death—a reality that does not render life meaningless, but rather prods us on to make the most of what short life we have through seeking happiness and tranquillity, peace and freedom, joy and contemplation, and the company of good friends.

Similarly, the ancient Jewish author of the book of Ecclesiastes declared that there is no certain life after death, that "all are from the dust, and all turn to dust again"—and yet we still should make the most of this life, to enjoy the brief time that we have, to eat our bread with enjoyment, drink our wine with a merry heart, find enjoyment in our labor, and love our spouses with gratitude. The medieval Persian poet and mathematician Omar Khayyám wrote in the early twelfth century that life is nothing but a bird's brief trill, a song that soon ends, and thus we must focus on the here and now, enjoying what we can, while we can. The bird's song may be short—but it still is. Existentialist philosopher Jean-Paul Sartre was emphatic on this point: there is no life after death, and thus to live maturely we need to be conscious of this fact, accept it, and in so doing wake ourselves up to what really matters in life and experience it more fully and more authentically. Similar sentiments were expressed by philosopher Martin Heidegger, who reasoned that the finitude of living is what gives it its immediate ultimacy, and it is only through soberly reckoning with our own mortality that we can truly, fully live.

Accepting the Finite

My wife, Stacy, harbors no fear of death—whatsoever. She has never believed in any sort of afterlife; she has always fully embraced her mortality. She was able to deal much better than I was with a mutual friend who was dying of cancer; she continues to mourn the death of her father to lung cancer, missing him and wishing he were still a part of our lives and yet understanding that he is gone forever; and as for any fear of flying—are you kidding? Even the most jolting turbulence doesn't cause her to stop reading her magazine article. The plane can be bouncing up and down hundreds of feet, careening this way and that, dropping, plunging—she doesn't even notice.

But while I am a nervous flier who does fear death and Stacy is a calm flier who doesn't fear death, what we share is an instinctual, immovable acceptance of it. I may worry about it, and she may not, but we both accept it. We are going to die. We are going to cease to exist. And in all honesty, that is not only fine, but simply and serenely natural. Neither of us wants to die anytime soon. Neither of us wants our death to be prolonged or violent. We'd both like to die at a ripe old age, and we'd like everybody else whom we know and love—heck, everyone at large—to have an easy death. But as for death itself, we both understand and accept its inevitability, and honestly can't imagine anything different.

If the acceptance of death as a natural and inevitable part of life is a visceral secular trait, then the virtue it tends to foster is a greater appreciation for life. For most of us, the lack of belief in immortality and the sober embracing of death's finality make living all the more urgent, love all the more important, authenticity all the more warranted, and time with friends and family all the more precious.

To the secular sensibility, life is not illusory, nor is it riddled with sin, nor is it the less significant precursor to some other more resplendent, pearly, or fiery realm. Rather, life is here, it is now, it is real, it is hard, it is soft, and it is ever so finite. And life's finiteness is the very essence of its glow and churning, the glow and churning that we feel coursing through the oxygen of our atria and tingling up the hair follicles on our ears and echoing through the very happiness of our teenage belly laughter, spurred on by little more than the *thwap* of a steak against a Cyclops's eye.

Chapter 8

—

Aweism

Life, this world, existence—it's all a surreal, pleasantly mind-blowing mystery. The depths of the infinite, the source of all being, the causes of the universe, the beginnings or ends of time and space—when it comes to such matters, we don't have a shred of a clue. And perhaps we never will.

What a funny and strange situation we find ourselves in: the only animals that exist with the simultaneous awareness that one day we won't; the only creatures that ponder and argue about the very nature of their essence and purpose; the only carbon-based life form with the ability to produce abstract art and hang it in a large building containing a café that offers free-range turkey burgers and a gift shop that sells cute little books on the philosophy of abstract art. And with all our admirable scientific advances that save lives and ease suffering and improve communication and increase mobility and harness energy and expand knowledge, we still have no real sense of what it all means, why there is anything to begin with, and how it is all actually possible. And we never will. "Humanity's destiny," acknowledges philosopher André Comte-Sponville, is "irreducible unknowingness."

Sure, we can hear the reverberating echoes of the Big Bang. Yet that cosmic vibration tells us nothing about what was before the Big Bang, or what was before that, or how or why there was even a bang to be binged at all. This mostly wet ball full of ptarmigans, ponytails, and poverty is floating in space among a billion other balls, and there are galaxies swirling and there is a universe expanding, which itself may actually just be an undulating freckle on the cusp of something we can't even conceive of, amid an endless soup of ever more unfathomables. And I find such a situation to be utterly, manifestly, psychedelically amazing—and far more spine-tinglingly awe-inspiring than any story I've ever read in the Bible, the Quran, the Vedas, the Upanishads, Dianetics, the Doctrine and Covenants, or the Tibetan Book of the Dead.

So smell that satchel of tangerines and nimbly hammer a dulcimer or pluck a chicken and listen to your conscience or master a new algorithm or walk to work or hitch a ride. Because we're here. And we will never, ever know why or exactly how this all comes about. That's the situation. Deal with it. Accept it. Let the mystery be.

IN THE BACKYARD of my grandparents' house there were bright swaths of yellow flowers that used to grow at certain times of the year. They were so stunning, sweet, beautiful, vivid, and friendly. When I was little, it just felt so good to look at them. I was told, at some point, that they were merely a common weed: *Oxalis compressa*. But to me, they were, and still are, the most wonderful flowers in the world. Grapes also grew in my grandparents' backyard; they covered the wooden lattice near the back brick patio, hanging down, drooping in abundance. Their skins were thick and deep blue and their insides felt like eyeballs in your mouth. I spent a lot of time playing in that backyard with the bright yellow flowers and the deep blue grapes, and I used to take a lot of naps at my grandparents' house as well, and I remember waking up one afternoon and watching all these tiny particles of dust floating listlessly in the sunlight that was pouring in through the window. It was really quiet. And then at some point my grandmother came in and gave me a snack: slices of crisp, green apples and flagrantly orange cheddar cheese.

One morning, alone, I drove from Whitefish, Montana, down past Big Fork, and then onward to Polson. It was early August. The road was mostly empty and the valley was vast and the massive mountains in the distance were stoic and serene and the fields were lonely and the air was still and smelled like dry pine as I drove alongside Flathead Lake. And when "Babe, I'm Gonna Leave You" by Led Zeppelin came on the radio, I felt my veins expand a bit, and when "He" by Moby Grape came on, I felt myself growing younger and older at the same time.

Like on a June night, years earlier, when I was in graduate school in Oregon in the 1990s, and my housemates and I threw a party. I danced a lot that night, wearing my faded jeans and my Fitzpatricks T-shirt. Stacy was wearing a chartreuse dress and clogs, and she even danced a little too, and then at around three in the morning we left the party and walked through our Eugene neighborhood, over to her place, the corner apartment with the giant redwood in front, and it felt like we were floating and then floating some more.

And there's that steady-sloped hill by the psychiatric hospital on the east coast of Jutland in Denmark, the one with the long and perfect downgrade. It was frozen over one January night so that its surface wasn't snowy anymore but purely icy and glassy and no one else was there, even with a half-moon glowing, and we all went down there with sleds in arms—Stacy, Flora, Ruby, August, and our friends Nancy, Louis, Lars, and Julie. But we didn't need the sleds because the icy hill was so glassy-slick that you could just fly down on your own, and we did, as a laughing snake, or in hand-holding pairs, or by ourselves, feet first on our backs or on our bellies with arms flying in front, with nothing below but soft snow and some hay bales farther on at the bottom, and we frolicked there for hours on that cold night, sliding, holding hands, breathing, sweating. Like the school night that I and my fourteen-year-old best friend, Hank, and our older brothers, David and Josh, played mud football in the rain up at the park, under the floodlights, in the fall.

Just the other day, Flora and I went to the beach near Santa Monica. The two of us got right into the water and the waves were lively and consistent and I clutched her left hand with my right and as each wave came closer, we made a split-second decision to jump up and over it, or dive down under it, or just stay put and let it smash us. Over and over again: the salt water, the oncoming waves, the splashing, the laughing, the sunshine, and Flora's face. Like my son August's face, similarly smiling in the misty hose water when it was a hot afternoon and we rigged up the hose to the top of the netting surrounding the trampoline in the backyard and we set it on "mist" and it gently sprayed all over us as we jumped and jumped.

And Ruby, now fourteen, recently described to me her desire to study space. She's always loved literature and music, but she recently took a one-week cosmology class at a nearby university, and she said that while much of the math was over her head, when the professor lectured about how we are made out of the same material as stars—that we are stardust made self-conscious—she got tears in her eyes, and tingles, and then a few weeks later she was camping with her friend Eloise and they were lying under the stars and there was a meteor shower above, and as she lay there taking it all in, she realized that she could imagine no music accompanying such a sight; she always likes to have music playing in the background—when she is in her room, or when we are driving, or when she is hanging out with friends—and she often finds herself in situations where she imagines certain music that would be good for accompanying certain moments, and she thinks that such-and-such a song would be perfect in the background, but when she was lying there camping, looking up at the stars, she realized that there was no song, no music, that could, would, or should make the moment any better or more deeply felt. The deep quietness of the space above her was amazing enough, utterly and needfully unaccompanied.

To Own the Awe

Occasionally I get asked "what I am." Most people I meet can tell that I'm a Jew by ethnicity, but if the conversation ever gets into the realm of faith, or specific religious beliefs and doctrines, or when people hear that I developed a Secular Studies program at Pitzer College, or when I am interviewing someone for my research and they can't quite tell where I am coming from, they will eventually ask me what I am, or how I identify myself. And I've always found the most common options lacking.

Take the label "atheist." Am I an atheist? Sure. Of course. I definitely do not believe that God—or any of the gods that have ever been created, concocted, or imagined by humans—actually exists. It's simply a matter of a lack of evidence. Do I know what created the universe? No. But that doesn't then translate into a belief in a God. It just means that I can acknowledge that there are some serious mysteries out there—awesome mysteries—that may not have any answers, ever. But again, the acknowledgment and recognition of such mystery does not then warrant belief in any sort of creator deity.

So, yeah, I'm lacking in theism. I'm an *a*-theist. But the term doesn't quite do me right, and I am hesitant to use the label "atheist" when people ask me what I am because, well, it is essentially a term of negation. It declares what I *don't* believe in, what I *don't* think is true, what

I *don't* accept. And that feels like a real loss to me, because when people ask me "what I am" I would prefer to offer a positive designation, an affirming description, not merely one that negates or denies what others believe in. To use an analogy, describing oneself as an atheist is a bit like describing oneself as "nonwhite" when in fact one is of Korean ancestry, or African American, or Choctaw.

Beyond that matter, I also don't like the label "atheist" because it doesn't adequately capture the joy of living I am fortunate enough to often experience, the general sense of amazement and deep appreciation that I regularly feel sweetly, wistfully, mournfully churning through my marrow when I frolic in the sea with Flora, or play football with best friends, or talk about stars with Ruby, or walk through the snowy woods with Stacy on a crystalline December night, or witness my children's births, or go with Harvs, Jelly, and Daniel P. up to the High Street café, or when I look at those yellow flowers, the same ones that used to grow in my grandparents' backyard.

Because I harbor a real love of life—not to mention a deep feeling for the profound mystery that is existence and the beauty that is being and the sublimity that is creation—the self-designation of "atheist" simply falls short, falls flat.

"Agnostic" is a bit better. I do like the term. I use it now and then. And yet it also has its shortcomings. First, in its most common usage, being agnostic means that you neither believe nor disbelieve in the existence of God. In the words of Julian Baggini, an agnostic "claims we cannot know whether God exists and so the only rational option is to reserve judgment." Maybe there is a God, and maybe there isn't—one just can't say. This is a fine position to take, I suppose. But on closer inspection, one must ask: is it even really a position? No. It is actually more like the *absence* of a position, for it is essentially nothing more than an admitted indecisiveness or embraced fence-sitting. For if a person cannot decide whether there is a God or not, or feels that it is impossible to say one way or the other, he isn't really anything at all, other than undecided, unsure. But when it comes to the question of God's existence, I'm not on such a fence. So that's one reason that I don't like to call myself agnostic.

But there's more on the agnostic front. There is actually a second, deeper, more philosophically nuanced meaning that is embedded in the term "agnostic." It is one that is much more in line with the literal Greek meaning of the term: to be "without knowledge." At this level, being agnostic means that one holds to the position that there are certain things, matters, subjects, or aspects of existence that simply cannot ever be known or understood; the human mind is inevitably limited, or the scientific method has its humble boundaries, and some aspects of reality may simply always transcend our understanding and comprehension. This form of agnosticism professes that, in the succinct words of Robert Ingersoll, "Nobody knows how it is. The human mind is not big enough to answer the questions of origin and destiny." Or in the words of philosopher Eric Maisel, an agnostic is one who believes that "no one has any special knowledge about the purpose or lack of purpose of the universe, that there is only scientific knowledge, with its limitations; the speculations of consciousness, with its limitations; and some amount of mystery, shared by us all and quite likely to remain unexplained until the end of time."

But even if some team of brilliant cosmologists can one day work out the answers to the perplexing questions of time and space and existence, there is still the unavoidable biggie, posed acutely by the German mathematician and philosopher Gottfried Wilhelm Leibniz: why is there something instead of nothing? For as Ludwig Wittgenstein put forth, the mystical mystery is not *how* the world is, but *that* it is.

That is the part of being agnostic that resonates deeply for me: I do believe that there are probably just some eternal unknowns out there, which suggests, to paraphrase Shakespeare, that "there are more things in heaven and earth" than can be dreamt of in *any* philosophy.

However, while considering myself agnostic in this vein, I prefer not to use that label too often simply because I find it to be so damn intellectual. It is too narrowly cognitive, too heady, too dustily philosophical. "Agnostic" implies an almost strictly contemplative position regarding life and its vexing questions and mysteries. But when I ponder the existence of certain existential questions and cosmic mysteries, I often have an *emotional* reaction beyond that of mere dry puzzlement or cold contemplation. I *feel* something. In fact, I would go so far as to say that sometimes I *experience* or *feel* existential questions and mysteries—concerning life, death, being, and the universe— much more than I merely ponder or contemplate them. And the label "agnostic" doesn't adequately capture or satisfactorily convey that experiential, emotional, or feeling dimension.

Okay, well, then what about the term "secular humanist"? I do like this label a lot—and I've tried to trumpet its worthiness throughout the pages of this book. Unlike "atheist," the label of secular humanist declares what I am *for*, and unlike "agnostic," it doesn't imply fence-sitting or abstract philosophical contemplation of existential unknowables. To declare oneself a secular humanist signals an optimistic belief in the potential of humans to solve problems and make the world a better, safer, and more just place. A secular humanist is someone who believes in reason, science, and rational inquiry, who is committed to democracy, tolerance, open debate, human rights, and so forth. So I do find the label "secular humanist" useful and appropriate now and then. On occasion. Like when I am invited to be part of a panel discussion on religion and politics. Or when I am debating a conservative Christian. Or when a secular parent asks me what she should call her religionless kids.

But I don't always like to use it as a self-designating label; it just doesn't always quite do the trick. To begin with, I find that secular humanism is more accurately a position or agenda that I *support*. Secular humanism entails a set of values, ideas, and practices that I *advocate*, such as the separation of church and state, the right to birth control, empowering the disabled, nourishing compassion, celebrating the arts. There is a decidedly political dimension to secular humanism—with its emphasis on tolerance, democracy, minority rights, environmentalism, women's rights, sexual rights, and so on—that I wholeheartedly embrace.

However, when describing what I *am*, I want to capture something else, something more personal than the values, ideas, and practices that I support and advocate. I want to describe what I feel and experience. After all, when I heard that Arthur Lee had just been released from prison and that he was going to be performing at the Knitting Factory that very night and I drove down there and even though it was sold out I somehow got in and I was right there in front of the stage and he played "Your Mind and We Belong Together," I didn't feel like a "secular humanist." What I felt was tearful joy and swelling wonder and utter rapture. When Robin Heckle, dressed up as a witch, donning black lipstick at the junior high Halloween party in the gymnasium, grabbed me and took me behind that curtain and kissed me, I didn't feel like a "secular humanist." I felt deeply tingly, aroused, elated. When Stacy and the kids and I had been hiking for too long on that hot, dry road up in the high mountains of Norway and we stumbled upon that ice-cold, azure-blue swimming hole, being fed by a waterfall that was in turn being fed by the glacial snow above, and we stripped off our clothes and dove in and drank the pure water as we swam in it, I didn't feel like a "secular humanist." I felt incredibly happy, sustained, embraced, loved, alive.

In sum, when I think of the most important, memorable, and meaningful moments of my life—moments when I feel simultaneously ephemeral and eternal, moments that define who I am and give me my deepest sense of self—I find that the title of "secular humanist" leaves a bit to be desired. Yes, I support and advocate the sane and noble goals of secular humanism. Yes, I am an atheist. Yes, I am an agnostic—at least the kind who suspects that there may be limits to the boundaries of human knowledge. But I am something more. I am often full of a profound, overflowing *feeling*. And the word that comes closest to describing that feeling is awe.

So at root, I'm an "aweist."

Granted, I'm obviously not always walking around in a constant, ever-flowing state of awe. I don't perpetually saunter about with my mouth wide open, my eyes glazed over, and my spine a-tingling. But I do experience a feeling of awe quite often enough. Sometimes it is fleeting and wispy. Sometimes it is deep and haunting. It can come from being in nature. It can come from interacting with people. Sometimes this feeling of awe can be kindled by reading Walt Whitman or listening to "Children of Darkness" by Richard and Mimi Fariña, or picking up my kids from school or taking them to a march downtown, with thousands of others, protesting against yet another unnecessary war. And of course, sometimes it comes from contemplating existential mysteries: time, space, beginnings, ends, and their—at least to me—unfathomability. Both the mundane things in life, as well as the profound can, at random times, stimulate a feeling of awe in me. But whatever the source, this awe is a feeling that constitutes an integral, visceral, and beloved part of my life experience.

Aweism encapsulates the notion that existence is ultimately a beautiful mystery, that being alive is a wellspring of wonder, and that the deepest questions of existence, creation, time, and space are so powerful as to inspire deep feelings of joy, poignancy, and sublime awe. Aweism humbly, happily rests on a belief that no one will ever really know why we are here or how the universe came into being, or why, and this insight renders us weak in the knees while simultaneously spurring us on to dance. An aweist is someone who admits that living is wonderfully mysterious and that life is a profound experience. An aweist agrees with the sentiments of historian Jennifer Michael Hecht, who, drawing from the insights of Gabriel Marcel and Alan Watts, suggests that while certain problems exist to be solved, deep mysteries exist to be enjoyed and unsolved—and we are happier when we accept that the universe and existence are just such mysteries. An aweist harkens to the words of Albert Einstein (a self-described agnostic), who suggested that "the most beautiful emotion we can experience is the mysterious. It is the fundamental emotion that stands at the cradle of all true art and science. He to whom this emotion is a stranger, who can no longer wonder and stand rapt in awe, is as good as dead, a snuffed-out candle."

MANY RELIGIOUS BELIEVERS can probably relate to such sentiments of Einstein's, and to aweism in general. And some may even see aweism as a manifestation of a sort of religious orientation to the world. But it is not. The similarities between various religions and aweism only go so far. As American philosopher Louise Antony explains, "Like theists, we affirm the limitations and fallibility of the human mind; like them, we acknowledge, with awe, the vastness and complexity of the natural world. Unlike theists, however, we have no master story to tell about the origins or the ultimate future of the world . . . we have no sacred texts, no authorities with definitive answers . . . no list of commandments." And, I would add, no gods.

After Charles Darwin lost his Christian faith and became an agnostic, he nonetheless retained a great feel and sense for the sublimity of creation, but he also said that "however difficult it may be to explain the genesis of this sense, it can hardly be advanced as an argument for the existence of God." But a religious or religiously spiritual person will do just that: interpret feelings or experiences of wonder, awe, and the sense of rapturous mystery as *evidence* of there being Something More, Something Else, Something Holy Out There. An aweist makes no such leap of faith. An aweist just feels awe from time to time, appreciates it, owns it, relishes it, and then carries on—without any supernatural or otherworldly baggage.

Joseph Conrad spoke of living in what he dubbed an "enchanted state." And yet for Conrad this enchantment is purely natural and wholly of this world. As he explained, "All my moral and intellectual being is penetrated by an invincible conviction that whatever falls under the dominion of our senses must be in nature, and however exceptional, cannot differ in its essence from all the other effects of the visible and tangible world of which we are a self-conscious part. The world of living contains enough marvels and mysteries as it is."

As French philosopher André Comte-Sponville has mused, "We live within the unfathomable." But while such a reality can often inspire oceanic feelings of transcendence, "there is nothing innately religious about this oceanic feeling. Indeed . . . when you feel 'at one with the All,' you need nothing more." Or as American atheist Sam Harris further expresses, though our universe is indeed "shot through with mystery . . . no myths need be embraced for us to commune with the profundity of our circumstance. No personal God need be worshipped for us to live in awe at the beauty and immensity of creation."

THUS AWEISM, THOUGH steeped in existential wonder and soulful appreciation, is still very much grounded in this world. It is akin to what philosopher Robert Solomon dubs a "naturalized" spirituality: a non-religious, nontheological, nondoctrinal orientation that is *"right here, in our lives and in our world, not elsewhere."*

I live this life in the here and now, and as the days and nights pass, I occasionally experience a profound sense of transcendent, swelling awe. And I simply enjoy that feeling. My awe stops there. As Einstein wrote, "We have to admire in humility the beautiful harmony of the structure of this world as far as we can grasp it. And that is all." I thus make little attempt to identify the source of my feelings of awe, and furthermore, I am perfectly content to explain my occasional sense of deep wonder or happiness or poignant joy in strictly naturalistic, neurological, or psychological terms. The source, in fact, is irrelevant to me. The awe is what I care about, and it is that feeling of awe which I consider a deeply important part of my personality and life experience.

A lack of belief in God does not render this world any less wondrous, lush, mystifying, or amazing. A freethinking, secular orientation does not mean that one experiences a cold, colorless existence, devoid of aesthetic inspiration, mystical wonder, unabashed appreciation, existential joy, or a deep sense of connection with others, with nature, and with the incomprehensible. Quite the contrary. One need not have God to feel and experience awe.

One just needs life.

Conclusion

A few years ago, while attending Cranston High School West in Rhode Island, Jessica Ahlquist took issue with the large Christian prayer banner that was affixed to the wall of the school auditorium. She felt that her public school should not be in the business of pushing religious faith, and so she sought to have the banner removed, insisting that it was a violation of the establishment clause of the First Amendment. In response to her activism on this issue, and the eventual lawsuit it inspired, Jessica was verbally harassed, received death threats, and ultimately had to have police protection while walking to and from class. The day after the U.S. District Court for the District of Rhode Island ruled in favor of Jessica and ordered that the banner be removed, Rhode Island state representative Peter Palumbo went on a local radio show and castigated her as an "evil little thing."

It still isn't easy being secular in America.

A clear majority of Americans—in fact two-thirds—say that they consider the United States to be a "Christian nation." This means that for many people, being an atheist or agnostic is seen as being somehow intrinsically un-American. Indeed, the current state constitutions of South Carolina, Arkansas, Maryland, Mississippi, Tennessee, and Texas bar atheists from holding public office. And given that the very Pledge of Allegiance includes the words "under God," and that leading American politicians often proclaim that it is our faith in God that unites us above all else as a nation, it makes sense that anyone who doesn't believe in God is clearly less than fully patriotic, right?

That was at least the first President Bush's position back in the 1980s, when he publicly said, "I don't know that atheists should be considered as citizens, nor should they be considered patriotic. This is one nation under God." Many Americans clearly agree with such a sentiment, as evidenced by the numerous surveys that reveal Americans' unwillingness to vote for an atheist for president. As we have seen, more Americans would be willing to vote for a Muslim, a homosexual, a Mormon, a Latino, a Jew, a Catholic, a woman, or an African American than for an atheist.

In the United States today, numerous pundits and politicians—usually Republican, but sometimes Democratic—insist that religious faith and being American go hand in hand. As the second President Bush—who claimed that Jesus was his favorite philosopher and that he consulted with God before invading Iraq—said in his 2003 State of the Union address, "We Americans have faith in ourselves, but not in ourselves alone—we do not claim to know all the ways of Providence, yet we can trust in them, placing our confidence in the loving God behind all of life, and all of history." The operative words in that passage are "we Americans." The unabashed implication of the nation's forty-third president is that if you don't place your confidence in a "loving God," then you aren't "we," and thus you aren't really American.

Such sentiments are quite mainstream these days. To list all the times that such an assertion has been put forth by some powerful person at a podium would take too many pages. So let me just offer one recent, all too typical example. On August 30, 2012, at the Republican

National Convention in Tampa, Florida, Senator Marco Rubio was given a very important, penultimate slot on the final night of the gathering: to give the speech just before Mitt Romney was to take the stage and accept his party's nomination. Youthful, articulate, and a very proud American, Marco Rubio embodies all that the current Republican Party stands for: a hatred of taxes and government bureaucracy, a love of family and freedom, and—perhaps above all else—faith in God. I say "perhaps above all else" because that's exactly what Senator Rubio stressed in his speech. As he declared that night, "Our national motto is 'In God We Trust,' reminding us that faith in our Creator is the most important American value of all." He additionally argued that America is a blessed and special nation "because we've been united not by a common race or ethnicity. We're bound together by common values . . . that almighty God is the source of all we have."

I couldn't disagree more. Nor could the facts of American history and demography.

Senator Rubio is simply wrong in his insistence that a shared faith in God is what unites us as Americans. It is not—for the obvious reason that such a faith is not embraced by all Americans. As I've reported in this book, millions of Americans—be they psychiatrists or nurses, veterans or secretaries, lawyers or stay-at-home moms, students or property managers, drug rehab directors or Holocaust survivors, receptionists or camera operators, truck drivers or police officers—live their lives without faith in God. And millions more live their lives without any interest in religion whatsoever. As touched upon in the introduction, the statistics are surprisingly clear on this front; with the current percentage of Americans identifying as nonreligious being somewhere between 20 and 30 percent, we're talking about tens of millions of Americans who are more secular than not.

What unites us as Americans, then, is clearly *not* our faith in God. And it never has been. From Thomas Jefferson to Ethan Allen, from

James Madison to Elizabeth Cady Stanton, from Thomas Paine to Margaret Sanger, from Frederick Douglass to Frances Wright, from John Henry Kagi to Charlotte Perkins Gilman, from Charles Knowlton to H. L. Mencken, from Robert Ingersoll to Susan B. Anthony, from William Howard Taft to A. Philip Randolph, from Clarence Darrow to Ayn Rand, from Felix Adler to Nella Larsen, from William Lloyd Garrison to Emma Goldman, from Andrew Carnegie to Matilda Joslyn Gage, from John Dewey to Betty Friedan, from Mark Twain to Pat Tillman, from Kyrsten Sinema to Juan Méndez, from Mary McCarthy to Charlie Parker, and from Mark Zuckerberg to Bill Gates, freethinkers, skeptics, agnostics, doubters, humanists, secularists, and atheists have always been an important contributing part of American culture.

What *does* and *should* unite us as Americans is our adherence to and respect for the U.S. Constitution—and that's about it. Love of, belief in, and a willingness to defend freedom, liberty, and democracy: government by the consent of the governed. But as for metaphysical, spiritual, otherworldly, religious, or transcendental matters—is there a God? What happens after we die? Why are we here? How does karma operate? Who was Jesus? Where does chi reside? What is the Holy Ghost? How can we best mollify jinn?—the answers to such questions, whatever they may be, are *not* what define us as Americans, as citizens, or as human beings. And to suggest—as more and more politicians seem to be doing—that to be a good, decent American requires faith in a Creator, or to imply that Christian values are the only values, or to argue that our laws are given to us solely by God, or to constantly denigrate nonbelievers as somehow less-than-welcome partners in the American enterprise . . . that's all, quite frankly, very un-American.

AFTER ALL, the brilliant founders of this nation made their new American vision quite clear, as they proclaimed in Article 11 of the

Treaty of Tripoli of 1797: "The government of the United States of America is not, in any sense, founded on the Christian religion." That's a very bold declaration to be made only ten years after the drafting of the Constitution. And what is even more amazing is that the treaty was passed *unanimously* by the U.S. Senate—only the third such unanimous vote in that body, out of 339 votes that had taken place up to that time. Although the Declaration of Independence of 1776 refers to God without apology, once American independence was won, and the arduous task of actually forming a new nation was under way, the writers of our Constitution deliberately left God out of the entire body of that foundational, brilliant, and oh so secular document. All authority was placed in the hands of "we the people"—not in a deity. Faith, prayer, Jesus, the Bible, a Creator, heaven, salvation, Christianity, the Ten Commandments, God—all were deliberately left out of America's official blueprint.

But there's more.

The founding fathers went out of their way to establish a clear "wall of separation" between religion and state, to quote Thomas Jefferson. They reasoned, as James Madison so cleverly articulated, that both religion and government exist in greater purity if kept apart. To this end, the creators of the United States explicitly stated that no "religious test" shall ever be required in order to hold public office. And they also stipulated that the presidential oath shall make no reference to God (or anything supernatural). And the congressional oath constructed by the nation's first lawmakers, and signed into law by George Washington in 1789, also left out any reference to God, or anything supernatural. Thus, as David Niose, recent past president of the American Humanist Association, concludes, the fact that the bodies of both the Bill of Rights and the U.S. Constitution are God-absent, the fact that the framers did not want to make presidents or members of Congress swear religious oaths upon taking office, and the fact that the

Senate unanimously approved the Treaty of Tripoli—all of this "would hardly reflect the handiwork of a Congress that was seeking to construct a Christian nation."

And as for the national motto of "One Nation Under God" that Senator Rubio referenced—that was not our original national motto! The actual founding American motto, adopted by an act of Congress in 1782, was "E Pluribus Unum" ("Out of many, one")—a decidedly secular motto if ever there was one. But in 1956, at the height of the Cold War, and in an effort to distinguish ourselves from those godless communists over in Russia, the motto was changed to "In God We Trust." And the words "under God" were also not in the original Pledge of Allegiance; they were added in 1954.

The founders of the United States knew the damage that religious fervor can cause a nation. They knew the problems that religious divisions, disagreements, and sectarian strife can stir up in a society. They knew the evil that can be done in the name of religion by those in power. They were fully cognizant of the threat religion can pose to a neonatal democracy. That said, however, most of them were personally religious to varying degrees, and they knew how important religion is to most people, how inspirational faith can be, how essential religious congregations can be, and that religious freedom is a necessary freedom. And so in the very first amendment to the U.S. Constitution—before getting to the issues of freedom of speech, freedom of the press, and freedom of assembly—they made their brilliant, biprincipled position on religion clear: "Congress shall make no law respecting an establishment of religion, or prohibiting the free exercise thereof." So, on the one hand, government should not be in the business of religion. There shall be no Church of America. There shall be no House Committee of God. The government should not promote, subsidize, or "establish" religion. No one should ever pay taxes to support religious beliefs that they do not share or religious activities that they oppose. However, government should definitely not take away people's right to be religious. It shall not suppress, destroy, persecute, or subvert religion. That is, government should not impinge on the "free exercise" of religion. What an enlightened, balanced position to take—and one that is originally, quintessentially American.

Thus when pundits and politicians such as Senator Marco Rubio conflate being American with being a religious believer, they do so not only in gross ignorance of the demographic realities of America, but in direct opposition to the vision of our founding fathers.

As President Ulysses Grant declared in 1875, "Leave the matter of religion to the family altar, the Church, and the private school, supported entirely by private contributions. Keep the Church and the State forever separate." Or as President Ronald Reagan declared a century later, in 1984, "We establish no religion in this country . . . church and state are, and must remain, separate." That is, in fact, exactly what political, Jeffersonian secularism is all about: keeping the public square, if not free from, then at least aggressively neutral when it comes to religion. In such a situation, both secular *and* religious Americans win.

BUT ACHIEVING SUCH a state of affairs has never been easy. As Professor Jacques Berlinerblau has observed, "Nonbelief is, and always has been, treated with contempt in the American public square." Many studies and opinion polls, such as those discussed in the introduction, bear this out. And while I definitely do not think that secular Americans have ever faced the kind of prejudice, exclusion, or hostility experienced by Native Americans, African Americans, Latino/a Americans, Asian Americans, Jews, Catholics, Mormons, Muslims, or homosexuals, there is still no question that atheists, agnostics, secularists, and others who eschew religion are often disliked and distrusted, or widely regarded as immoral, or not considered fully American.

Heck, we aren't even allowed in the Boy Scouts, the American Legion, or the Veterans of Foreign Wars. Humanist chaplains are barred from serving in our nation's military. Charities regularly reject donations that are offered by secularist organizations. And the only way that this cultural exclusion, political stymieing, and social stigmatization will ever change is if nonbelieving, nonreligious Americans straighten up their secular spines a bit, clear their humanist throats, and assert their position with knowledge, confidence, and pride. Our secular humanism is not something to be hidden from family, friends or colleagues; it is something to be proud of, explained, and discussed. And our secular humanist values should propel us to get actively involved in shaping our schools, our cities, our nation, our world. And we should work with other secular humanists—as well as those religious Americans out there who share our values and vision—in an organized fashion.

It is essential to assert, both publicly and privately, that religion is clearly not the sole source, arbiter, or purveyor of morality and values. For to equate religion with morality, or to conflate theism with "having values," is to commit a grave historical, sociological, and philosophical fallacy. Historically, some of the greatest moral and ethical advances have been predicated upon strictly secular ideologies championed by the nonreligious. The Enlightenment push for democracy, the modern movement for women's rights, the fight against caste in India, and the acceptance of homosexuality are but four obvious examples. The creation of the Universal Declaration of Human Rights is another. As for technological, medical, and scientific advances—the contributions of secularism on these fronts are truly enormous and awesomely unparalleled.

Sociologically, we know that religion is far from a guarantor of morality. After all, as discussed in chapter 2, those societies today with the highest proportion of secular men and women tend to be among the most humane, moral societies on earth. And conversely, those societies that are the most religious, well, they tend to be beset by a greater degree of societal ills, from inequality to corruption to murder.

Philosophically, secular morality is not based on obedient faith in a mysterious deity, nor is it linked to eternal heavenly reward or hellish damnation. Rather, secular morality—to paraphrase philosopher Emmanuel Levinas—is based on the faces of others. Our moral compasses flicker, calibrate, and adjust themselves in relation to the suffering we may or may not cause other people. We soberly acknowledge the subjectivity of others, and try to treat them the way we would like to be treated. This Golden Rule requires no leap of faith. It is simple, clear, and universally intelligible—probably as a result of our neurological capacity for empathy and our biological evolution as social animals over so many thousands of years.

The longer we keep quiet at dinner table discussions for fear of offending someone, the longer we shy away from joining school boards and allow creationists to set our nation's educational agenda, and the longer we allow the religious right to claim to be the sole proprietors of "values," the longer will our cultural marginalization continue, the longer will we be ignored in the halls of political power, and the longer will we live in a country that fails to incorporate, respect, or even understand our worldview.

But it is a worldview that is not only legitimate, humane, and honorable—it is a worldview that is sorely needed, perhaps now more than ever. Global warming, increasing inequality, terrorism, despotism, extremism, international disputes, hunger, wanton violence— these problems will best be solved by the very things that secularity is intrinsically predicated upon and ultimately grounded in: a this-worldly, empirically driven, rational frame of reference. Economic crises, melting ice caps, threats to democracy, domestic violence, sex trafficking, a lack of adequate funding for hospitals, corruption, genocide, the destruction of the rain forest, drug addiction, violence in schools, corporate crime, street crime, children dying of AIDS—all of these are problems of this world, and their only solutions will come from this world as well, namely: human willpower, rational inquiry, critical thinking, scientific discovery, data-based decision making, evidence-based policy making, and frequent dashes of hope, empathy, optimism, and creativity. Humanity is certainly a major source of much brutality, suffering, and destruction, but at the same time, humanity is a major source of kindness, compassion, and reparation. We have no gods to appeal to for help, no avatars, no saviors, and no prophets to do our work for us. Just our all-too-human selves: our minds, our reason, our bodies, our love, and our camaraderie.

ATHEISTS ARE OFTEN accused of striking an indignant tone; as best-selling author, presidential inaugurator, and evangelical pastor Rick Warren once declared, "I've never met an atheist who wasn't angry." Strange that Pastor Warren has never met people like the ones I've profiled in this book, and the hundreds of others whom I've interviewed over the years: nonbelievers who are anything but angry.

Most secular men and women are definitely not out to destroy religion. Being secular does not mean hating religion or seeing religion as the problem. We just don't see it as the solution, either in the realm of politics or in our personal lives. While there are admittedly some secular people out there who are hostile to religion, most secular men and women can and do accept it, and even appreciate various aspects of it, from time to time.

Thus while I deeply admired him, I didn't agree with Christopher Hitchens when he acerbically proclaimed that religion "poisons everything." No way. Religion provides so much sustenance, support, inspiration, and hope for millions of people every day.

Alain de Botton recognized in his wonderful book *Religion for Atheists* that there is much in religion that is beautiful, touching, effective, and wise. Religion allows people to feel loved in a world that is often loveless. Faith allows people to feel special in a world that often treats them as worthless. Religious congregations provide social support, child care, counseling. Religious heritage links people to their parents, grandparents, children, and grandchildren. Religious life is often full of music, food, festivity, tradition, and joy. Religion, both its theism as well as its communal dynamics, can often inspire altruism and charity, goodwill and humility. Religion provides guidelines for how to live, it strengthens links to one's culture and ethnic group, it eases difficult transitions in life as well as providing comfort in the face of pain, suffering, and death. As social psychologist Bob Altemeyer has acknowledged, "Believing intensely in a religion brings an enormous number of rewards. You know who you are, you know what life is about, you know what you are supposed to do, you know you will have friends all your life, you know you will never really die, and you know you will rejoin all the loved ones who died before and after you. It is all laid out for you." Clearly, countless people find religion attractive and rewarding, and so, as yet another atheist author, Dale McGowan, has written, anyone who fails to understand the religious impulse doesn't fully grasp the human condition.

But while happily admitting all of the above, it is nonetheless the reality that more and more people prefer to live their lives without religion. This does not render them any less normal, natural, American, human, or humane than their religious counterparts. And it does not mean that they are "nothing," that they lack something essential, or meaningful, or purposeful. Not even close. The stories I've shared are illustrative of hundreds of millions of secular people—in America and around the world—who experience their secularity in an affirmative, positive, sustaining manner, replete with its own comforts, benefits, and rewards. Such secular men and women value reason over faith, action over prayer, existential ambiguity over unsupportable certitude, freedom of thought over obedience to authority, the natural over the supernatural, and hope in humanity over hope in a deity.

I've written this book to explore and illuminate the lives, values, and experiences of just such people, and to offer a glimpse at how we raise our kids with love, optimism, and a predilection for independence of thought, how we foster a practical, this-worldly morality based on empathy, how we employ self-reliance in the face of life's difficulties, how we handle and accept death as best we can, how and why we do or do not engage in a plethora of rituals and traditions, how we create various forms of community while still maintaining our proclivity for autonomy, and what it means for us to experience awe in the midst of this world, this time, this life.

Acknowledgments

I would like to sincerely thank the following for their help, assistance, support, and input: Miriam Altshuler, Ahmed Alwishah, Jacques Berlinerblau, Sami Cleland, Michael DeLuise, Ian Dodd, Charlotte Eulette, Emilio Ferrer, Ryan Falcioni, Sara Grand, Sandy Hamilton, Arthur Lee, Ami Mezahav, David Moore, Frank Pasquale, Karen Peris, Pitzer College, Benjamin Platt, Dan Paul Rose, Elizabeth Saft, Suzette Soto, Trish Vawter, Susan Warmbrunn, Chantal Yacavone, and Marvin Zuckerman.

Notes

Introduction

5 **Back in the 1950s:** For the figure of 30 percent, see Frank Newport, "Mississippi Most Religious State, Vermont Least Religious," Gallup, February 3, 2014, gallup.com/poll/167267/mississippi-religious-vermont-least-religious-state.aspx and Global Index of Religiosity and Atheism, WIN–Gallup International, 2012, www.wingia.com/web/files/news/14/file/14.pdf. For the figure of 20 percent, see Hout, Fischer, and Chaves (2013). For the figure of nearly 19 percent, see "'Nones' on the Rise," Pew Research Center's Religion & Public Life Project, October 9, 2012, pewforum.org/2012/10/09/nones-on-the-rise. For the 18 percent figure, see Merino (2012). See also Putnam and Campbell (2010); Grossman (2012); and the American Religious Identification Survey (2008), commons.trincoll.edu/aris/publications/2008-2.

5 **This means that the number:** Kosmin et al. (2009).

5 **a third of Americans:** "'Nones' on the Rise," Pew Research Center's Religion & Public Life Project, October 9, 2012, pewforum.org/2012/10/09/nones-on-the-rise.

5 **In the early 1970s:** Cragun (2013), 173.

5 **helps explain why *Time* magazine:** Amy Sullivan, "The Rise of the Nones," *Time,* March 12, 2012.

9 **This assumption is so widespread:** Edgell, Gerteis, and Hartmann (2006).

9 **And a recent national poll:** Jeffrey Jones, "Atheists, Muslims See Most Bias

as Presidential Candidates," Gallup, June 21, 2012, gallup.com/poll/155285 /atheists-muslims-bias-presidential-candidates.aspx.

9 **Many other studies:** Hwang, Hammer, and Cragun (2011); Jenks (1986).

9 **psychology professor Adrian Furnham:** Furnham, Meader, and McClelland (1998).

9 **legal scholar Eugene Volokh:** Volokh (2006).

9 **psychologist Marcel Harper:** Harper (2007).

9 **psychology professor Will Gervais:** Gervais, Shariff, and Norenzayan (2011).

9 **sociologist Penny Edgell:** Edgell, Gertais, and Hartmann (2006).

Chapter 1: Morality

12 **Supreme Court justice Antonin Scalia recently:** Quoted in Daniel Burke, "Scalia Says Atheism 'Favors the Devil's Desires,'" CNN.com, October 7, 2013, religion.blogs.cnn.com/2013/10/07/scalia-says-satan-is-a-real-person.

12 **various national surveys consistently report:** Bloom (2012).

13 **As he explained in a publication:** On Holyoake, see *English Secularism* (1896) and "George Holyoake," Wikipedia, en.wikipedia.org/wiki/George_ Holyoake.

13 **For contemporary secular people:** Wattles (1996).

13 **Though it was undoubtedly articulated:** Richard Jasnow, *A Late Period Hieratic Wisdom Text (P. Brooklyn 47.218.135)* (Chicago: University of Chicago Press, 1992).

14 **The Golden Rule was also recorded:** Wattles (1996), 16–17.

14 **In ancient Greece, Thales:** Ibid., 29–31.

14 **The rabbi Hillel:** Ibid., 48.

14 **Although we find other versions:** Epstein (2005), 115.

14 **As the great English philosopher:** John Stuart Mill, "Moral Influences in Early Youth," from *Autobiography,* in Hitchens, ed. (2007), 61.

15 **As Kai Nielsen, author of:** Nielsen (1990), 17.

16 **One comes from a man named Milton Newcombe:** These are not their real names. Throughout this book, the names of many individuals and their key identifying characteristics have been changed, for obvious reasons.

16 **In the words of philosopher and humanist:** Law (2011), 2.

20 **In order to see the real-world benefits:** Shook (2013); Didyoung, Charles, and Rowland (2013).

20 **The most interesting finding:** Hall, Matz, and Wood (2009); see also Jackson and Hunsberger (1999).

20 **As psychologists Ralph Wood:** Hood, Hill, and Spilka (2009), 411.

21 **why secular white people:** Eckhardt (1970).

21 **why secular white South Africans:** Beit-Hallahmi (2010, 2007). See also Jacoby (2004).

21 **in a national survey from 2009:** "The Religious Dimensions of the Torture Debate," Pew Research Center's Religion & Public Life Project, April 29, 2009, pewforum.org/2009/04/29/the-religious-dimensions-of-the-torture· -debate.

21 **support of the death penalty:** Joseph Carroll, "Who Supports the Death Penalty?," Death Penalty Information Center, November 16, 2004, deathpenalty info.org/gallup-poll-who-supports-death-penalty; see also Beit-Hallahmi (2007). One major exception to this assertion is African Americans—they tend to be quite religious and yet generally oppose the death penalty. So the correlation between greater religiosity and greater support for the death penalty exists most prominently among white Americans.

21 **less likely to be racist or vengeful:** Cota-Mckinley, Woody, and Bell (2001).

21 **less likely to be strongly nationalistic:** Greeley and Hout (2006), 83; see also Tobin Grant, "Patriotism God Gap: Is the U.S. the Greatest Country in the World?" *Christianity Today Politics Blog,* August 5, 2011, blog.christiani tytoday.com/ctpolitics/2011/08/patriotism_god.html.

21 **when we look specifically at militarism:** Smidt (2005); see also Guth et al. (2005); Hamilton (1968); Connors, Leonard, and Burnham (1968).

21 **Secular people are also much more tolerant:** Putnam and Campbell (2010), 482–84; see also Froese, Bader, and Smith (2008); Gay and Ellison (1993).

21 **protecting the environment:** "Religion and the Environment: Polls Show Strong Backing for Environmental Protection Across Religious Groups," Pew Research Center's Religion & Public Life Project, November 2, 2004, pewforum.org/2004/11/02/religion-and-the-environment-polls-show-strong -backing-for-environmental-protection-across-religious-groups.

21 **threat of global warming:** McCright and Dunlap (2011).

21 **support women's equality:** Petersen and Donnenwerth (1998); Hoffman and Miller (1997); Brinkerhoff and Mackie (1993, 1985); Hayes (1995).

22 **believe that wives should obey:** Cragun (2013), 113.

22 **gay rights:** Pew Research Center's Religion & Public Life Project, "Religion

and Attitudes Toward Same-Sex Marriage," February 7, 2012, pewforum
.org/2012/02/07/Religion-and-Attitudes-Toward-Same-Sex-Marriage/; see also
Rowatt et al. (2006); Linneman and Clendenen (2009); Schulte and Battle
(2004).

22 **corporal punishment:** Ellison (1996); Ellison and Sherkat (1993a).

22 **status of illegal immigrants:** "Few Say Religion Shapes Immigration,
Environment Views," Pew Research Center's Religion & Public Life Project,
September 17, 2010, pewforum.org/2010/09/17/few-say-religion-shapes-immi
gration-environment-views.

22 **suffering of animals:** Peek, Konty, and Frazier (1997); DeLeeuw et al. (2007).

22 **when it comes to generosity:** When it comes to goodness and morality, there
is one significant area where secular folk simply fall short, and the religious shine: generosity. In their comprehensive analysis of contemporary religious life in the United States, *American Grace: How Religion Divides and
Unites Us* (2010), Robert Putnam and David Campbell found that religious
people are far more likely than secular people to donate their time and their
money. Religious Americans are more likely to volunteer (for religious as well
as nonreligious causes), to donate blood, to help the homeless, to give to charities, and to give in greater amounts than their nonreligious counterparts—
and this is all the more striking given the fact that religious Americans tend
to be slightly poorer on average than secular Americans. Even when control-
ling for such variables as race, gender, education, marital status, and age, the
correlation remains the same: religiously observant Americans are more generous, both with their time and their money, than demographically similar
secular Americans. Similar findings have been reported in the popular book
Who Really Cares? by Arthur Brooks and James Q. Wilson (2007).

How do we explain this? As it turns out, and as Putnam and Campbell's
own data shows, God is actually not the secret to religious people's generosity
edge. It isn't faith in the Lord that propels most religious people to be so charitable. Nor is it specific religious teachings, beliefs, or precepts. Rather, it is the
community aspect of religious life—being part of a social group. Much current
research indicates that church membership is the undisputable key to religious
charity, not theism. Theological views simply do not correlate with increased
generosity or volunteering. Nor do the actual content of people's beliefs, or the
depth of their piety. It is tempting, Putnam and Campbell acknowledge, to assume that religious people are more charitable "because of their fear of God or
their hope of salvation . . . but we find no evidence for those conjectures." What
does make a difference is communal connectedness. The real impact of religi-

osity on generosity and overall good neighborliness, as Putnam and Campbell explain, "comes through chatting with friends after service or joining a Bible study group, not from listening to the sermon or fervently believing in God."

Being socially integrated, being socially involved, being with other people—these dynamics seem to breed altruistic, charitable tendencies. But since secular people are much less likely to be communally engaged to the degree that the religious are, certain charitable aspects of their moral lives may suffer, and their ability to do good in the world, as individuals, may be less than optimal.

22 **violent crime:** "Percentage of atheists," Freethoughtpedia, freethought pedia.com/wiki/Percentage_of_atheists, note 6; see also Golumbaski (1997).

22 **A similar underrepresentation:** "UK Prison Population 2009," Wikipedia, en.wikipedia.org/wiki/File:UK_Prison_Population_2009.jpg.

22 **professor of psychology Benjamin Beit-Hallahmi:** Beit-Hallahmi (2010), 134; see also Bonger (1943).

27 **Such research is mushrooming:** J. Anderson Thomson and Clare Aukofer, "Science and Religion: God Didn't Make Man; Man Made Gods," *Los Angeles Times,* July 18, A11.

27 **psychology professor James Waller:** Waller (2007), 156–58.

30 **number of people raised without any religion:** Merino (2012).

30 **Benjamin Beit-Hallahmi has observed:** Beit-Hallahmi (2010), 134–35.

Chapter 2: The Good Society

42 **when we compare these types of nations:** Rees (2009b); Zuckerman (2013).

42 **University of London professor Stephen Law has observed:** Law (2011), 81.

43 **"No God, no moral society":** Dennis Prager, "No God, No Moral Society," *Jewish Journal,* February 2, 2011, jewishjournal.com/dennis_prager/article /no_god_no_moral_society_20110202.

43 **according to Gingrich, a secular society:** Steve Benen, "Gingrich's Nightmare." *Political Animal* blog, *Washington Monthly,* November 20, 2011, washingtonmonthly.com/political-animal/2011_11/gingrichs_nightmare 033613.php.

43 **A few years earlier, in his 2006 book:** Gingrich (2010).

43 **in the aftermath of the wanton massacre:** Melissa Jeltsen, "Newt Gingrich: Sandy Hook Shooting Tied to Godless Society," *Huffington Post,* December 19, 2012, huffingtonpost.com/2012/12/19/newt-gingrich-sandy-hook-_n_2330506 .html.

44 **Voltaire, the celebrated Enlightenment philosopher:** Lewy (2008), 13.

44 **Alexis de Tocqueville, in his 1835 classic:** Tocqueville (1969), 544.

44 **O'Reilly made the traditional argument:** "Bill O'Reilly Confronts Richard Dawkins," YouTube, youtube.com/watch?v=qVWxo3fspew.

44 **he's written similar sentiments:** O'Reilly (2006).

44 **Pundit Tammy Bruce concurs:** Bruce (2003), 58.

44 **In a prominently placed op-ed:** Larry Alex Taunton, "My Take: When Bedford Falls Becomes Pottersville, Belief blog, CNN.com, December 24, 2011, religion.blogs.cnn.com/2011/12/24/my-take-when-bedford-falls-becomes -pottersville.

45 **furthermore, the obvious case could be made:** Norris and Inglehart (2004).

46 **Drawing on numerous international surveys:** Drawn from Ingelhart's (2004) international survey analyses; Inglehart and Norris's (2003) multivariate "Strength of Religiosity Scale"; as well as Steve Crabtree and Brett Pelham, "What Alabamians and Iranians Have in Common," Gallup, February 9, 2009, gallup.com/poll/114211/alabamians-iranians-common.aspx. See also Diener, Tay, and Myers (2001); Keysar and Navarro-Rivera (2013); and my own calculations of rates of theism worldwide based on numerous national and international surveys (Zuckerman, 2007).

48 **Additional research by sociologists and criminologists:** Jensen (2006); Paul (2005); Fajnzylber, Lederman, and Loayza (2002); Fox and Levin (2000).

48 **Robert Brenneman is a sociologist:** Brenneman (2012), 158.

48 **various studies that measure subjective happiness:** Georgia McCafferty, "World's Happiest Nations Are . . . ," CNN.com, September 9, 2013.

49 **One scholar who has researched this:** Paul (2010, 2009, 2005).

49 **The ten states that report:** Pew Research Center's Religion & Public Life Project, U.S. Religious Landscape Survey, religions.pewforum.org.

50 *Forbes* **magazine recently ranked:** Rebecca Ruiz, "America's Best States to Live," Forbes.com, March 11, 2009, forbes.com/2009/03/11/united-states -healthy-lifestyle-health-healthy-living.html.

50 **child-abuse fatality rate in Mississippi:** "U.S. Rates of Child Abuse Fatalities," NPR, March 2, 2010, npr.org/templates/story/story.php?storyId=123891714.

51 **There are many, many factors:** Rees (2009b).

51 **it is quite likely that when societies become wealthy:** See, for example, Solt, Habel, and Grant (2012).

51 **secularity does not necessarily cause societal goodness:** This is the position of Norris and Inglehart (2004).

51 **Independent researcher R. Georges Delamontagne's studies:** Delamontagne (2010).

52 **major historical-political improvement in the West:** Schulman (2011).

52 **divorcing of religious authorities:** Berlinerblau (2012).

52 **Women's rights is another obvious societal improvement:** See Keysar (2013); Quack (2012).

52 **fight against caste in India:** Quack (2012).

52 **sane, effective sex education:** Sanger (1971).

52 **the enviably successful welfare state in Scandinavia:** Nordstrom (2000).

52 **Adolf Hitler, a Catholic:** Hitler repeatedly declared himself a Christian, believed in Jesus as his savior, couched his genocidal goals in distinctly religious/theistic terms, and wrote explicitly in *Mein Kampf* that he felt that he was acting in accordance with the will of God. In fact, the very oath of loyalty to Hitler, sworn by all Nazi officers, soldiers, and civil servants, began with the words "I swear by God." See Steigmann-Gall (2003); Mannheim (1999); Baynes (1969); see also Jim Walker, "Hitler's Religious Beliefs and Fanaticism," November 28, 1996, nobeliefs.com/hitler.htm.

53 **In the totalitarian situation, religion is demonized:** Froese (2008).

54 **It may not be *because* they are religious:** For one last example of how high degrees of religion do not guarantee societal well-being, just think of Rwanda in 1994—the most thoroughly Catholic nation in all of Africa, with nary an atheist to be found. And yet in the span of a hundred days, some 800,000 men, women, and children were butchered, an unimaginably horrific genocide. The widespread, fervent, and deep religiosity of Rwandan society certainly did not cause the genocide—but it most definitely didn't prevent it either. And on the other side of the planet, at the same time that the Hutus of Rwanda were slaughtering their countrymen with machetes, with clergy often facilitating the slaughter, the Japanese—a people who exhibit some of the lowest rates of religious belief in the world—were enjoying all the benefits of a safe, sane social order, with one of the lowest rates of murder ever seen in history.

Chapter 3: Irreligion Rising

55 **The views and teachings of the Carvaka:** I am especially indebted to the work of Jennifer Michael Hecht (2003) for this entire section; see also Bremmer (2007); Thrower (2000).

56 **"Only the perceived exists":** Hecht (2003), 96, 98; see also Quack (2012), chapter 5.

56 **the unknown author of the book of Job:** Malkin (2007).

56 **Lucretius argued that the gods did not exist:** Hecht (2003); Lucretius (1995).

57 **Democritus rejected the existence:** Thrower (2000).

57 **Protagoras articulated a proto-agnosticism:** Hecht (2003).

57 **Carneades, a true skeptic:** Hecht (2003); Thrower (2000).

57 **Anaximander sought to understand:** Couprie, Hahn, and Naddaf (2003).

57 **the critical rationalism of Muhammad al-Warraq:** Warraq (2003).

57 **"Men talk of heaven":** Quote in Hitchens, ed. (2007), 8.

57 **evidence of various nascent forms:** Hecht (2003), Thrower (2000).

58 **hundreds of millions of people:** Keysar and Navarro-Rivera (2013).

58 **there are now more people leaving:** Skirbekk, Kaufmann, and Goujon (2010).

58 **while secularization is in no way inevitable:** Bruce (2011).

58 **in Canada one hundred years ago:** Bruce (2011), 14; see also Ron Csillag, "'No Religion' Is Increasingly Popular for Canadians: Report," *Huffington Post,* May 15, 2013, huffingtonpost.com/2013/05/15/no-religion-is-increasingly -popular-for-canadians-report_n_3283268.html.

59 **approximately one in five Canadians:** Altemeyer (2009); see also Bibby (2002).

59 **consider Australia:** Bruce (2011), 14. As for Gillard being an atheist, see "Gillard Won't Play Religion Card," ABC News (Australia), June 29, 2010, abc .net.au/news/2010-06-29/gillard-wont-play-religion-card/885142.

59 **even more dramatic in Europe:** Bruce (2011, 2002).

59 **A century ago in Holland:** Bruce (2011), 10; see also Halman (2010).

59 **In contemporary Great Britain:** Bagg and Voas (2010), 97; see also Voas and Day (2007); Crockett and Voas (2006); Gil, Hadaway, and Marler (1998).

59 **British historian Callum Brown:** Brown (2001), 1.

59 **a similar situation in Sweden:** Ahlin (2005), 94.

59 **Furthermore, 61 percent of Czechs:** Inglehart et al. (2004).

59 **Thirty-three percent of the French:** Eurobarometer report, *Social Values, Science, and Technology* (2005), ec.europa.eu/public_opinion/archives/ebs /ebs_225_report_en.pdf; see also Shand (1998).

59 **survey information from Japan:** Reader (2012).

59 **Uruguay:** Jenkins (2013).

59 **Chile:** Rossi and Rossi (2009).

59 **South Korea:** Eungi (2003).

59 **Israel:** See "Israel 2010: 42% of Jews Are Secular," *Ynetnews,* May 18, 2010, ynetnews.com/articles/0,7340,L-3890330,00.html; also Dashefsky, Lazerwitz, and Tabory (2003).

59 **Azerbaijan:** Cornell (2006).

60 **For many years, the United States:** Berger, Davie, and Fokas (2008).

60 **secularity has nonetheless increased significantly:** Chaves (2011); Laurie Goodstein, "Percentage of Protestant Americans Is in Steep Decline, Study Finds." *New York Times,* October 9, 2012, http://www.nytimes.com/2012/10/10 /us/study-finds-that-percentage-of-protestant-americans-is-declining.html.

60 **Harvard professor Robert Putnam:** Putnam and Campbell (2010), 3.

60 **The percentage of Americans who claim "none":** For the figure of 30 percent, see Global Index of Religiosity and Atheism, WIN–Gallup International, 2012, wingia.com/web/files/news/14/file/14.pdf. For the figure of 20 percent, see "More Americans Have No Religious preference: Key Finding from the 2012 General Social Survey," sociology.berkeley.edu/sites/default/files/faculty /fischer/Hout%20et%20al_No%20Relig%20Pref%202012_Release%20Mar%20 2013.pdf. For the figure of nearly 19 percent, see "'Nones' on the Rise," Pew Research Center's Religion & Public Life Project, October 9, 2012, pewforum .org/2012/10/09/nones-on-the-rise. For the 18 percent figure, see Merino (2012); see also Putnam and Campbell (2010). See also Cathy Lynn Grossman, "Survey Finds 19% Without Religious Affiliation," *USA Today,* July 20, 2012; and the American Religious Identification Survey (2008), commons.trincoll .edu/aris/publications/2008-2.

60 **The number of "nones" in America has increased:** Kosmin et al. (2009).

60 **In absolute numbers:** see Kosmin (2013); Kosmin et al. (2009).

60 **nonreligious Americans are now the second largest:** Goodstein, "Number of Protestants Is in Steep Decline"; see also Putnam and Campbell (2010), 17.

60 **the only "religious" group growing:** Abrams, Yaple, and Wiener (2011).

60 **Between one-third and one-half of all "nones":** Cragun et al. (2012); see also Baker and Smith (2009b); Kosmin et al. (2009); see also Public Religion Research Institute, "2012 Pre-election American Values Survey," October 22, 2012, publicreligion.org/research/2012/10/american-values-survey-2012.

60 **between 9 percent and 21 percent:** Kosmin et al. (2009). See also Hout, Fischer, and Chaves (2013); Humphrey Taylor, "While Most Americans Believe in God, Only 36% Attend a Religious Service Once a Month or More Often," Harris Poll #59, October 15, 2003, harrisinteractive.com/vault /Harris-Interactive-Poll-Research-While-Most-Americans-Believe-in-God -Only-36-pct-A-2003-10.pdf.

61 **Twenty-seven percent of Americans:** "Spirituality in America," *Parade,* October 4, 2009, parade.com/news/2009/10/04-spirituality-poll-results.

61 **Rates of secularity are markedly stronger:** See "'Nones' on the Rise," Pew Research Center's Religion & Public Life Project, October 9, 2012, pewforum .org/2012/10/09/nones-on-the-rise/. See also Nona Willis Aronowitz, "The Rise of the Atheists: 1 in 4 Millennials Don't Identify with Any Religion," *Good,* November 7, 2011, magazine.good.is/post/the-rise-of-the-atheists-1-in-4 -millennials-don-t-identify-with-any-religion. See also Kosmin et al. (2009).

61 **This is a significant change:** Putnam and Campbell (2010), 125.

61 **The vast majority of nonreligious Americans:** "'Nones' on the Rise," Pew Research Center's Religion & Public Life Project, October 9, 2012, pewforum .org/2012/10/09/nones-on-the-rise.

63 **"fuzzy fidelists":** Voas (2009).

63 **"liminals":** Lim, MacGregor, and Putnam (2010).

63 **"believing without belonging":** Davie (1990); Winter and Short (1993).

64 **"belong without believing":** Riis (1994).

64 **folks who are active in religious congregational life:** Kelly (1997).

64 **I even personally know some actual pastors:** Dennett and LaScola (2010).

64 **And closely related to this last type:** Demerath (2000).

64 **"apatheists":** Shook (2010).

64 **various types of apostates:** Zuckerman (2011); Bromley (1988).

65 **the simple binary of religious/secular:** See Zuckerman, Galen, and Pasquale (2015).

65 **social psychologists Bruce Hunsberger and Bob Altemeyer:** Hunsberegr and Altemeyer (2006), 12.

67 **What all of this this has done is alienate:** Hout and Fischer (2002).

68 **sociologist Mark Chaves:** Chaves (2011), 21.

68 **A second factor that helps account:** Michael D'Antonio, "What Went Wrong in the Catholic Church?," *Los Angeles Times,* February 10, 2013, A32.

68 **After the extent of the crimes:** Barry Kosmin, "One Nation, Losing God," *Point of Inquiry* radio interview, December 31, 2010, http://www.pointof inquiry.org/barry_kosmin_one_nation_losing_god.

68 **The result has been clear:** G. Jeffrey MacDonald, "Who's Filling America's Church Pews?," *Christian Science Monitor,* December 23, 2012, 26–31.

68 **In 1990, 54 percent of Massachusetts residents:** Barton (2012).

69 **And according to an "American Values" survey:** Public Religion Research Institute, "2012 Pre-election American Values Survey," October 22, 2012, publicreligion.org/research/2012/10/american-values-survey-2012.

69 **But a very important third possible factor:** Brown (2001).

69 **as women grew less religious:** See Hertel (1998) and Riis (1994).

69 **We've seen a similar pattern:** De Vaus and McAllister (1987) and Dubach (2009).

69 **Today, more than 40 percent of American families:** Emily Alpert, "More U.S. Women Than Ever Are Breadwinners, Pew Study Finds," *Los Angeles Times*, May 28, 2013.

70 **Since the days of Stonewall and Harvey Milk:** Zuckerman (2011).

70 **Next, the Internet has had a secularizing:** For further discussion, see Armfield and Holbert (2003).

71 **Debunking on the Internet abounds:** Laurie Goodstein, "Some Mormons Search the Web and Find Doubt," *New York Times,* July 20, 2013, nytimes .com/2013/07/21/us/some-mormons-search-the-web-and-find-doubt.html.

71 **For example, in her ongoing research:** See Dennett and LaScola (2010).

71 **In another study:** Winston (2005).

71 **the Internet allows people:** See, for example, Cimino and Smith (2011) and Smith and Cimino (2012).

72 **Dr. Barry Kosmin is the founding director:** Personal communication (telephone interview).

73 **But it is a line of human culture:** Pasquale (2007b).

73 **Consider Christian Smith:** Smith (2012).

74 **And Professor Smith is far from alone:** Wilson (2002); Barrett (2004); Bering (2010); Murray (2009).

74 **Sociologist Paul Froese characterizes religiosity:** Froese (2008).

74 **Psychology professor Justin Barrett further:** Barrett (2012, 2004).

74 **For example, 42 percent of the Dutch:** Global Index of Religiosity and Atheism, WIN–Gallup International, 2012, wingia.com/web/files/news/14/file/14 .pdf; see also Grotenhuis and Scheepers (2001).

75 **anthropologists such as Daniel L. Everett:** Everett (2008).

75 **As nineteenth-century abolitionist and feminist:** Quoted in Hecht (2003), 388.

75 **approximately 450 to 700 million nonbelievers:** Keysar and Navarro-Rivera (2013); Zuckerman (2007).

75 **sociologists Marta Trzebiatowska and Steve Bruce:** Trzebiatowska and Bruce (2012), 171.

76 **Third, even if we can recognize that:** Boyer (2011).

76 **skeptical, agnostic, atheist, religiously indifferent, or affirmatively secular:** See, for example, Thomson and Aukofer (2011).

76 **So while the author Nicholas Wade writes:** Wade (2009).

76 **As cognitive psychologists Armin Geertz:** Geertz and Markusson (2010).

76 **The truth is that many societies today:** Amanda Marcotte, "Eight Countries Where Atheism Is Accepted, Even Celebrated, Instead of Demonized," Alternet.com, August 28, 2012, alternet.org/8-countries-where-atheism -accepted-even-celebrated-instead-demonized; Bruce (2011).

77 **Some societies are very religious for centuries:** Brown (2001).

77 **Some societies are relatively secular:** For example, the situation in modern Israel: Assaf Inbari, "The End of the Secular Majority," Haaretz.com, February 3, 2012. See also Efron (2003).

77 **Many individuals are strongly religious:** Altemeyer and Hunsberger (1997).

Chapter 4: Raising Kids

87 **41 percent of atheists have experienced discrimination:** Hammer et al. (2012).

91 **it is intrinsically less stable:** For instance, Oliner and Oliner (1992) found that secular people were more likely than religious people to help Jews during the Holocaust.

91 **Deborah's reflections on the moral instruction:** Kohlberg, Levine, and Hewer (1983).

92 **Kohlberg outlined six stages:** See also Mercer (2007) and Cottone, Drucker, and Javier (2007).

92 **And what many people think:** Nunn (1964); Nelsen and Kroliczak (1984).

93 **But what else do we know about secular parenting:** Merino (2012), 13.

93 **However, it does look like:** Baker and Smith (2009a); Bruce (2011), 204.

93 **The data backs this up:** Merino (2012), 12.

93 **According to Professor Nelsen's analysis:** Nelson (1990).

93 **This research was confirmed:** Bruce and Glendinning (2003).

94 **in his impressive study of sex and religion:** Regnerus (2007), 66–81.

94 **Vern Bengtson, a professor:** Bengtson (2013), 163–64.

94 **And what are some of their values:** Starks and Robinson (2007).

94 **according to various national surveys:** Cragun (2013), 87.

95 **The secular emphasis on cultivating autonomy:** Pearce and Denton (2010), 67.

95 **And sociologists Christopher Ellison:** Ellison and Sherkat (1993b).

95 **social psychologists Bruce Hunsberger and Bob Altemeyer:** Hunsberger and Altemeyer (2006).

96 **Finally, confirming Professor Bengtson's research:** Manning (2010).

96   **For many nonreligious parents:** Merino (2012).

97   **Americans born between the years 1925 to 1943:** Ibid.

105   **As sociologist Lynn Davidman argues:** Davidman (1993).

105   **Danièle Hervieu-Léger's apt phrase:** Hervieu-Legér (2000).

Chapter 5: Creating Community

107   **But then one day I happened upon:** For more on Camp Quest, see Metskas and Brunsman (2007).

109   **Such communities are springing up everywhere:** Cimino and Smith (2007).

109   **From Seattle Atheists:** "AHA Reaches 100,000 on Facebook," *Free Mind* 57, no. 1 (2013).

114   **The U.S. military has a reputation:** Chris Rodda, "Mandatory U.S. Army Survey Says Non-believers Unfit to Serve," *Huffington Post,* January 1, 2011.

114   **A couple of years before that:** Patrick O'Driscoll, "Plaintiffs Say Air Force Recruiters Told to Use Religion as Tool," *USA Today,* March 10, 2006.

114   **And while serving in Iraq:** Neela Banerjee, "Soldier Sues Army, Saying His Atheism Led to Threats," *New York Times,* April 26, 2008.

114   **And although there are hundreds of thousands:** Zucchino (2013).

119   **While there have certainly been many:** Allen (1991).

119   **most African Americans are very religious:** Taylor (1988); Taylor et al. (1996); Baker and Smith (2009a).

119   **For example, according to recent findings:** "A Religious Portrait of African-Americans," Section II: Religious Beliefs and Practices, Pew Research Center's Religion & Public Life Project," January 30, 2009, pewforum.org/A -Religious-Portrait-of-African-Americans.aspx.

119   **Furthermore, only 8 percent:** Kosmin et al. (2009).

122   **Whatever the disparate reasons:** Smith (2010).

122   **but being secular is also high on their list:** For further discussion of irreligious identity construction, see the work of Smith (2010).

124   **As an ethnographer:** Pasquale (2010, 2007a).

125   **Psychological studies back this up:** Saroglou, (2010); Farias and Lalljee (2008).

125   **And a recent Pew study:** "'Nones' on the Rise," Pew Research Center's Religion & Public Life Project, October 9, 2012, pewforum.org/2012/10/09/nones -on-the-rise.

126   **Other scholars agree with this assessment:** Nelson (2012), 55.

126   **Georgetown University professor Jacques Berlinerblau:** Berlinerblau (2012), 113; see also Bainbridge (2005).

127   **Some of the key differences:** Caldwell-Harris (2012).

127   **"less in need of social support":** Ibid., 17.

128   **If secularism is to be understood:** See Kurtz (1994) for further elaboration.

129   **the proclamation of the Ethical Culture movement:** Quoted in McGowan, ed. (2007), 255.

130   **"There is no Eastern solution":** Hitchens (2007).

Chapter 6: Trying Times

139   **Given these undeniably comforting aspects:** See, for example, Krause et al. (2001).

140   **For example, numerous studies have shown:** Myers (1992).

140   **it can help parents cope:** McIntosh, Silver, and Wortman (1993).

140   **it can help people seeking:** Zemore and Kastukas (2004).

140   **it can help people deal with chronic illness:** Mattlin, Wethington, and Kessler (1990).

140   **and pain:** Hayden (1991).

140   **it can help people cope with cancer:** Gall, de Renart, and Boonstra (2000).

140   **it can help comfort refugees:** Ai et al. (2005).

140   **it can help the victims:** Kennedy, Davis, and Taylor (1998).

140   **and in still more ways:** See, for example, Pargament (1997).

140   **leading psychologist of religion Ralph Hood:** Hood, Hill, and Spilka (2009), 461.

140   **As the leading expert on religious coping:** Pargament (1997), 301.

147   **In the absence of God:** Laden (2007), 132.

148   **Just another day in the Tomaszów ghetto:** Neumark (2006).

161   **So what do secular people do:** Hilary Wells isn't the only therapist out there to emphasize secularity in her practice. Hans Hils of North Carolina has spearheaded seculartherapy.org, which went live in 2012; as of last count, they had 112 registered therapists from all over the country, with over 1,300 clients (Ray, 2013).

162   **In her pioneering research:** Hwang (2008).

162   **Rather than questioning the "meaning":** Ibid.

162   **Other studies bolster Dr. Hwang's assertions:** Thompson and Vardaman (1997).

163   **And Kenneth Pargament found:** Pargament et al. (1994).

163 **And as Judith Herman argues:** Herman (1997), 51.

163 **Luke Galen is a professor of psychology:** Galen (2009).

164 **When I asked Professor Galen:** McCullough and Smith (2003); Brown (1994).

Chapter 7: Don't Fear the Reaper

179 **Although the phenomenon is most likely explained:** McGowan (2013); Woerlee (2004).

179 **much has been made of near-death experiences:** Rivas (2003).

179 **Many people have spoken of:** See, for example, Sabom (1998).

180 **And while her reluctance to embrace:** Croog and Levine (1972).

180 **And related studies indicate:** See Beit-Hallahmi and Argyle (1997), 196.

180 **psychologists Benjamin Beit-Hallahmi:** Ibid., 193.

180 **But not everyone buys it:** Inglehart et al. (2004), 338.

181 **In fact, approximately 25 percent of Americans:** Pew Research Center's Religion & Public Life Project, U.S. Religious Landscape Survey, "Summary of Key Findings," religions.pewforum.org/pdf/report2religious-landscape -study-key-findings.pdf.

185 **And we are seeing that more and more Americans:** American Religious Identification Survey (2008), commons.trincoll.edu/aris/publications/2008 -2; Kosmin and Keysar (2009).

191 **For instance, in Oregon, about 40 percent:** Pew Research Center's Religion & Public Life Project, U.S. Religious Landscape Survey, religions.pewforum.org; Kosmin et al. (2009); Joseph Carroll, "Public Divided over Moral Acceptability of Doctor-Assisted Suicide," Gallup, May 31, 2007, gallup.com/poll/27727/public -divided-over-moral-acceptability-doctorassisted-suicide.asp.

191 **And according to a recent census study:** Jahnabi Barooah, "Most and Least Christian Cities in America," *Huffington Post,* October 8, 2012, huffing tonpost.com/2012/10/08/most-and-least-christian-cities_n_1915050 .html.

192 **Indeed, according to the research:** Hamil-Luker and Smith (1998); see also Burdette, Hill, and Moulton (2005).

197 **As Dan Barker, a onetime Christian preacher:** Barker (2008), 343.

198 **Existentialist philosopher Jean-Paul Sartre:** Sartre, *Being and Nothingness.*

198 **Similar sentiments were expressed by:** Heidegger, *Being and Time.*

Chapter 8: Aweism

200 **"Humanity's destiny":** Comte-Sponville (2006), 72.

204 **it is essentially a term of negation:** Eller (2010).

205 **In the words of Julian Baggini:** Baggini (2003), 4.

205 **Maybe there is a God:** See also Le Poidevin (2010), 2.

206 **This form of agnosticism professes:** Quoted in Wakefield (1951), 274.

206 **Or in the words of philosopher Eric Maisel:** Maisel (2009), 4.

206 **For as Ludwig Wittgenstein put forth:** Wittgenstein (1922), sect. 6.44–6.45.

210 **An aweist agrees with the sentiments:** Hecht (2003), xiii.

210 **An aweist harkens to the words of Albert Einstein:** Quoted in Walter Isaacson, *Einstein: His Life and Universe* (New York: Simon and Schuster, 2007), 387.

210 **As American philosopher Louise Antony explains:** Antony (2007), xiii; see also Laden (2007).

210 **After Charles Darwin lost his Christian faith:** Quoted in Hitchens, ed. (2007), 96.

211 **Joseph Conrad spoke of living:** Quoted in Hitchens, ed. (2007), 123.

211 **French philosopher André Comte-Sponville:** Comte-Sponville (2006), 145.

211 **But while such a reality can often inspire:** Ibid., 150.

211 **as American atheist Sam Harris further expresses:** Harris (2004), 227.

211 **It is akin to what philosopher Robert Solomon dubs:** Solomon (2002), xvi.

212 **"We have to admire in humility":** Quoted in Hitchens, ed. (2007), 163.

Conclusion

213 **A clear majority of Americans:** Straughn and Feld (2010).

213 **Indeed, the current state constitutions:** Heiner (1992); West (2006).

214 **the first President Bush's position:** Quoted in Heiner (1992), 6.

214 **Many Americans clearly agree:** Hunter (1990).

214 **As we have seen, more Americans:** Jones (2012).

214 **the second President Bush:** Bush on Jesus: Stephen Buttry, "Candidates Focus on Christian Beliefs," *Des Moines Register,* December 15, 1999, archives.cnn.com/1999/ALLPOLITICS/stories/12/15/religion.register; Bush on God and Iraq: "Robert Scheer, "With God on His Side," *Los Angeles Times,* April 20, 2004, available at commondreams.org/views04/0420-01 .htm.

215 **the statistics are surprisingly clear:** Of course, not all Americans who claim to be nonreligious are atheists or agnostics. As discussed in chapter 2, secularity comes in a variety of shades; the continuum is broad, and not every nonreligious person is a nonbeliever. But a very significant proportion is nonbelieving; about half of all Americans who are nonreligious are atheist or agnostic in orientation. For details, see the American Religious Identification Survey (2008), commons.trincoll.edu/aris/publications/2008-2.

215 **What unites us as Americans:** Jacoby (2004).

216 **After all, the brilliant founders of this nation:** Niose (2012).

217 **as David Niose, recent past president:** Ibid., 54.

219 **As President Ulysses Grant declared:** Quoted in Berlinerblau (2012), 85.

219 **Or as President Ronald Reagan declared:** Quoted at "Ronald Reagan on Separation of Church and State," *Atheist Revolution,* atheistrev.com/2012/03 /ronald-reagan-on-separation-of-church.html.

219 **what political, Jeffersonian secularism is all about:** Berlinerblau (2012).

219 **But achieving such a state of affairs:** Ibid., 89.

220 **we aren't even allowed in the Boy Scouts:** Hammer et al. (2012).

222 **Atheists are often accused of striking an indignant tone:** "The God Debate," *Newsweek,* April 9, 2007, web.archive.org/web/20100328002309/http://www .newsweek.com/id/35784/page/1.

223 **Thus while I deeply admired him:** Hitchens (2007).

223 **Alain de Botton recognized:** de Botton (2012).

223 **As social psychologist Bob Altemeyer:** Altemeyer (2010).

223 **Clearly, countless people find religion attractive:** McGowan, ed. (2007).

Bibliography

Abrams, Daniel M., Haley A. Yaple, and Richard J. Wiener. 2011. "A Mathematical Model of Social Group Competition with Application to the Growth of Religious Non-affiliation." *Physical Review Letters* 107, no. 8: id. 088701.

Ahlin, Lars. 2005. *Pilgrim, Turist Eller Flykting? En Studie av Individuell Religiös Rörlighet i Senmoderniteten*. Stockholm: Brutus Östlings Bokförlag Symposium.

Ai, A. L., et al. 2005. "Wartime Faith-Based Reactions Among Traumatized Kosovar and Bosnian Refugees in the United States." *Mental Health, Religion, and Culture* 8: 291–308.

Allen, Norm R., Jr., ed. 1991. *African-American Humanism: An Anthology*. Buffalo, NY: Prometheus.

Altemeyer, Bob. 2009. "Non-belief and Secularity in North America." In *Atheism and Secularity*, vol. 2, edited by Phil Zuckerman. Santa Barbara, CA: Praeger.

Altemeyer, Bob, and Bruce Hunsberger. 1997. *Amazing Conversions: Why Some Turn to Faith and Others Abandon Religion*. Amherst, NY: Prometheus.

Antony, Louise M., ed. 2007. *Philosophers Without Gods: Meditations on Atheism and the Secular Life*. New York: Oxford University Press.

Armfield, Greg G., and R. Lance Holbert. 2003. "The Relationship Between Religiosity and Internet Use." *Journal of Media and Religion* 2, no. 3: 129–44.

Bagg, Samuel, and David Voas. 2010. "The Triumph of Indifference: Irreligion in British Society." In *Atheism and Secularity*, vol. 2, edited by Phil Zuckerman. Santa Barbara, CA: Praeger.

Baggett, Jerome. 2011. "Protagoras's Assertion Revisited: American Atheism and Its Accompanying Obscurities." *Implicit Religion* 14, no. 3: 257–93.

Baggini, Julian. 2003. *Atheism: A Very Short Introduction*. New York: Oxford University Press.

Baier, Kurt. 2008 [1957]. "The Meaning of Life," in *The Meaning of Life: A Reader*, edited by E. D. Klemke and Steven M. Cahn. New York: Oxford University Press.

Bainbridge, William Sims. 2005. "Atheism." *Interdisciplinary Journal of Research on Religion* 1: 2–26.

Baker, Joseph, and Buster Smith. 2009a. "The Nones: Social Characteristics of the Religiously Unaffiliated." *Social Forces* 87, no. 3: 1251–63.

———. 2009b. "None Too Simple: Examining Issues of Religious Nonbelief and Nonbelonging in the United States." *Journal for the Scientific Study of Religion* 48, no. 4: 719–33.

Barker, Dan. 2008. *Godless: How an Evangelical Preacher Became One of America's Leading Atheists*. New York: Ulysses Press.

Barrett, Justin L. 2012. *Born Believers: The Science of Children's Religious Belief*. New York: Free Press.

———. 2004. *Why Would Anyone Believe in God?* Lanham, MD: AltaMira.

Barton, Bernadette C. 2012. *Pray the Gay Away: The Extraordinary Lives of Bible Belt Gays*. New York: New York University Press.

Baynes, Norman H., ed. 1969. *Speeches of Adolf Hitler: April 1922–August 1939*. New York: Howard Fertig.

Beit-Hallahmi, Benjamin. 2010. "Morality and Immorality Among the Irreligious." In *Atheism and Secularity,* vol. 1, edited by Phil Zuckerman. Santa Barbara, CA: Praeger.

———. 2007. "Atheists: A Psychological Profile." In *The Cambridge Companion to Atheism*, edited by Michael Martin. New York: Cambridge University Press.

Beit-Hallahmi, Benjamin, and Michael Argyle. 1997. *The Psychology of Religious Behaviour, Belief, and Experience*. London: Routledge.

Bellah, Robert. 2003. "The Ritual Roots of Society and Culture." In *Handbook of the Sociology of Religion*, edited by Michele Dillon. New York: Cambridge University Press.

Bengtson, Vern L., with Norella Putney and Susan Harris. 2013. *Families and Faith: How Religion Is Passed Down Across Generations*. New York: Oxford University Press.

Berger, Peter, Grace Davie, and Effie Fokas. 2008. *Religious America, Secular Europe? A Theme and Variations*. Burlington, VT: Ashgate.

Bibliography

Bering, Jesse. 2010. *The God Instinct: The Psychology of Souls, Destiny, and the Meaning of Life*. London: Nicholas Brealey.

Berlinerblau, Jaques. 2012. *How to Be Secular: A Call to Arms for Religious Freedom*. New York: Houghton Mifflin Harcourt.

Bibby, Reginald W., 2002. *Restless Gods: The Renaissance of Religion in Canada*. Toronto: Stoddart.

Bloom, Paul. 2012. "Religion, Morality, Evolution." *Annual Review of Psychology* 63: 179–99.

Boehm, Christopher. 2012. *Moral Origins: The Evolution of Virtue, Altruism, and Shame*. New York: Basic Books.

Bonger, W. A. 1943. *Race and Crime*. New York: Columbia University Press.

Boyer, Pascal. 2001. *Religion Explained*. New York: Basic Books.

Braun, Claude. 2012. "Explaining Global Secularity: Existential Security or Education?" *Secularism and Nonreligion* 1: 68–93.

Bremmer, Jan. 2007. "Atheism in Antiquity." In *The Cambridge Companion to Atheism*, edited by Michael Martin. New York: Cambridge University Press.

Brenneman, Robert. 2012. *Homies and Hermanos: God and Gangs in Central America*. New York: Oxford University Press.

Brinkerhoff, Merlin B., and Marlene M. Mackie. 1993. "Casting Off the Bonds of Organized Religion: A Religious-Careers Approach to the Study of Apostasy." *Review of Religious Research* 34: 235–58.

———. 1985. "Religion and Gender: A Comparison of Canadian and American Student Attitudes." *Journal of Marriage and the Family* 47: 415–29.

Bromley, David. 1988. *Falling from the Faith: Causes and Consequences of Religious Apostasy*. Beverly Hills, CA: SAGE.

Brooks, Arthur C., and James Q. Wilson. 2007. *Who Really Cares: The Surprising Truth About Compassionate Conservatism*. New York: Basic Books.

Brown, Callum G. 2001. *The Death of Christian Britain: Understanding Secularisation, 1800–2000*. New York: Routledge.

Brown, Laurence B., ed. 1994. *Religion, Personality, and Mental Health*. New York: Springer-Verlag.

Bruce, Steve. 2011. *Secularization: In Defence of an Unfashionable Theory*. New York: Oxford University Press.

———. 2002. *God Is Dead: Secularization in the West*. Malden, MA: Blackwell.

———. 2001. "Christianity in Britain, R.I.P." *Sociology of Religion* 62, no. 2: 191–203.

Bruce, Steve, and Anthony Glendinning. 2003. "Religious Beliefs and Differences." In *Devolution: Scottish Answers to Scottish Questions*, edited by Catherine

Bromley, John Curtice, Kerstin Hinds, and Alison Park. Edinburgh University Press, 86–115.

Bruce, Tammy. 2003. *The Death of Right and Wrong*. New York: Three Rivers Press.

Burdette, Amy M., Terrence D. Hill, and Benjamin E. Moulton. 2005. "Religion and Attitudes Toward Physician-Assisted Suicide and Terminal Palliative Care." *Journal for the Scientific Study of Religion* 44, no. 1: 79–93.

Caldwell-Harris, Catherine. 2012. "Understanding Atheism/Non-belief as Expected Individual-Differences Variable." *Religion, Brain, and Behavior* 2, no. 1: 4–47.

Chaves, Mark. 2011. *American Religion: Contemporary Trends*. Princeton, NJ: Princeton University Press.

Cimino, Richard, and Christopher Smith. 2011. "The New Atheism and the Formation of the Imagined Secularist Community." *Journal of Media and Religion* 10, no. 1: 24–38.

———. 2007. "Secular Humanism and Atheism Beyond Progressive Secularism." *Sociology of Religion* 68, no. 4: 407–24.

Comte-Sponville, André. 2006. *The Little Book of Atheist Spirituality*. Translated by Nancy Huston. New York: Viking.

Connors, John F., Richard C. Leonard, and Kenneth E. Burnham. 1968. "Religion and Opposition to War Among College Students." *Sociological Analysis* 29: 211–19.

Cornell, Svante. 2006. *The Politicization of Islam in Azerbaijan*. Central Asia-Caucasus Institute Silk Road Studies Program, October. silkroadstudies .org/new/docs/Silkroadpapers/0610Azer.pdf.

Cota-McKinley, Amy, William Douglas Woody, and Paul A. Bell. 2001. "Vengeance: Effects of Gender, Age, and Religious Background." *Aggressive Behavior* 27: 343–50.

Cottone, John, Philip Drucker, and Rafael A. Javier. 2007. "Predictors of Moral Reasoning: Components of Executive Functioning and Aspects of Religiosity." *Journal for the Scientific Study of Religion* 46, no. 1: 37–53.

Couprie, Dirk L., Robert Hahn, and Gerard Naddaf. 2003. *Anaximander in Context: New Studies in the Origins of Greek Philosophy*. Albany: State University of New York Press.

Cragun, Ryan T. 2013. *What You Don't Know About Religion (but Should)*. Durham, NC: Pitchstone Publishing.

Cragun, Ryan T., et al. 2012. "On the Receiving End: Discrimination Toward the Non-religious in the United States." *Journal of Contemporary Religion* 27, no. 1: 105–27.

Crockett, Alasdair, and David Voas. 2006. "Generations of Decline: Religious

Change in 10th Century Britain." *Journal for the Scientific Study of Religion* 45, no. 4: 567–84.

Croog, Sydney H., and Sol Levine. 1972. "Religious Identity and Response to Serious Illness: A Report on Heart Patients." *Social Science and Medicine* 6: 17–32.

Dashefsky, Arnold, Bernard Lazerwitz, and Ephraim Tabory. 2003. "A Journey of the 'Straight Way' or the 'Roundabout Path': Jewish Identity in the United States and Israel." In *Handbook of the Sociology of Religion*, edited by Michele Dillon. New York: Cambridge University Press.

Davidman, Lynn. 1993. *Tradition in a Rootless World: Women Turn to Orthodox Judaism*. Berkeley: University of California Press.

Davie, Grace. 1990. "Believing Without Belonging: Is This the Future of Religion in Britain?" *Social Compass* 37, no. 4: 455–69.

de Botton, Alain. 2012. *Religion for Atheists: A Non-believer's Guide to the Uses of Religion*. New York: Pantheon.

Delamontagne, R. Georges. 2010. "High Religiosity and Societal Dysfunction in the United States During the First Decade of the Twenty-First Century." *Evolutionary Psychology* 8, no. 4: 617–57.

DeLeeuw, Jan, et al. 2007. "Support for Animal Rights as a Function of Belief in Evolution and Religious Fundamentalism." *Animals and Society* 15: 353–63.

Demerath, Nicholas Jay. 2000. "The Rise of 'Cultural Religion' in European Christianity: Learning from Poland, Northern Ireland, and Sweden." *Social Compass* 47, no. 1: 127–39.

Dennett, Daniel, and Linda LaScola. 2010. "Preachers Who Are Not Believers." *Evolutionary Psychology* 8, no. 1: 122–50.

de Vaus, David, and Ian McAllister. 1987. "Gender Differences in Religion: A Test of the Structural Location Theory." *American Sociological Review* 52, no. 4: 480.

de Waal, Frans. 2013. *The Bonobo and the Atheist: In Search of Humanism Among Primates*. New York: W. W. Norton.

———. 1997. *Good Natured: The Origins of Right and Wrong in Humans and Other Animals*. Cambridge, MA: Harvard University Press.

Dewey, John. 1929. *The Quest for Certainty*. New York: Minton, Balch.

Didyoung, Justin, Eric Charles, and Nicholas Rowland. 2013. "Non-theists Are No Less Moral Than Theists: Some Preliminary Results," *Secularism and Nonreligion* 2: 1–20.

Diener, Ed, Louise Tay, and David Myers. 2011. "The Religion Paradox: If Religion Makes People Happy, Why Are So Many Dropping Out?" *Journal of Personality and Social Psychology* 101, no. 6: 1278–90.

Douglas, Emily. 2006. "Familial Violence Socialization in Childhood and Later Life Approval of Corporal Punishment: A Cross-cultural Perspective." *American Journal of Orthopsychiatry* 76, no. 1: 23–30.

Dubach, Alfred. 2009. "The Religiosity Profile of European Catholicism." In *What the World Believes,* edited by Martin Rieger. Gütersloh, Germany: Bertelsmann Stiftung.

Durkheim, Emile. 1965 [1912]. *The Elementary Forms of the Religious Life*. New York: Free Press.

Eckhardt, K. W. 1970. "Religiosity and Civil Rights Militancy." *Review of Religious Research* 11, no. 3: 197–203.

Edgell, Penny, Joseph Gerteis, and Douglas Hartmann. 2006. "Atheists as 'Other': Moral Boundaries and Cultural Membership in American Society." *American Sociological Review* 71, no. 2: 211–34.

Efron, Noah. 2003. *Real Jews: Secular vs. Ultra-Orthodox and the Struggle for Jewish Identity in Israel*. New York: Basic Books.

Eliade, Mircea. 1968. *The Sacred and the Profane: The Nature of Religion*. New York: Harvest.

Eller, Jack David. 2010. "What Is Atheism?" In *Atheism and Secularity,* vol. 1, edited by Phil Zuckerman. Santa Barbara, CA: Praeger.

Ellison, Christopher. 1996. "Conservative Protestantism and the Corporal Punishment of Children: Clarifying the Issues." *Journal for the Scientific Study of Religion* 35, no. 1: 1–16.

Ellison, Christopher, and Darren Sherkat. 1993a. "Conservative Protestantism and Support for Corporal Punishment." *American Sociological Review* 58: 131–44.

———. 1993b. "Obedience and Autonomy: Religion and Parental Values Reconsidered." *Journal for the Scientific Study of Religion* 32, no. 4: 313–29.

Epstein, Greg. 2005. *Good Without God: What a Billion Nonreligious People Do Believe*. New York: William Morrow.

Eungi, Kim. 2003. "Religion in Contemporary Korea: Change and Continuity." *Korea Focus,* July–August: 133–46.

Everett, Daniel. 2008. *Don't Sleep, There Are Snakes: Life and Language in the Amazonian Jungle*. New York: Vintage.

Fajnzylber, Pablo, Daniel Lederman, and Norman Loayza. 2002. "Inequality and Violent Crime." *Journal of Law and Economics* 45, no. 1: 1–40.

Farias, Miguel, and Mansur Lalljee. 2008. "Holistic Individualism in the Age of Aquarius: Measuring Individualism/Collectivism in New Age, Catholic, and

Atheist/Agnostic Groups." *Journal for the Scientific Study of Religion* 47, no. 2: 277–89.

Flynn, Tom. 2012. "Does Secular Humanism Have a Political Agenda?" *Free Inquiry* 32, no. 6: 18–21.

Fox, James, and Jack Levin. 2000. *The Will to Kill: Making Sense of Senseless Murder*. Boston: Allyn and Bacon.

Froese, Paul. 2008. *The Plot to Kill God: Findings from the Soviet Experiment in Secularization*. Berkeley: University of California Press.

Froese, Paul, Christopher Bader, and Buster Smith. 2008. "Political Tolerance and God's Wrath in the United States." *Sociology of Religion* 69, no. 1: 29–44.

Freud, Sigmund. 1927. *The Future of an Illusion*. New York: W. W. Norton.

Furnham, Adrian, Nicholas Meader, and Alastair McClelland 1998. "Factors Affecting Nonmedical Participants' Allocation of Scarce Medical Resources." *Journal of Social Behavior and Personality* 13, no. 4: 735–46.

Galen, Luke W. 2009. "Profiles of the Godless: Results from a Survey of the Nonreligious." *Free Inquiry* 29, no. 5: 41–45.

Gall, Terry Lynn, Rosa Maria Miguez de Renart, and Bonnie Boonstra. 2000. "Religious Resources in Long-Term Adjustment to Breast Cancer." *Journal of Psychosocial Oncology* 18, no. 2: 21–37.

Gay, David A., and Christopher G. Ellison. 1993. "Religious Subcultures and Political Tolerance: Do Denominations Still Matter?" *Review of Religious Research* 34, no. 2: 311–32.

Geertz, Armin, and Guðmundur Ingi Markússon. 2010. "Religion Is Natural, Atheism Is Not: On Why Everybody Is Both Right and Wrong." *Religion* 40, no. 3: 152–65.

Gervais, Will, Azim Shariff, and Ara Norenzayan. 2011. "Do You Believe in Atheists? Distrust Is Central to Anti-atheist Prejudice." *Journal of Personality and Social Psychology* 101, no. 6: 1189–206.

Gil, Robin, C. Kirk Hadaway, and Penny Long Marler. 1998. "Is Religious Belief Declining in Britain?" *Journal for the Scientific Study of Religion* 37, no. 3: 507–16.

Gilman, Charlotte Perkins. 2003 [1922]. *His Religion and Hers*. Walnut Creek, CA: AltaMira.

Gingrich, Newt. 2010. *To Save America: Stopping Obama's Secular-Socialist Machine*. Washington, DC: Regnery.

Golumbaski, Denise. 1997. "Appendix: 1997 Federal Bureau of Prisons from Denise

Golumbaski, as Formatted in Rice/Swift." In "Prison Incarceration and Religious Preference," adherents.com/misc/adh_prison.html#altformat.

Greeley, Andrew, and Michael Hout. 2006. *The Truth About Conservative Christians: What They Think and What They Believe.* Chicago: University of Chicago Press.

Grotenhuis, Manfred Te, and Peer Scheepers. 2001. "Churches in Dutch: Causes of Religious Disaffiliation in the Netherlands, 1937–1995." *Journal for the Scientific Study of Religion* 40, no. 4: 591–606.

Guth, James, et al. 2005. "Faith and Foreign Policy: A View from the Pews." *Review of Faith and International Affairs* 3: 3–10.

Hall, Deborah, David Matz, and Wendy Wood. 2009. "Why Don't We Practice What We Preach? A Meta-analytic Review of Religious Racism." *Personality and Social Psychology Review* 14, no. 1: 126–39.

Halman, Loek. 2010. "Atheism and Secularity in the Netherlands." In *Atheism and Secularity*, vol. 2, edited by Phil Zuckerman. Santa Barbara, CA: Praeger.

Hamil-Luker, Jenifer, and Christian Smith. 1998. "Religious Authority and Public Opinion on the Right to Die." *Sociology of Religion* 59, no. 4: 373–91.

Hamilton, Richard F. 1968. "A Research Note on the Mass Support for 'Tough' Military Initiatives." *American Sociological Review* 33, no. 3: 439–45.

Hammer, Joseph, et al. 2012. "Forms, Frequency, and Correlates of Perceived Antiatheist Discrimination." *Secularism and Nonreligion* 1: 43–67.

Harper, Marcel. 2007. "The Stereotyping of Nonreligious People by Religious Students: Contents and Subtypes." *Journal for the Scientific Study of Religion* 46, no. 4: 539–52.

Harris, Sam. 2004. *The End of Faith.* New York: W. W. Norton.

Hayden, J. J. 1991. "Rheumatic Disease and Chronic Pain: Religious and Affective Variables." Paper presented at the annual convention of the American Psychological Association, San Francisco, CA, August 18.

Hayes, Bernadette. 1995. "Religious Identification and Moral Attitudes: The British Case." *British Journal of Sociology* 46, no. 3: 457–74.

Hecht, Jennifer Michael. 2004. *Doubt: A History.* New York: HarperCollins.

Heiner, Robert. 1992. "Evangelical Heathens: The Deviant Status of Freethinkers in Southland." *Deviant Behavior* 13, no. 1: 1–20.

Herman, Judith. 1997. *Trauma and Recovery.* New York: Basic Books.

Hertel, Bradley. 1988. "Gender, Religious Identity, and Work Force Participation." *Journal for the Scientific Study of Religion* 27, no. 4: 574–92.

Hervieu-Léger, Danièle. 2000. *Religion as a Chain of Memory.* New Brunswick, NJ: Rutgers University Press.

Hitchens, Christopher. 2007. *God Is Not Great: How Religion Poisons Everything.* New York: Twelve.

——, ed. 2007. *The Portable Atheist: Essential Readings for the Nonbeliever.* New York: Da Capo.

Hoffman, John P., and Alan S. Miller. 1997. "Social and Political Attitudes Among Religious Groups: Convergence and Divergence over Time." *American Sociological Review* 36, no. 1: 52–70.

Hood, Ralph, Peter Hill, and Bernard Spilka. 2009. *The Psychology of Religion.* New York: Guilford Press.

Hout, Michael, and Claude S. Fischer. 2002. "Why More Americans Have No Religious Preference: Politics and Generations." *American Sociological Review* 67, no. 2: 165–91.

Hout, Michael, Claude S. Fischer, and Mark Chaves. 2013. "More Americans Have No Religious Preference: Key Finding from the 2012 General Social Survey." Institute for the Study of Societal Issues, University of California, Berkeley.

Hunsberger, Bruce, and Bob Altemeyer. 2006. *Atheists: A Groundbreaking Study of America's Nonbelievers.* Amherst, NY: Prometheus.

Hunter, James Davison. 1990. "The Williamsburg Charter Survey: Methodology and Findings." *Journal of Law and Religion* 8, nos. 1–2: 257–72.

Hwang, Karen. 2008. "Atheists with Disabilities: A Neglected Minority in Religion and Rehabilitation Research." *Journal of Religion, Disability, and Health* 12, no. 2: 186–92.

Hwang, Karen, Jospeh Hammer, and Ryan Cragun. 2011. "Extending Religion-Health Research to Secular Minorities: Issues and Concerns." *Journal of Religion and Health* 50, no. 3: 608–22.

Inglehart, Ronald, Pippa Norris, and Christian Welzel. 2003. "Gender Equality and Democracy." In *Human Values and Social Change,* edited by Ronald Inglehart, 91–116. Boston: Brill.

Inglehart, Ronald, et al. 2004. *Human Beliefs and Values: A Cross-Cultural Sourcebook Based on the 1999–2002 Values Surveys.* Mexico City: Siglo Veintiuno Editores.

Jackson, Lynne M., and Bruce Hunsberger. 1999. "An Intergroup Perspective on Religion and Prejudice." *Journal for the Scientific Study of Religion* 38, no. 4: 509–23.

Jacoby, Susan. 2004. *Freethinkers: A History of American Secularism.* New York: Metropolitan Books.

Jenkins, Philip. 2013. "A Secular Latin America?" *Christian Century*, March 12.

Jenks, Richard J. 1986. "Perceptions of Two Deviant and Two Nondeviant Groups." *Journal of Social Psychology* 126, no. 6: 783–90.

Jensen, Gary F. 2006. "Religious Cosmologies and Homicide Rates Among Nations." *Journal of Religion and Society* 8: 1–13.

Kanazawa, Satoshi. 2010. "Why Liberals and Atheists Are More Intelligent." *Social Psychology Quarterly* 73, no. 1: 33–57.

Kelly, James. 1997. *Skeptic in the House of God*. New Brunswick, NJ: Rutgers University Press.

Kennedy, James, Robert Davis, and Bruce Taylor. 1998. "Changes in Spirituality and Well-Being Among Victims of Sexual Assault." *Journal for the Scientific Study of Religion* 37, no. 2: 322–28.

Keysar, Ariela. 2013. "Freedom of Choice: Women and Demography in Israel, France, and the US." Paper presented at the "Secularism on the Edge" conference, Georgetown University, Washington, DC, February 20–22.

Keysar, Ariela, and Juhem Navarro-Rivera. 2013. "A World of Atheism: Global Demographics." In *The Oxford Handbook of Atheism*, edited by Stephen Bullivant and Michael Ruse. Oxford: Oxford University Press.

King, Barbara. 2007. *Evolving God: A Provocative View of the Origins of Religion*. New York: Doubleday.

Klemke, Elmer D., and Steven M. Cahn. 2008. *The Meaning of Life: A Reader*. New York: Oxford University Press.

Kohlberg, Lawrence, Charles Levine, and Alexandra Hewer. 1983. *Moral Stages: A Current Formulation and a Response to Critics*. Basel: Karger.

Kosmin, Barry. 2013. "The Vitality of Soft Secularism in the U.S. and the Rise of the Nones." Paper presented at the "Secularism on the Edge" Conference, Georgetown University, Washington, DC, February 20–22.

Kosmin, Barry, et al. 2009. *American Nones: The Profile of the No Religion Population*. Hartford, CT: Trinity College. commons.trincoll.edu/aris/files/2011/08/NONES_08.pdf.

Krause, Neal, et al. 2001. "Church-Based Social Support and Religious Coping." *Journal for the Scientific Study of Religion* 40, no. 4: 637–56.

Kurtz, Paul. 1994. *Living Without Religion: Eupraxophy*. Amherst, NY: Prometheus.

Laden, Anthony Simon. 2007. "Transcendence Without God: On Atheism and Invisibility." In *Philosophers Without Gods: Meditations on Atheism and the Secular Life,* edited by Louise M. Antony. New York: Oxford University Press.

Law, Stephen. 2011. *Humanism: A Very Short Introduction*. New York: Oxford University Press.

Le Poidevin, Robin. 2010. *Agnosticism: A Very Short Introduction.* New York: Oxford University Press.

Lewy, Guenter. 2008. *"If God Is Dead, Everything Is Permitted?"* New Brunswick, NJ: Transaction.

Lim, Chaeyoon, Carol MacGregor, and Robert Putnam. 2010. "Secular and Liminal: Discovering Heterogeneity Among Religious Nones." *Journal for the Scientific Study of Religion* 49, no. 4: 596–618.

Linneman, Thomas J., and Margaret Clenenden. 2009. "Sexuality and the Secular." In *Atheism and Secularity,* vol. 1, edited by Phil Zuckerman. Santa Barbara, CA: Praeger.

Lucretius. *On the Nature of Things.* Translated and edited by Anthony M. Esolen. Baltimore: Johns Hopkins University Press.

McCullough, Michael, and Timothy Smith. 2003. "Religion and Health: Depressive Symptoms and Mortality as Case Studies." In *Handbook of the Sociology of Religion,* edited by Michele Dillon. New York: Cambridge University Press.

McCright, Aaron M., and Riley E. Dunlap. 2011. "The Politicization of Climate Change and Polarization in the American Public's Views of Global Warming, 2001–2010." *Sociological Quarterly* 52, no. 2: 155–94.

McGowan, Dale. 2013. "Humanism and the Big Problem." In *What Is Humanism and Why Does It Matter?,* edited by Anthony Pinn. Durham, NC: Acumen.

———. 2007. "Seven Secular Virtues: Humility, Empathy, Courage, Honesty, Openness, Generosity, and Gratitude." In *Parenting Beyond Belief,* edited by Dale McGowan. New York: Amacom.

———, ed. 2007. *Parenting Beyond Belief.* New York: Amacom.

McIntosh, Daniel N., Roxane C. Silver, and Camille B. Wortman. 1993. "Religion's Role in Adjustment to a Negative Life Event: Coping with the Loss of a Child." *Journal of Personality and Social Psychology* 65, no. 4: 812–21.

Maisel, Eric. 2009. *The Atheist's Way: Living Well Without Gods.* Novato, CA: New World Library.

Malkin, Yaakov. 2007. *Epicurus and Apikorsim: The Influence of the Greek Epicurus and Jewish Apikorsim on Judaism.* Detroit: Milan Press.

Mannheim, Ralph, ed. 1999. *Mein Kampf.* New York: Mariner.

Manning, Christel. 2010. "Atheism, Secularity, the Family, and Children." In *Atheism and Secularity,* vol. 1, edited by Phil Zuckerman. Santa Barbara, CA: Praeger.

Marler, Penny Long, and C. Kirk Hadaway. 2002. "'Being Religious' or 'Being Spiritual' in America: A Zero-Sum Proposition?" *Journal for the Scientific Study of Religion* 41, no. 2: 289–300.

Mattlin, J. A., E. Wethington, and R. C. Kessler. 1990. "Situational Determinants of Coping and Coping Effectiveness." *Journal of Health and Social Behavior* 31, no. 1: 103–22.

Mercer, Jean. 2007. "Behaving Yourself: Moral Development in the Secular Family." In *Parenting Beyond Belief*, edited by Dale McGowan. New York: Amacom.

Merino, Stephen M. 2012. "Irreligious Socialization? The Adult Religious Preferences of Individuals Raised with No Religion." *Secularism and Nonreligion* 1: 1–16.

Metskas, Amanda, and August Brunsman. 2007. "Summer Camp Beyond Belief." In *Parenting Beyond Belief*, edited by Dale McGowan. New York: Amacom.

Moore, Sally Falk, and Barbara G. Myerhoff, eds. 1977. *Secular Ritual*. Assen, Netherlands: Van Gorcum and Co.

Murray, Michael. 2009. "Evolutionary Explanations of Religion." In *God Is Great, God Is Good: Why Believing in God Is Reasonable and Responsible*, edited by William Lane Craig and Chad Meister. Downers Grove, IL: InterVarsity Press.

Myers, David G. 1992. *The Pursuit of Happiness: Discovering the Pathway to Fulfillment, Well-Being, and Enduring Personal Joy*. New York: William Morrow.

Nall, Jeff. 2010. "Disparate Destinations, Parallel Paths: An Analysis of Contemporary Atheist and Christian Parenting Literature." In *Religion and the New Atheism*, edited by Amarnath Amarasingam. Boston: Brill.

Nelsen, Hart. 1990. "The Religious Identification of Children of Interfaith Marriages." *Review of Religious Research* 32, no. 2: 122–34.

Nelsen, Hart M., and Alice Kroliczak. 1984. "Parental Use of the Threat 'God Will Punish': Replication and Extension." *Journal for the Scientific Study of Religion* 23, no. 3: 267–77.

Nelson, John K. 2012. "Japanese Secularities and the Decline of Temple Buddhism." *Journal of Religion in Japan* 1, no. 1: 37–60.

Neumark, Zenon. 2006. *Hiding in the Open: A Young Fugitive in Nazi-Occupied Poland*. Portland, OR: Vallentine-Mitchell.

Nielsen, Kai. 1990. *Ethics Without God*. Amherst, NY: Prometheus.

Niose, David. 2012. *Nonbeliever Nation: The Rise of Secular Americans*. New York: Palgrave Macmillan.

Nordstrom, Byron. 2000. *Scandinavia Since 1500*. Minneapolis: University of Minnesota Press.

Norris, Pippa, and Ronald Inglehart. 2004. *Sacred and Secular: Religion and Politics Worldwide*. New York: Cambridge University Press.

Nunn, Clyde. 1964. "Child-Control Through a 'Coalition with God.'" *Child Development* 35, no. 2: 417–32.

Obama, Barack. 2006. *The Audacity of Hope.* New York: Crown.

Oliner, Samuel P., and Pearl M. Oliner. 1992. *The Altruistic Personality: Rescuers of Jews in Nazi Germany.* New York: Touchstone.

O'Reilly, Bill. 2006. *Culture Warrior.* New York: Broadway.

Ozment, Katherine. 2013. "Losing Our Religion." *Boston* 51, no. 1: 70–79.

Pasquale, Frank. 2010. "A Portrait of Secular Group Affiliates." In *Atheism and Secularity*, vol. 1, edited by Phil Zuckerman. Santa Barbara, CA: Praeger.

———. 2007a. "The 'Nonreligious' in the American Northwest." In *Secularism and Secularity: Contemporary International Perspectives*, edited by Barry A. Kosmin and Ariela Keysar. Hartford, CT: Institute for the Study of Secularism in Society and Culture, Trinity College.

———. 2007b. "Unbelief and Irreligion, Empirical Study and Neglect of." Entry in *The New Encyclopedia of Unbelief,* edited by Tom Flynn. Amherst, NY: Prometheus.

Paul, Gregory S. 2010. "The Evolution of Popular Religiosity and Secularism: How First World Statistics Reveal Why Religion Exists, Why It Has Become Popular, and Why the Most Successful Democracies are the Most Secular." In *Atheism and Secularity*, vol. 1, edited by Phil Zuckerman. Santa Barbara, CA: Praeger.

———. 2009. "The Chronic Dependence of Popular Religiosity upon Dysfunctional Psychosociological Conditions." *Evolutionary Psychology* 7, no. 3: 398–441.

———. 2005. "Cross-National Correlations of Quantifiable Societal Health with Popular Religiosity and Secularism in the Prosperous Democracies." *Journal of Religion and Society* 7: 1–17.

Pargament, Kenneth I. 1997. *The Psychology of Religion and Coping.* New York: Guilford.

Pargament, Kenneth I., et al. 1994. "Methods of Religious Coping with the Gulf War: Cross-Sectional and Longitudinal Analyses." *Journal for the Scientific Study of Religion* 33, no. 4: 347–61.

Pearce, Lisa, and Melinda Lundquist Denton. 2010. *A Faith of Their Own: Stability and Change in the Religiosity of America's Adolescents.* New York: Oxford University Press.

Peek, Charles W., Mark A. Konty, and Terri E. Frazier. 1997. "Religion and Ideological Support for Social Movements: The Case of Animal Rights." *Journal for the Scientific Study of Religion* 36, no. 3: 429–39.

Petersen, L. R., and G. V. Donnenwerth. 1998. "Religion and Declining Support for Traditional Beliefs About Gender Roles and Homosexual Rights." *Sociology of Religion* 59, no. 4: 353–71.

Putnam, Robert D., and David E. Campbell. 2010. *American Grace: How Religion Divides and Unites Us*. New York: Simon and Schuster.

Quack, Johannes. 2012. *Disenchanting India: Organized Rationalism and Criticism of Religion in India*. New York: Oxford University Press.

Rappaport, Roy A. 1999. *Ritual and Religion in the Making of Humanity*. Cambridge: Cambridge University Press.

Ray, Darrel W. 2013. "The Secular Therapy Project." *Free Inquiry* 33, no. 4 (June/July): 31–32.

Raymo, Chet. 1999. "Celebrating Creation." *Skeptical Inquirer* 23, no. 4: 21–23.

Reader, Ian. 2012. "Secularisation R.I.P.? Nonsense! The 'Rush Hour away from the Gods' and the Decline of Religion in Contemporary Japan." *Journal of Religion in Japan* 1, no. 1: 7–36.

Rebhun, Uzi, and Shlomit Levy. 2006. "Unity and Diversity: Jewish Identification in America and Israel, 1990–2000." *Sociology of Religion* 67, no. 4: 391–414.

Rees, Tomas James. 2009a. "Is Personal Insecurity a Cause of Cross-National Differences in the Intensity of Religious Belief?" *Journal of Religion and Society* 11: 1–24.

———. 2009b. "Why Some Countries Are More Religious Than Others." Epiphenom, July 8. http://epiphenom.fieldofscience.com/2009/07/why-some-countries-are-more-religious.html.

Regnerus, Mark, Christian Smith, and David Sikkink. 1998. "Who Gives to the Poor? The Influence of Religious Tradition and Political Location on the Personal Generosity of Americans Toward the Poor." *Journal for the Scientific Study of Religion* 37, no. 3: 481–93.

Ridley, Matt. 1998. *The Origins of Virtue: Human Instincts and the Evolution of Cooperation*. New York: Penguin.

Riis, Ole. 1994. "Patterns of Secularization in Scandinavia." In *Scandinavian Values: Religion and Morality in the Nordic Countries*, edited by Thorleif Pettersson and Ole Riis. Uppsala: ACTA Universitatis Upsaliensis.

Rivas, Titus 2003. "The Survivalist Interpretation of Recent Studies into the Near-Death Experience." *Journal of Religion and Psychical Research* 26, no. 1: 27–31.

Roemer, Michael. 2009. "Religious Affiliation in Contemporary Japan: Untangling the Enigma." *Review of Religious Research* 50, no. 3: 298–320.

Rossi, Ianina, and Máximo Rossi. "Religiosity: A Comparison Between Latin Europe and Latin America." In *The International Social Survey Programme, 1984-2009: Charting the Globe*, edited by Max Haller, Roger Jowell, and Tom W. Smith, 302-12. New York: Routledge, 2009.

Rowatt, Wade, et al. 2006. "Associations Between Religious Personality Dimensions and Implicit Homosexual Prejudice." *Journal for the Scientific Study of Religion* 45, no. 3: 397-406.

Sabom, Michael. 1998. *Light and Death: One Doctor's Fascinating Account of Near-Death Experiences*. Grand Rapids, MI: Zondervan.

Sanger, Margaret, 1971 [1938]. *The Autobiography of Margaret Sanger*. Mineola, NY: Dover.

Saroglou, Vassilis. 2010. "Religiousness as a Cultural Adaptation of Basic Traits: A Five-Factor Model Perspective." *Personality and Social Psychology Review* 14, no. 1: 108-25.

Schulman, Alex. 2011. *The Secular Contract: The Politics of Enlightenment*. New York: Continuum.

Schulte, Lisa, and Juan Battle. 2004. "The Relative Importance of Ethnicity and Religion in Predicting Attitudes Towards Gays and Lesbians." *Journal of Homosexuality* 47, no. 2: 127-41.

Shand, Jack D. 1998. "The Decline of Traditional Christian Beliefs in Germany." *Sociology of Religion* 59, no. 2: 179-84.

Shermer, Michael. 2004. *The Science of Good and Evil*. New York: Holt.

Shook, John R. 2013. "With Liberty and Justice for All." *Humanist*, January/February, 21-24.

———. 2010. *The God Debates: A 21st Century God for Atheists and Believers (and Everyone in Between)*. Hoboken, NJ: Wiley-Blackwell.

Skirbekk, Vegard, Eric Kaufmann, and Anne Goujon. 2010. "Secularism, Fundamentalism, or Catholicism? The Religious Composition of the United States to 2043." *Journal for the Scientific Study of Religion* 49, no. 2: 293-310.

Smidt, Corwin. 2005. "Religion and American Attitudes Toward Islam and an Invasion of Iraq," *Sociology of Religion* 66, no. 3: 243-61.

Smith, Christian. 2012. "Man the Religious Animal." Paper presented at the Berkley Center for Religion, Peace, and World Affairs, Georgetown University, February 12.

Smith, Christian, et al. 2003. "Mapping American Adolescent Subjective Religiosity and Attitudes of Alienation Toward Religion: A Research Report." *Sociology of Religion* 64, no. 1: 111-33.

Smith, Christopher, and Richard Cimino. 2012. "Atheisms Unbound: The Role of

New Media in the Formation of a Secularist Identity." *Secularism and Nonreligion* 1: 17–31.

Smith, Jesse. 2010. "Becoming an Atheist in America: Constructing Identity and Meaning from the Rejection of Theism." *Sociology of Religion* 72, no. 2: 215–37.

Solomon, Robert C. 2002. *Spirituality for the Skeptic: The Thoughtful Love of Life.* New York: Oxford University Press.

Solt, Frederick, Philip Habel, and J. Tobin Grant. 2011. "Economic Inequality, Relative Power, and Religiosity." *Social Science Quarterly* 92, no. 2: 447–65.

Stark, Rodney, and Roger Finke. 2000. *Acts of Faith: Explaining the Human Side of Religion.* Berkeley: University of California Press.

Starks, Brian, and Robert V. Robinson. 2007. "Moral Cosmology, Religion, and Adult Values for Children." *Journal for the Scientific Study of Religion* 46, no. 1: 17–35.

Steigmann-Gall, Richard. 2003. *The Holy Reich: Nazi Conceptions of Christianity, 1919–1945.* New York: Cambridge University Press.

Straughn, Jeremy Brooke, and Scott L. Feld. 2010. "America as a 'Christian Nation'? Understanding Religious Boundaries of National Identity in the United States." *Sociology of Religion* 71, no. 3: 280–306.

Tamney, Joseph, Shawn Powell, and Stephen Johnson, 1989. "Innovation Theory and Religious Nones." *Journal for the Scientific Study of Religion* 28, no. 2: 216–29.

Taylor, Robert Joseph, et al. 1996. "Black and White Differences in Religious Participation: A Multisample Comparison." *Journal for the Scientific Study of Religion* 35, no. 4: 403–10.

———. 1988. "Correlates of Religious Non-involvement Among Black Americans." *Review of Religious Research* 30, no. 2: 126–39.

Thompson, Martie P., and Paula J. Vardaman. 1997. "The Role of Religion in Coping with the Loss of a Family Member to Homicide." *Journal for the Scientific Study of Religion* 36, no. 1: 44–51.

Thrower, James. 2000. *Western Atheism: A Short History.* Amherst, NY: Prometheus.

———. 1980. *The Alternative Tradition: A Study of Unbelief in the Ancient World.* The Hague: Mouton.

Tocqueville, Alexis de. 1969 [1835]. *Democracy in America.* Edited by J. P. Mayer. New York: Harper Perennial.

Trzebiatowska, Marta, and Steve Bruce. 2012. *Why Are Women More Religious Than Men?* New York: Oxford University Press.

Van Doren, Carl. 2007 [1926]. "Why I Am an Unbeliever." In *The Portable Atheist,* edited by Christopher Hitchens. Philadelphia: Da Capo.

Voas, David. 2009. "The Rise and Fall of Fuzzy Fidelity in Europe." *European Sociological Review* 25, no. 2: 155–68.

Voas, David, and Abby Day. 2007. "Secularity in Great Britain." In *Secularism and Secularity*, edited by Barry A. Kosmin and Ariela Keysar. Hartford, CT: Institute for the Study of Secularism in Society and Culture, Trinity College.

Volokh, Eugene. 2006. "Parent-Child Speech and Child Custody Speed Restrictions." *New York University Law Review* 81, no. 2: 631–733.

Wade, Nicholas. 2009. *The Faith Instinct: How Religion Evolved and Why It Endures.* New York: Penguin.

Wakefield, Eva Ingersoll, ed. 1951. *The Letters of Robert Ingersoll.* New York: Philosophical Library.

Waller, James. 2007. *Becoming Evil: How Ordinary People Commit Genocide and Mass Killing.* New York: Oxford University Press.

Walsh, A. 2002. "Returning to Normalcy." *Religion in the News* 5, no. 1: 26–28. trincoll.edu/depts/csrpl/rinvol5no1/returning%20normalcy.htm.

Warraq, Ibn, ed. 2003. *Leaving Islam: Apostates Speak Out.* Amherst, NY: Prometheus.

Wattles, Jeffrey. 1996. *The Golden Rule.* New York: Oxford University Press.

West, Ellis M. 2006. "Religious Tests of Office-Holding (Article 6, Cl. 3)." In *Encyclopedia of American Civil Liberties,* edited by Paul Finkelman, 1314–15. New York: Routledge.

Willson, Jane Wynne. 2007. "Humanist Ceremonies." In *Parenting Beyond Belief,* edited by Dale McGowan. New York: Amacom.

Wilson, David Sloan. 2002. *Darwin's Cathedral: Evolution, Religion, and the Nature of Society.* Chicago: University of Chicago Press.

Winston, Hella. 2005. *Unchosen: The Hidden Lives of Hasidic Rebels.* Boston: Beacon.

Winter, Michael, and Christopher Short. 1993. "Believing and Belonging: Religion in Rural England." *British Journal of Sociology* 44, no. 4: 635–51.

Wittgenstein, Ludwig. 1922. *Tractatus Logico-Philosophicus.* London: Routledge and Kegan Paul.

Woerlee, G. M. 2004. "Darkness, Tunnels, and Light." *Skeptical Inquirer* 28, no. 3: 28–32.

Zemore, S. E., and L. S. Kastukas. 2004. "Helping, Spirituality, and Alcoholics Anonymous in Recovery." *Journal of Studies on Alcohol* 65, no. 3: 383–91.

Zucchino, David. 2013. "He Wants to Be the Navy's First Humanist Chaplain." *Los Angeles Times,* August 17.

Zuckerman, Phil. 2013. "Atheism and Societal Health." In *The Oxford Handbook of*

Atheism, edited by Stephen Bullivant and Michael Ruse. Oxford: Oxford University Press.

———. 2011. *Faith No More: Why People Reject Religion*. New York: Oxford University Press.

———. 2009a. "Atheism, Secularity, and Well-Being: How the Findings of Social Science Counter Negative Stereotypes and Assumptions." *Sociology Compass* 3, no. 6: 949–71.

———. 2009b. "Aweism." *Free Inquiry,* April/May, 52–55.

———. 2007. "Atheism: Contemporary Numbers and Patterns." In *The Cambridge Companion to Atheism*, edited by Michael Martin. New York: Cambridge University Press.

Zuckerman, Phil, Luke Galen, and Frank Pasquale. Forthcoming. *Being Secular: What We Know About the Non-religious*. New York: Oxford University Press.

Index

Index